NONE
Call Me
D♥D

NONE Call Me D♥D

Ky Owen

Interrobang Collective | Portland, OR

To Dave Owen

CONTENTS

CONTENTS

PROLOGUE

THE BALL RICOCHETED OFF the edge of the racquet and spun off at an angle before dropping just short of the net. I slammed the racquet face against my left hand, looking down to avoid my partner's glare.

"Come on, Ky," the coach shouted as I took my position on the service line. "Show some Mateen!"

The reference to Michigan State's point guard invigorated me. When the coach put another ball in play, I ignored the tension in my left hamstring. Charging forward at an angle, I squarely volleyed a shot into the front corner, well outside the opponent's reach.

"Now that's Spartan tennis!" the coach exclaimed.

"Not bad for a guy who turned 41 yesterday," I said with a grin.

Monday night tennis was part of my routine, followed by a late-night dinner. Tammy, my wife of 11 years, accepted being a tennis widow.

I'd become so committed to my tennis game that two years earlier we built a tennis court at our house, situated in the woods just minutes from our office in downtown Charleston, West Virginia. We designed the house to fit our lifestyle, complete with a library, formal dining room and wide-open basement with black and white tiles across the floor.

"You must not have kids," the painter said when I showed him the paint chips for the basement walls. "Red makes children hyper."

"No, just a dog," I said. Needless to say our beagle, Samantha, was more interested in the wildlife than the basement walls.

Tammy and I had long ago grown accustomed to our "dual income, no kids," aka DINK, status. We focused on our law practice in a mid-sized firm. Being in the capital city, the practice attracted a fair amount of business—transactional work for Tammy and significant litigation for me. I worked out almost every day, played tennis four days a week, and constantly trained for distance runs with Tammy. And as a faithful Michigan State University alum, I religiously followed Spartan sports.

I'd given up on any notion of becoming a father, being satisfied with my role as Uncle Ky—and that role by virtue of marriage. Aaron's biological father was Tammy's brother. Six years old, Aaron lived with his grandparents, Tammy's mother and stepfather.

Aaron often spent weekends with us. We chauffeured him to soccer and t-ball, occasionally helping practice his sight words or complete other school work. I took Aaron to see his first NFL game at Soldier Field and baseball games at Camden Yards and Three Rivers Stadium. And, of course, there were the usual trips to McDonalds.

Y2K arrived without incident, with Tammy and I content in our role as fun-loving Uncle Ky and Aunt Tammy, focusing on our law practice and enjoying the freedom of our DINK status. I christened the New Year with a Miller Lite and Tombstone pizza, watching the Spartans kick a field goal as time expired to win the Citrus Bowl, then turning my attention to the Spartan basketball team that stood in the top 10.

TWO WEEKS NOTICE

IT WAS THE FIRST Monday of March 2000. I was downstairs in the exercise room going through my hour-long workout routine. Tammy was at the hospital with her mother, who had suffered a stroke on Sunday afternoon.

Tammy came in a few minutes before six o'clock. The strain was evident in her face. She let out a long sigh, taking comfort in knowing she didn't have to worry about putting up a front.

I continued jumping rope and asked, "What's the prognosis?"

"She'll have to go to a rehab facility," Tammy said, powering up the treadmill to four miles an hour for a brisk walk. "Hopefully she can go home eventually, but Jack is going to have to take care of her around the clock."

I stopped short of 300 reps to ask the obvious.

"What about Aaron?"

"I'm not sure Jack can handle both my mom and Aaron," Tammy said.

Before she could say any more, I interrupted her. "I know what's coming. And I'm willing to do it." I added one condition. "We adopt him. I'm not in this just to be a guardian."

"That goes without saying," Tammy said, nodding in agreement. "We've got to do what's in his best interest. Aaron needs to have a stable environment, with people he knows to be his parents and raise him."

I resumed jumping rope, overwhelmed by excitement and anxiety at the prospect of transitioning from uncle to father, with absolutely no concept of what was to come.

◆ ◆ ◆

Over the next two weeks, Tammy's family considered our adoption plan. All acknowledged that Tammy's stepfather couldn't realistically care for both a stroke victim and a six-year-old boy. Aaron's biological father was not in a position to take on custodial responsibilities, and Aaron's biological mother had her hands full with Aaron's half-siblings, Robert and Sierra, ages 13 and 11.

In the meantime, I brought Aaron over each Friday night and kept him occupied during the weekend so his grandfather could spend time at the hospital. That's how movie night came to be. I needed a plan to feed and entertain Aaron, while at the same time feeding Samantha and completing mundane household tasks like sorting the mail.

"How about we rent a movie and eat pizza?" I suggested. Little did I know that I was creating a family tradition that continued when Tammy was able to stay home on weekends. All three of us ate pizza and watched movies on Friday night for years to come.

◆ ◆ ◆

Aaron knew that his grandmother was in the hospital, but he didn't know the severity of her condition. On the second weekend following the stroke, Tammy took a break from the hospital so we could talk to Aaron. We sat down on the edge of the twin beds in the front bedroom.

"Hey buddy," Tammy said with a mix of cheer and concern. "We need to talk."

"About what?"

"It's about your Nan," Tammy said. "She's hurt and her brain is not working right. We hope she'll be OK, but she's going to need a lot of help. Grandpa needs to take care of her, and it's best for you to come and live with us."

I braced for an emotional outburst. Instead, Aaron just focused his eyes on Tammy, listening intently. He asked a few more questions about his Nan, but otherwise seemed remarkably calm as we outlined the logistics.

"You'll stay with Grandpa for the next two weeks so you can finish the grading period at Nitro Elementary," she explained. "Then you'll move here and go to a new school." Aaron just nodded and asked if he and I were still going out to a movie.

On Sunday I packed up Aaron's clothes, planning to take him back to his grandparents' house that afternoon and then return home to enjoy one last Tombstone pizza and Miller Lite before beginning parenthood.

"What are you doing with that?" Aaron asked when he saw me with his bag. "I live here now."

"Just taking everything to your room," I improvised.

◆ ◆ ◆

Coming home from the office on Monday, I realized that my routine would change. Rather than working out and practicing my serve and volley, I'd be eating supper at the kitchen table and running bath water. Nevertheless, I hopped out of the car with a spring in my step. I was Dad—just like the TV dads from the 1960s sitcoms I watched as a kid. I burst through the garage door like Dick Van Dyke, looking forward to my family cheerily greeting me.

I was met by Aaron standing in the middle of the basement, just below the stairwell. "Now that I'm living here, I'm calling you Ky and Tammy," he announced in a voice loud enough for both of us to hear.

Thinking like a lawyer, I immediately considered this a challenge to our parental authority. "Shouldn't he be calling us 'Mom and Dad'?" I asked myself.

Title or no title, when we sat down at the kitchen table for supper that first night, I reached over and turned the television off.

"Hey," Aaron said. "What are you doing?"

"We're having supper together so we can talk," Tammy said. Aaron opened his mouth to respond, but Tammy cut off debate.

"Because we said so. We're your parents."

Later that evening she privately confided in me. "I'm beginning to sound like my mother. I swore I'd never say that to a child of mine."

◆ ◆ ◆

Two days later I opened the door from the garage to find Aaron sitting in a chair midway down the hallway. Aaron furrowed his brows and stared straight ahead, working his shoulders back and forth between a sulk and a defiant arch.

Tammy appeared in the laundry room door with a stoic face. "He's in time-out," she said. Her tone was measured—not too stern, not too frantic. "I told him if he could tell me what he did wrong and what he would do differently next time, I'd release him early." According to "the book," a time-out should last one minute per year of age, and Tammy had offered to release him three minutes early.

Aaron's response to Tammy's offer of clemency was unequivocal. Gritting his teeth like my dad on the golf course, he looked up and said, "I'll take the minutes."

"Well," I said, working hard to adopt Tammy's moderated, parental tone, "then he can have the minutes." I was ready to call our counselor for advice. Tammy had to focus on removing the lint from the dryer so Aaron wouldn't see her laughing.

◆ ◆ ◆

My baptism came the following night. Michigan State had reached the Sweet 16 in the NCAA basketball tournament. I turned on the game and left Tammy in charge of getting Aaron ready for bed.

Aaron threw a tantrum.

"I want Ky to help me!"

"Ky's watching his game," Tammy said.

"I want Ky!" Aaron repeated.

The first half was coming to an end and the Spartans were down by 10. Between the game and the tantrum, I was beginning to feel physically sick to my stomach. The need to change my priorities was obvious, and with a heavy sigh I turned off the television and went to help Aaron get ready for bed.

An hour later I turned the television back on to discover that while I had been reading to Aaron, Mateen Cleaves had rallied the Spartans to victory!

Missing the championship game was not an option. I decided to go watch the game with Tammy's grandfather. "He needs some company," I told Tammy and Aaron on my way out the door. "Don't worry buddy, maybe you can stay up and watch with me when you're older."

I thoroughly enjoyed seeing my team win the national championship in peace, the only shouting coming from me. When I arrived back home shortly before midnight, I was still wired and charged inside ready to relive the game. Tammy greeted me with a finger to her mouth, her expression clearly signaling, "Be quiet!"

So much for cracking open that bottle of Dom Perignon.

◆ ◆ ◆

Sam quickly grew accustomed to having Aaron around. But the more she let him pet her the more he missed Dolly, his six-month-old beagle/basset puppy. We told Aaron that Dolly needed to keep Jack company.

That worked for almost a week.

On Sunday we agreed that Dolly could come up to visit that afternoon. Aaron sat in the front seat of my Celica—probably in violation of state law, but the Celica didn't really have a back seat— and held Dolly up to let her lick his face. Dolly was the runt of the litter. At six months she weighed no more than 15 pounds. She had long ears and short legs. And she had those brown eyes, the ones that look right into your heart. My sister used to say that God gave dogs those eyes so they wouldn't go hungry. When I looked over and saw the smile on Aaron's face and Dolly's tail wagging across the windshield, I told myself, "That dog isn't going back."

Sam adapted to Dolly's arrival with ease. After just a few vicious snarls, Dolly learned her boundaries.

If only I could have redrawn Aaron's boundaries with such ease.

◆ ◆ ◆

"You know what I order—a cheeseburger, fries and nuggets," Aaron used to say with a sigh. I thought this was a bit much for a six-year-old, but when I was an uncle I didn't fight it.

"I'm not going to let him run into traffic," I told Tammy. "But if his grandparents allow him to eat half the value menu, who am I to say no?"

Having become Aaron's dad, however, I decided that he was going to cut back. I made the announcement as we pulled into the drive-thru lane.

"You can have a cheeseburger and either fries or nuggets," I told him. "Which do you want?"

"I want a burger, fries and nuggets!" he shouted.

"You can have either fries or nuggets, not both," I replied in a calm, but firm, tone.

"I want my regular meal!" he yelled.

"I'm almost to the speaker," I answered. "You need to decide."

"Take me back to Grandpa's."

"We'll talk about that later. For now, fries or nuggets?"

"I hate you!"

"I'll stipulate to that," I said, my calm tone belying my frayed nerves. "Fries or nuggets?"

◆ ◆ ◆

Not surprisingly, by this time Aaron had seen enough to conclude that "Ky and Tammy" weren't as much fun as "Uncle Ky and Aunt Tammy." When I came home after work on Friday night, I saw Aaron walking down the driveway.

"I'm going back to Grandpa's," he told me in a calm, even tone.

"OK," I intoned, equally calm, as Tammy glared at me.

I parked and took Tammy aside. "I don't know what to do," I said. "My mom would let me go, knowing I'd come back."

The plan worked, perhaps because Aaron knew I'd brought pizza.

The second time Aaron tried this stunt, Tammy casually walked a short distance behind him, telling Aaron she was just taking a walk. Once again, he quickly changed his mind and turned around. We were getting the hang of this parenting gig.

Or so we thought.

On his sixth attempt in as many days, Aaron crossed the interstate bridge just down the road from our house. Tammy stopped, and within a few feet Aaron turned back as well. But the next time he crossed the bridge, continued to the top of the hill, and started down Crestwood Road.

Recognizing that we had not figured out this parenting gig, we sought professional advice. The counselor instructed us to stop Aaron at the bottom of the driveway and physically turn him around. "Do it every time he walks out until he stops." Tammy rolled her eyes, but I suggested we give it a try.

"I know it sounds ridiculous, and I agree with you that pushing a 100-pound kid back up the hill presents an uphill battle," I said, with no pun intended. "But I don't know what else to do."

The following day I came home to find Aaron starting down the driveway. Per our instructions, I stopped immediately and got out of the car. I caught up with him at the bottom of the driveway. "That's far enough," I said as I took his hand. "We're going back inside. You live here now."

He stayed 15 years.

GOLF, "IT'S TRADITION"

AARON AMBLED AROUND THE pro shop with his team-mates. The kids fidgeted with tees in their fingers, tossed balls between hands, pulled the velcro on and off their golf gloves. All five were outfitted in khaki pants and white collared shirts. Aaron and his friend Justin had their shirts tucked in. I was tempted to ask Aaron about the upcoming match. After all, golf is a father-son tradition in the Owen family. But I held back and left Aaron alone to fidget with the rest of the Elkview Middle School golf team, aka the Elk Herd. Drifting back to a corner, I recalled what my dad used to say when I honed my golf game: "Your grandfather would be proud."

◆ ◆ ◆

I only had two weeks to prepare to be a father. No time for self-help books; no time to ask my dad for advice. All I knew was that I needed to get Aaron a set of golf clubs.

Easter Sunday came within five weeks and I gave Aaron his first set of golf clubs—a modern driver with a graphite head, four irons and a putter—with a red and black nylon bag. Quite a contrast to my first set of clubs, which came loaded haphazardly in a tattered bag patterned after the interior of a London Fog raincoat.

My dad had learned the game from his father—though from the stories he told me, it sounded like my dad spent more time as a caddy than a playing partner. When I finally showed an interest in the game at age 14, Dad decided to bequeath his clubs to me, taking the opportunity to buy a new set for himself.

"Your grandfather gave me these clubs," Dad told me. My grandfather was a pretty good golfer. He played both for recreation and business. Being a public relations guy for the Hormel Company presented opportunities to mix business and golf. On one such outing, he met a club designer. The guy gave my grandfather a prototype of a new club, nattily named "Power Plus."

"This set is one of only 300," my dad told me as I examined the unique structure of the club face.

The following season he told me the rest of the story. "There were only 300 made because no one could play with them," he admitted. "Why do you think your grandfather gave them to me?"

I couldn't master the club any better than my grandfather's cronies back in the '50s, and after a year I received a set of modern irons. The Power Plus set remained in the back of the garage storage closet along with a few antique wooden clubs.

In the years that followed, I spent countless summer afternoons on the golf course with my dad. I looked forward to giving my son the same opportunity.

The opportunity came the day after Easter. After work, I found Aaron standing at the top of the stairs with the golf bag slung over his shoulder.

"Will you come out and practice with me?" he asked.

I tossed my suit coat on the banister and headed out the door. "Let's start with the nine iron," I suggested.

Aaron pulled out the driver and teed up a ball. "Watch this!"

Wearing a tie and dress shoes, I shagged balls across the front yard and into the woods for nearly an hour. I tried to offer some semblance of instruction and managed to hit a few practice shots of my own.

The following year Aaron was ready to venture on the golf course. For Father's Day my dad took Aaron and me to play a round at the Parkersburg Country Club. I quickly realized that my role involved more than bridging the generation gap. Aaron was starting to get the hang of the game, but he still hit some errant shots. My dad was an admitted duffer whose shots usually went to the left of the intended target. Aaron just swung at will without looking for the trajectory of the ball and my dad always looked straight ahead like his dad had taught him. As a result, neither one had any idea where their shot might actually land. I found myself serving as caddy to both father and son, stopping in between to advance my own ball.

Like any golfers, on occasion we found our groove. Late one Saturday afternoon, we stood on the tee box at the fifth hole, a par 3 measuring just under 100 yards. The short fairway lay in between railroad tracks on the left and River Road on the right.

Aaron teed off first, using his driver. Adopting my nomenclature, he called it the "Big Cuhuda." He struck the ball right on the sweet spot and it sailed in a straight line toward the green.

"Great shot!" my dad shouted as the ball rolled up on the green.

"Not bad, buddy," I added.

Aaron smiled triumphantly as he carefully put the head cover back on the Cuhuda.

Dad went next. He stood over his ball and took at least a dozen short practice swings. I looked over at Aaron and shook my head before Aaron could make some smart remark like, "Is there a shot in our future?" Finally, Dad took a full swing and the ball took off in a line drive just a few feet over the ground, coming to rest on the front edge of the green.

"Yes!" Aaron shouted, pumping his fist.

"Nice shot," I said.

I relaxed with the knowledge that no caddy duties would be required. I took a soft swing with my wedge and pitched a perfect lob to the center of the green. We took our putters out of the cart and walked to the green.

"Your putt is downhill, so take it easy," I told Aaron. He rolled the putt close to the hole and then walked over to mark his ball with a degree of fanfare. My dad putted close enough to the hole that he was able to tap in his putt for par. I left my putt just outside of Aaron's ball and then putted in for par as well.

Aaron took his time placing the ball down, studying the putt. Then he carefully tapped the ball with the putter head.

The sound of the golf ball dropping in for par was melodic.

We strutted off the green, each casually swinging a putter in our right hand. We looked like real golfers.

My grandfather would have been proud.

I'm not sure if the following hole would have caused him to laugh or cringe.

◆ ◆ ◆

The sixth hole is a long par 5 running along the railroad track. I put my tee shot over the rails, then took a mulligan. Over the next 540 yards, I scuttled back and forth to help Aaron and my dad. As we neared the green, I sent Dad ahead, rushed over to hit my shot and hopped in the cart on the passenger side.

"You're up that way too," I told Aaron. "Drive up the right side and pull up behind my dad." Aaron hit the gas too hard and we took off with a jolt. "Hey buddy," I said, "you might want to slow down." Three seconds later Aaron locked up the brakes and the cart skidded to a stop just inches behind Dad's cart.

My father turned to his grandson and gritted his teeth so hard that the lower plate of his dentures moved forward. "Damnit!" he shouted. "Be careful!"

Aaron's face turned pale as he looked over to me. "Aaron, I think Dave missed the sand trap after all—he's in great position to win the hole," I said with a forced smile. My ploy worked and the tension passed.

◆ ◆ ◆

We continued the tradition the following summer. One Saturday we played nine holes and then returned home for beverages on the patio and steaks on the grill, just as Dad and I had done when I was growing up.

After dinner, Aaron started asking my dad about the Navy. Dad brought down his *USS Kearsarge* yearbook and showed Aaron pictures while reminiscing about his Navy days. "I was a steward," Dad explained. To this day, Aaron brags that his grandfather served as a bartender in the Navy.

I relished seeing my dad feel the joy of being a grandfather. Aaron began telling his friends that "Dave" had not been his grandfather at first, but he had become his grandfather.

A few weeks later, Aaron visited Dave, now his grandfather, in the ICU unit at Charleston Area Medical Center. I had to leave the room when I saw Dad raise his eyebrows to acknowledge his grandson's visit. Dad died an hour later.

Aaron loves to tell people that he played golf with his grandfather, who had played with his father and then with me. Borrowing a line from *Fiddler on the Roof*, Aaron exclaims, "It's tradition!"

◆ ◆ ◆

In March of Aaron's sixth grade year he came home from school and announced that he was joining the middle school golf team. My only regret was that I couldn't tell my dad.

Early in the season, the team practiced after school in the gym. Since this was golf, I insisted that I be the one to pick Aaron up after practice.

One day Aaron came walking across the gym floor with a teammate. They were both smiling, walking with a casual stride. Each was swinging a golf club. Aaron's faded jeans and hoodie provided a stark contrast to his teammate's creased khaki pants and collared golf shirt.

"This is Justin," Aaron said. "Can we give him a ride home?"

A few weeks later, I gave Aaron and Justin a ride to their first match for the Elk Herd. When Aaron prepared to tee off, I watched patiently from the gallery. The other players looked on with curiosity as Aaron pulled out a driver with a steel shaft and wooden face, remnants of the "Power Plus" logo etched across the club head.

"This belonged to my great-grandfather," he boasted.

I beamed with pride as Aaron took his backswing.

Aaron's grandfather would have been proud. As would mine.

"COACH"

TWO DAYS AFTER AARON signed up for fall soccer the league president called.

"We've placed Aaron on a team," he told me.

"That's great," I said. "He's looking forward to it."

"Well, the reason I'm calling is... we need a coach."

"I'd be glad to help," I stammered. "But I've never played soccer, much less coached."

"That's not a problem," he said. "We can help you."

"Seriously," I said. "I don't know anything about soccer."

"You're the fifth person I've called."

My coaching career was underway.

◆ ◆ ◆

While Aaron had played soccer before, with his size I thought he'd be better off playing football. As a matter of fact, two weeks earlier we'd taken Aaron to sign up for midget league football.

"We practice four nights a week and on Saturday until the season starts," the football coach said. "Practice starts at 5:45 p.m. sharp and runs until about eight o'clock." As if that weren't enough, the coach made a passing reference to the weight limits. "110 pounds for C league," he noted.

Tammy and I tried to talk to Aaron, but he just ran by with the other kids saying, "We're going to get our helmets!"

One of the assistants told us that Aaron weighed in at 112 pounds. He must have noticed Tammy and I exchanging worried looks. "Don't worry, he'll work it off in practice," he said assuredly.

We couldn't risk Aaron spending every evening at practice and then ride the bench because he couldn't meet the weight limit. We took advantage of the one night off to talk to Aaron. Tammy laid out the pros and cons, stressing the lack of free time to ride his bike, hit golf balls or play with friends, much less watch television. We breathed a collective sigh of relief when Aaron said he'd rather stick with soccer.

◆ ◆ ◆

My first order of business as a soccer coach was a trip to Books-A-Million. I read *Soccer for Dummies* from cover to cover.

Aaron was thrilled to hear I'd be his coach. "What's the name of our team?" he asked.

"We don't have one yet," I said. "Maybe you can come up with a name. Just keep in mind that the team colors will be green and white. That's not negotiable, by the way." Green Lightning was born.

The first practice was organized chaos, nothing like the model practices outlined in *Soccer for Dummies*. Tammy assisted by occupying five kids while I tried to show the other five some technique from Chapter One.

Eventually, one of the other parents who had played soccer offered to help. Practices improved, although it wasn't until the final practice that I discovered that using one soccer ball instead of giving each kid a ball dramatically increased their attention span.

We didn't win a game, but the kids had fun. And no one quit. That may have been my finest hour.

Midway through the fall season, Tammy talked to the grandparent of one of our players, Christopher. His mom was a single parent and his grandmother usually brought him to practice. She explained that Christopher wanted to quit, but she and his mother wanted him to keep playing. Tammy mentioned the conversation to me and when I came to the field for the next practice, I kept my eye out for Christopher. He hopped out of the car while his grandmother stayed back, keeping her distance. Christopher walked straight to me, looked up with doleful eyes, and said, "Coach, I'm quitting the team."

Looking down at him, with his shin guards, cleats and goalie gloves, a plan came to mind. "Sorry to hear that," I said. "We'll sure miss you."

Christopher just stood there, looking up at me with his lips quivering.

"Hey, I see you've got your goalie gloves on today," I said. "I need a goalie for a drill today. Since you're here, maybe you can stay and help."

"Sure," he replied.

After practice I gave Christopher a high-five and said, "Thanks for helping out. If you can make the game Saturday we can use you."

The following Saturday several players couldn't make the game and we had just enough to field a team. At half-time Christopher came running off the field. While the others reached for Gatorades, Christopher made a beeline toward me. Standing directly in front of me with sweat dripping off his face, he exclaimed, "Coach, you are not taking me out of this game!" Rather than telling him we only had seven players and no substitutes, I simply said, "OK, you're my goalkeeper."

We finished our winless season with a pizza party. A lawyer's billboard across the street was emblazoned with the slogan "Been Through Hell?" A couple of the kids saw it at the same time I did, and they finished the season with a burst of laughter and smiles on their faces.

◆ ◆ ◆

No sooner had soccer ended than I found myself at the middle school gymnasium registering Aaron for basketball. When I arrived I saw a former associate from the law firm and discovered that he was one of the organizers.

"Second graders can play as long as their parent coaches," he said with a grin. My jaw dropped. "You probably want to watch the players as they warm up," he added.

The kids went through various drills—dribbling, passing, lay-ups—and then lined up against the wall. Aaron broke into a smile when he realized that I was one of the coaches. I joined the other coaches, all of whom had clipboards and copious notes, to pick a team. I hadn't picked a team since I was in sixth grade, and that was on the playground.

With my first pick I took a third grader named Matt. He was wearing a Cavaliers jersey, and that was good enough for me. Matt turned out to be our best player, leading us to an exciting last-minute victory over the other team from our elementary school.

At our first practice I asked the players to introduce themselves and asked each to tell everyone their favorite sport. Turns out I had picked three baseball players, two football players, a soccer player and a four-wheel racer to go along with Matt, who said he liked to play basketball.

Any visions I had of being the next Tom Izzo—Michigan State's legendary basketball coach—were dashed early. Organized plays were out of the question. That required five kids knowing where to go on the court. "Right side on the block," I yelled across the court. "By the soda machine," I added, pointing to the machine located at the entrance to the gym. Next thing I knew, the referee was telling the kid to come out from beside the Coke machine and onto the court.

Lest there be any doubt, my efforts to employ Coach Izzo's famous "War Drill" backfired. The essence of the drill is to encourage players to be more aggressive when fighting for a rebound. Neither the league's budget nor the scope of the release permitted me to outfit the players in football pads like they do at Michigan State practices, but I employed the concept. I lined up four players on either side of the basket, intentionally missed a shot, and encouraged the kids to be aggressive.

The following game I had to pull out Austin, my tallest player, because he had committed four fouls. "One more and you can't finish the game," I told him as he came over to the bench.

He summoned me a few minutes later. "Coach," he said with a mischievous grin, "put me back in with two minutes to go. I got a plan!"

"Just don't hurt anybody."

Austin simply smiled.

I substituted him for Aaron with just over two minutes left in the game.

"Why are you taking me out?" Aaron asked.

"Just hold on a sec," I said. Before Aaron could respond, the referee blew the whistle. "We've got a hold on 6 green," he said. I signaled to Aaron to go back in as Austin walked off the court, grinning ear to ear.

◆ ◆ ◆

We lost one game that year, a close loss. Matt sat down on the bench and voiced his displeasure with the officials. I looked over and saw from Aaron's body language that he was about to follow suit. In that second, I decided that I might not be able to control my team, but I could control my kid.

"That ref was lousy," Aaron said as I came over.

"Listen up," I said sternly. "We're not blaming the referee. He gave his time today so we could play the game. You're not going to blame him. In fact, you're going to shake hands and thank him."

For the rest of Aaron's playing career—in basketball, soccer, baseball and hockey—he always shook hands with the official after the game. As he grew older, Aaron included the opposing coach in his post-game ritual. After one hotly contested baseball game, players and coaches from both teams stormed off the field. Aaron tracked down the opposing coach in the concession line to congratulate him on the win.

I didn't always exhibit such perspective. One year we led 18–8 with less than two minutes to play. Despite having excellent math skills, it didn't occur to me that a team that had scored 8 points in 22 minutes was not going to score 10 points in 2 minutes. When our best ball handler asked to come out of the game, I said we needed him in the game. Quoting Mateen Cleaves, I shouted, "Leave it all on the court!"

In the midst of our victory celebration I noticed the key player was absent. "He's getting a breathing treatment," another kid said. "He's got asthma."

From that day forward I inquired of any medical conditions.

◆ ◆ ◆

I reached the pinnacle of my coaching career in third grade, when I coached the all-star team. At the first practice I became convinced we had a good team. After all, 8 of the 10 kids could dribble a basketball. Maybe I'd be the Tom Izzo of youth basketball yet.

We opened on a Friday night against a team from Charleston's west side. While the kids from our area looked forward to baseball and riding four-wheelers, the kids on the west side shot hoops on the playground.

Down 36–4 at the half, I realized that I'd violated the Peter Principle. I'd gone one step too far up the coaching ladder. Somehow I found something positive to say to the team. Years later, I ran into a kid who'd played for me. "You always had something positive to say," he said, recalling that each year I ended the season with the same speech.

"I played little league baseball, and I got two hits in four years," I told the teams. "But I never quit. That's what I learned in little league baseball. So, I just want to say I'm proud of you kids for sticking out the season. You didn't quit."

BECOMING
SIERRA'S DAD

THE FAMILY COURT ADJOURNED. I buttoned my suit jacket with one hand while picking up the guardianship papers with my other hand. "Should we go to the mall and get lunch?" I asked.

"Sure," Sierra said. "Can we go to Hot Topic first?"

The walls inside the Hot Topic store were painted pitch black, the darkness accentuated by the dim lighting. An assortment of black clothing adorned the walls: t-shirts emblazoned with red skulls, mini-skirts, lace stockings. "I love their incense," Sierra said. With my limited sense of smell, I hadn't noticed the odor of the burning incense. "You can buy me anything from here," she added as she headed over to a rack of black jeans.

The store throbbed to the heavy metal beat of Slipknot blaring from the speakers mounted in all four corners. The lyrics of "Duality" by Slipknot seemed apropos:

> Tell me the reality is better than the dream
> But I found out the hard way,
> Nothing is what it seems!

For the first time in my life, I was claustrophobic. I felt like I was suffocating. Standing there, in the middle of Hot Topic, I realized that I wasn't in Kansas anymore.

I was becoming Sierra's dad.

◆ ◆ ◆

Four months earlier, we got a call from Aaron's biological mother saying that Sierra wanted to see him. Aaron had not seen or talked to Sierra since his fifth birthday party six years earlier. We picked Sierra up for dinner one night, and soon she started joining Aaron for church youth group activities. In no time, she was staying over on weekends.

Sierra was a pretty girl, petite with long black hair and warm green eyes. She looked thin and somewhat pale, though, so Tammy made it a point to serve plenty of protein and vegetables. Peas covered with cheese was one of Sierra's favorites.

One night she walked into the family room and speaking to no one in particular said, "Someday I'm going to live here." Tammy and I glanced at each other, both of us with a slight smile, saying nothing.

Later that evening when we had retired to our bedroom, I said, "I take it you heard Sierra."

"Yes," Tammy replied. "That would be good for both of them."

◆ ◆ ◆

"Someday" came the week before Christmas. Tammy was on the treadmill on Saturday morning when Sierra called in a panic. She had been living with a cousin, but her mother was insisting she come back home. "I'd like to live with you guys," she said. Tammy and I had surmised that Sierra was not doing well with her mom, and immediately agreed that she could stay. Tammy and Aaron picked her up later that day.

With all the commotion, I hadn't had a chance to tell my mom any of this, naively thinking I'd find a good time to break the news. Instead, Aaron abruptly announced the news when he called from the hospital two days later.

"Hey Frieda," he said. "I have diabetes and we're adopting Sissy."

When I took the phone, my mom asked, "Are you trying to save the world?"

"No, just one kid at a time."

◆ ◆ ◆

The following week Tammy and I petitioned the court to be appointed as guardians for Sierra. We were thrilled for Aaron to have a sister and looked forward to having a teenager in the house. On Christmas Eve, I set four place settings for our traditional family dinner.

After we finished eating, everyone went to change clothes for the candlelight service. Sierra came out of her bedroom wearing boots and stockings from Hot Topic, with a black dress topped off by a floral shawl.

Had I had time to confer with Tammy, I would have admitted that the boots weren't standard attire at the First Presbyterian Church of Charleston, established 1819. But by comparison to Hot Topic's other offerings, Sierra's outfit constituted church attire. Plus, we usually sit in the back.

As soon as we entered the sanctuary, an elder recruited Sierra to serve as an usher. At five minutes before 11 o'clock, Sierra, boots and all, seated Congresswoman Shelley Moore Capito and her family.

"You do realize that you just seated a member of Congress," I said when she returned to her seat.

"Huh?" Sierra replied.

If I hadn't been in the sanctuary, I might have laughed out loud.

The next morning Sierra found a skirt and blouse from Macy's under the Christmas tree and, most important, her first cell phone. She spent most of the morning sitting by the tree in her new outfit entering contacts into the Nokia phone.

◆ ◆ ◆

After the holidays, we turned our attention to getting Sierra back on track. We were also focused on learning to manage Aaron's diabetes, but that's another chapter. Sierra had dropped out of South Charleston High School a few months earlier, but we were able to get her enrolled as a sophomore at Capital High School. We started a new routine, dropping Aaron off at the bottom of the hill to catch the school bus and then taking Sierra to the high school.

Tammy once again began impersonating her mother. Many days I heard her firmly say, "You're not wearing that to school."

I stayed out of the fray. To this day, I deny all knowledge of what happened to the chain-laden black jeans that Sierra had put down the laundry chute.

"I can't believe you guys won't let me wear what I want to school," Sierra told me one night. I insisted that as long as her clothes met the dress code, they were okay with me. And that included the jeans, should they be located.

Tammy and I had guessed that Sierra's prior house rules were lenient, but we were beginning to discover that we had underestimated the situation. Sierra wasn't accustomed to any semblance of structure. The task of parenting a teenage girl was becoming more daunting than expected.

◆ ◆ ◆

Sierra spent many evenings on the computer playing an online game and talking with friends via AOL instant messaging. I didn't even know we had instant messaging. One evening when I was using the computer to revise a brief, a message popped up in the lower right hand corner.

"Hey, what's up?"

I ignored the message and continued working.

"Hey," the screen blinked again.

I realized that Sierra was showing up as being online. If I told Sierra she had a message she'd take over the computer, but with no response her friend might think Sierra was ignoring the message. So I clicked on the message and typed a reply.

"Sierra's off the computer for a few."

"Who are you?" came the reply.

I thought about paraphrasing Ronald Reagan—"I paid for this computer"—but I figured Sierra's generation wouldn't appreciate a line from the 1980 presidential primary. Instead, I responded, "Her dad, Ky."

"Oh, lol. How are you?"

"Fine. And you?"

"OK. Gotta go."

"Nice chatting with you."

When I was finished on the computer, I came in the family room and bragged that I'd had my first "IM" conversation.

"Really," Tammy said.

"Yeah, I was talking to some girl named Cassie."

"Oh my God!" Sierra screamed as she jumped up from the table and ran to the computer. "What did you say?"

I assured her that nothing embarrassing occurred, and she eventually learned to laugh about it. But she never left the IM program open again.

At a parent-teacher conference a few weeks later, we mentioned that Sierra and Cassie were friends. The chorus teacher frowned. "Oh, I know," she said. "But Cassie's an alto." I wasn't sure why it mattered that my soprano daughter was friends with an alto.

I met Cassie later that spring. I was delivering ice cream for an after school party. I stood in the courtyard, listening to the birds chirp on the warm spring day. The solitude was broken by the ringing bell and a rush of teenagers, many who shop at Hot Topic. They seemed oblivious to the man in a navy blue suit holding a carton of Neapolitan ice cream. I heard Sierra and turned to see her walking toward me, accompanied by a short girl wearing shorts and socks that looked like they were borrowed from Pippi Longstocking. But most striking was her hair. The color was patterned after the ice cream in my hand. As my jaw dropped, Sierra said, "This is Cassie."

◆ ◆ ◆

That spring Sierra and I went out on our inaugural "father-daughter date." We started the evening with dinner at the Tidewater, an upscale seafood restaurant.

"So, is your dad taking you to see Natalie Cole?" the waitress asked as she filled our water glasses.

"I guess so," Sierra said, looking over at me excitedly.

"Oh, I'm sorry," the waitress said. "I guess you were going to surprise her."

"Well, now you know," I laughed. "So, how was school today?"

"My cell phone went off in algebra class," she confessed.

Unbeknownst to me, having a cell phone in class violated a sacred policy at Capital High School.

Her defense still makes me laugh.

"It was a wrong number," she pleaded. "They were looking for some guy named Joe Manchin," she added, obviously unaware that a guy named Joe Manchin was the sitting governor of West Virginia.

"What?"

"I guess I have his old number," she said with a shrug.

While Sierra shrugged off the significance of the wrong number, I couldn't help but imagine the look on some politico's face when he called for the governor and heard Sierra's voice. "Hey... No, this is Sierra... Oh, it's okay sweetie. No problem."

◆ ◆ ◆

Sierra had correctly determined that I was the softer touch of her new parents. Maybe it's genetic. When my sister was 11 years old, she escaped out a window after being grounded by the babysitter and rode her bike down to my dad's office, where she was promptly treated to a chocolate malt.

Not surprisingly, Sierra hatched a plan to ensure that I'd be the first one to see her initial report card. On the day grades were issued, Tammy left a message explaining that the school called because Sierra was ill and Tammy had picked her up early. "She left her report card in her locker," the voicemail said. "So don't worry that she doesn't have it."

After supper, Tammy and Aaron left on an errand while Sierra and I finished eating.

"Just out of curiosity," I said, "do you know any of your grades?"

"Uh..."

"Listen, Sierra," I said. "Last semester you didn't have any grades, so having a report card is an improvement."

Sierra looked down for a moment, then sat forward and said, "You want to see my report card?"

"I take it the report card is not in your locker?"

"It's in my backpack."

"Let me see it," I said. I looked at the report card and nodded as I read passing grades for each class.

"That's a good start," I said, handing back the card. "But let's wait until tomorrow to show Tammy, when you get it from your locker."

◆ ◆ ◆

Outside of school, Sierra stayed busy during the spring rehearsing for the musical *Honk!*, which was being put on by a local theater group. Sierra preferred that I drive, probably because I was more tolerant of her musical tastes. And I was willing to take the long way home to allow time for Sierra to listen to "one more song, just one more."

By the time the show went live for two weekends in April, I knew the script by heart. Still, Tammy and I didn't miss a performance. I beamed with pride every time Sierra came on stage,

more so when random members of the audience stopped to compliment her after the show.

No sooner had *Honk!* finished than Sierra prepared to audition
for *Bye Bye Birdie*, which was being produced as part of a youth
summer theater workshop in Parkersburg. Sierra didn't need my
help for the musical audition, but I insisted that she allow me
to coach her on the dramatic reading. "I was a Thespian in high
school, in case you didn't know," I told her. "And the director is
John Lee. I know this is hard to believe, but he was my high school
drama teacher." Sierra garnered a role as one of the teenie bop-
pers who worshipped Conrad Birdie, probably based more on her
soprano voice than my tutelage.

While Sierra was staying at my mom's house in Parkersburg,
I investigated my suspicion that Sierra was sneaking cigarettes
in her bedroom. I was secretly hoping to prove her innocence.
I decided to put away Sierra's laundry—I saw no signs of the
jeans—and lingered in the room as I went about the task. Eyeing
a wastebasket in the corner, I recalled a law school case study in
which the FBI had searched a suspect's trash. At first I casually
peered into the basket as I emptied it into a larger bag. Then I
noticed a Hot Topic bag that was tied off. My senses heightened,
I kneeled down on the floor and opened the bag.

I instantly became nauseous. Not because of the smell—smoking was permitted in bars during my college days—but by the
reality that my girl was smoking on the sly. As I sifted through
the bag I found a receipt. The date of the purchase confirmed
that the disposed cigarette butts were of recent vintage.

"So that's why she likes to burn incense," I said to myself.

Tammy and I discussed the situation. "Let's wait until after the
show," Tammy suggested. "I don't want your mom to take the
brunt of this." We decided to wait until Sierra returned home the
following Sunday.

One of the scenes Mr. Lee included in *Bye Bye Birdie* had one
of the wholesome teenagers take a drag on a cigarette. Yes, that
role was played by none other than Sierra. All around us the

crowd burst out laughing. Tammy and I looked at one another. Tammy managed to curl her lips ever so slightly and tapped my arm, reassuring me that we'd make it.

Our talk on Sunday evening went about as well as could be expected. Sierra offered no defense, choosing instead to look away with a blank stare. After a few minutes, I concluded that Sierra had tuned us out and ended the lecture.

Becoming Sierra's dad was no easy task.

◆ ◆ ◆

Sierra passed all of her spring semester classes. She was still behind in credits, so she enrolled in summer school, attending physical education class and taking English online. The key to passing PE was arriving on time and changing in and out of gym clothes. English, however, required reading and writing. Sierra worked diligently on the daily assignments. She didn't ask me to do any writing assignments, however, pointing out that my prior writing assistance had cost her a letter grade.

I'd helped her out on a writing assignment once during the spring semester. Sierra had been overloaded trying to catch up on the semester of world history she'd missed at South Charleston and she had to write a dramatic critique. I suggested that she dictate her thoughts while I typed, implying that I'd do nothing more than put her words into complete sentences.

"This won't work," she said, handing the paper back to me. "A paragraph has to have at least three sentences."

"Sierra," I responded. "I'm a writer. I've got a journalism degree, you know. Sometimes a one-sentence paragraph works."

"The teacher says each paragraph has to have at least three sentences," she argued.

"But this is perfect as one sentence," I countered.

"Whatever," she sighed and rolled her eyes as she took the paper and stuffed it in her backpack. "Oh, and we're not supposed to begin a sentence with 'but either, but whatever."

A few days later she slapped the paper down in front of me. The red markings indicated that at Capital High School a paragraph needs three sentences, none of which should begin with "but."

For summer school I only volunteered to help with the online quizzes. This required that I read the assigned short stories. Sometimes we took turns reading aloud to save time. With ten days to go before the course deadline, Sierra still needed to complete a report on George Orwell's *Animal Farm*.

"I'm afraid I managed to graduate from high school without reading *Animal Farm*," I admitted. Sierra focused her eyes on mine and held her mouth in a straight line. "I tell you what," I said. "Read as much as you can and I'll read the book to back you up."

Sierra finished with an A in the course. And I could say with a clear conscience that I too had completed the required reading for 10th grade English.

◆ ◆ ◆

One night Sierra mentioned that she'd met a guy in class and wanted to hang out with him sometime. She had learned that we wouldn't let her go on a date without at least knowing the guy's name, if not more. She suggested that I could meet the guy when I picked her up after PE.

The next day I was sitting in the parking lot when Sierra appeared with a male teenager in tow. His hair reached his shoulders and he wore a black t-shirt emblazoned with the logo of what I assumed to be a heavy metal band. He extended his right hand confidently.

"I'm Danny Jones's boy."

My first thought was, "Sierra's dating the mayor's son." I admired the kid's style. Mitigating the hair and the shirt by introducing himself as the son of Charleston's longtime mayor was a nice touch.

"Nice to meet you, Zac," I said.

One day when I picked up the kids after class, Zac mentioned that he had a third ticket to the baseball game. Though clearly a ruse to get a ride, I accepted the offer. My seat was directly behind home plate, just a few rows up from the kids' seats. Between innings Sierra apologized that Zac's dad had made him switch one of the tickets.

"No worries," I assured her.

"By the way, you do know who that is sitting next to you, don't you?"

"Yeah, why?" she said.

"He's the governor."

"Oh," she replied nonchalantly. "He just said his name is Joe."

Sierra had to leave early for rehearsal, so she didn't get a chance to tell the governor that she'd been taking his calls.

That summer she was in the cast of Anything Goes. Zac never complained, but I could tell he was unhappy that Sierra was often busy. Zac joined us for opening night. Upon seeing the marquee, he burst out laughing.

"Anything Goes is the name of the play? Whenever Sierra told me couldn't go out because it was her 'anything goes' time, I thought it was her free time. I always wondered why she wouldn't spend her 'anything goes' time with me."

The summer fling ended after summer school as Zac went to high school at Riverside High School, about 30 miles away. I played an impromptu role in the break-up scene. I answered the telephone and as soon as I said, "Hey Zac," Sierra started motioning with her hand across her neck. "She's not here," I said, much to Sierra's relief.

A couple of days later, Sierra remembered that she'd left her swimsuit at the mayor's house. "I did my part the other night," I told her when she looked at me with her puppy dog eyes and curled lip. "I'm not going to pick up the swimsuit." We did, however, laugh out loud when imagining the political implications of Sierra showing up at the mayor's office to ask for her bikini.

❖ ❖ ❖

Tammy and I assumed Sierra would return to Capital, the magnet school for the performing arts, but after one of her performances in *Anything Goes*, the music teacher at George Washington High School approached us. He waxed eloquently about Sierra's talents and talked about how she would be a fine addition to the GW show choir.

"Now I know how the parents of athletes feel," I told Tammy. "She's being recruited!" The following month she sang a solo with the show choir at the Clay Center, Charleston's marquee performance hall.

The drive to GW was 25 minutes, more than long enough for Sierra to complete her makeup. On the other hand, only a five-minute window existed in which we could drop off Sierra a block away and get out before traffic snarled. Missing the window of opportunity meant that Tammy or I sat in traffic for another half hour.

Tammy laid down a firm rule: "We leave the house by 7:18 in the morning or you listen to AM radio on the way to school." Sierra immediately tested Tammy's resolve and found herself listening to traffic and weather on 580 AM.

A few days later a disagreement over skirt length caused a delay, so Sierra asked me if I'd drive. "It's 7:25," Tammy said with a stern look directed at me as Sierra and I walked out the door, "so it's AM radio."

Sierra was not amused when I tuned into ESPN's *Mike & Mike in the Morning*. Rather than voicing her displeasure openly, she scowled until we reached the interstate, which had become her cue to start putting on makeup. The sound of silence was only broken when the radio talk turned to a dress code being imposed on NBA players. "What?" she exclaimed. "That's so freaky!"

That spring Sierra auditioned for a part in *Oklahoma!* I was out of town on business when she called to report that she'd once again be a chorus girl.

"It's okay," she told me on our call.
"But you deserved more," I insisted.

◆ ◆ ◆

Summer school that year consisted of an online health class. I was of virtually no assistance whatsoever, even on the diabetes chapter. Sierra managed to complete enough of the assignments to get a passing grade.

The highlight of the summer was a two-week music workshop at Ithaca College in upstate New York. I handled the 12-hour drive on my own since Sierra had yet to get her driver's license. Somewhere outside of Harrisburg, Pennsylvania, Sierra grew tired of her music and spent a couple of hours in conversation with me.

The next day I experienced a fraction of the emotions my parents felt when they dropped off their 18-year-old son at Michigan State University.

Sierra turned 18 in August. We celebrated her birthday at the beach, serving cake and allowing her to go down to the arcade on her own. That fall Sierra started her senior year. She started missing classes and chafed at our efforts to monitor her attendance and grades. The final straw came in late October.

The kids were out on Sunday afternoon when I logged on to check my email. My jaw dropped and tears welled in my eyes when I saw the picture Sierra had downloaded to send to her boyfriend. Looking back on it, the photograph was no more revealing than a magazine ad for Chanel No. 5 or Victoria's Secret. But when it's your daughter, it's a different story. We confronted Sierra about the photograph and made clear that posting this kind of photograph on the internet was unacceptable. A few days later, the church youth group leader called to tell us that Sierra was moving out.

Sierra's birth mom picked her up on a Monday night. When they pulled in the driveway, Aaron was walking out to go with a friend to the ice rink. Tammy and I waited in the family room while Sierra came back and forth to her bedroom. When Sierra took out the final load, she walked back in the house. Watching her place the Nokia cell phone on the counter, there was no denying she was leaving. I gave her a brief hug and said goodbye. "We'll be here if you need us."

As she walked out the door, I remained at the counter and fought back tears. The lyrics of Saliva's "Rest in Pieces," which I'd heard countless times on the car radio over the past 20 months, flooded my mind:

> Look at me, my depth perception must be off
> again
> Cause this hurts deeper than I thought it did.

I'd become Sierra's dad.

"DX 12 / 21 / 2004"

"**A**ARON'S GOT SOME NEWS!" Tammy's exuberant tone had an edge, which I realized meant she was not entirely pleased.

I stopped in the parking garage, anxiously waiting for Aaron to come on the line.

"Hey," he said. "I'm getting an insulin pump."

I took a deep breath and put my hand on the wall to maintain my balance as I fought back tears.

"There's no denying it," I told myself. "My son has Type 1 diabetes."

Until that moment I had held out hope that Aaron's blood sugar might be managed through diet and exercise, maybe by adding a daily pill. But the insulin pump signified that the diagnosis of Type 1 diabetes was conclusive. Aaron would be forever dependent on insulin injections.

In the Type 1 diabetes community, Aaron would remain classified as "Dx 12/21/2004."

◆ ◆ ◆

Ten months earlier, on December 21, 2004, Tammy called from the emergency room. By the time I reached the hospital, Aaron had been admitted to the pediatric unit. He sat up in the hospital bed and calmly announced, "I have diabetes."

Aaron had been complaining of constantly needing to urinate. On Monday morning, he insisted we drive him to school because the 20-minute bus ride was too long. He needed to go so often that he didn't want to go to his Monday night Boy Scout meeting. I insisted he attend.

"Aaron, you're not going to die," I said sternly. "Get in there for crying out loud."

Fourteen hours later the doctor instructed Tammy to go directly to the emergency room without stopping to pay the bill. Aaron's blood glucose level exceeded 600. High enough to be fatal. What Tammy had diagnosed as a minor bladder infection turned out to be Type 1 diabetes.

Kevin, a physician's assistant, walked in the room and directed his attention to Aaron. Kevin said, "Everyone who might give you an insulin injection should learn how to give the shot." He handed Aaron an orange and a syringe and asked, "Will both your parents be giving you shots?"

Without hesitation, Aaron said, "You better show Tammy."

Aaron and Tammy practiced drawing up saline and plunging the needle into the orange. "Remember, it needs to go straight in," Tammy instructed.

"I know!" Aaron said.

Tammy turned to me and said, "You really should know how to do this."

I looked at Aaron and asked, "Do you want me giving you shots?"

"No!" he shouted.

"Me neither," I said with a firm nod. "Tammy, he's 11 years old. He can administer his own shots," I added with false bravado. My dad had Type 2 diabetes, which I now know is an entirely different condition, and he had warned me that diabetes runs in the family. He told horror stories about giving his mother her insulin shots. But my dad never took a shot—well, at least not of insulin.

When I was in junior high, I used up my allotted D in health class. I didn't know about the difference between Type 1 and

Type 2 diabetes. I had no idea that "normal" blood sugar runs between 80 and 120. I couldn't tell the difference between Lantus (long-acting insulin) and Novalog (short-acting insulin). I was clueless when it came to carbohydrates, known to Type 1 families as "carb counting."

Aaron was placed on a low-carb diet—45 carbs per meal and 15 carbs for a snack. "Only half of that baked potato," Tammy instructed at dinner one night.

"Baked potatoes have carbs? I thought only candy and ice cream were off limits." And to think I had prided myself on insisting that Aaron opt for a baked potato in lieu of fries.

At meal times, a defined protocol was established. Aaron would wipe his finger with an alcohol swab, load a new lancet to prick his finger to draw blood and then check his blood sugar on the meter. If it was below 150, he did not need to take an insulin shot. He was doing well, with readings in the 140s, but at supper one night his meter read 155. I was as disappointed as Aaron. Then I remembered that physical activity decreases blood sugar levels.

"Dinner won't be ready for a few minutes," I said. "Go walk a few laps around the tennis court and check again." Five minutes later he clocked in at 148.

For the first couple of weeks, we had been eating at home under Tammy's supervision, but both Aaron and Sierra were anxious to get out of the house. One Saturday we decided to eat lunch at Wendy's, and I took my first solo adventure.

Aaron was hesitant about administering a shot in public, so he checked his blood sugar in the car. He was running too far above the 150 level for laps to make a difference, so I calculated the required amount of insulin. Sierra and I sat quietly and patiently while Aaron drove the needle in like he'd practiced on the orange and pushed the plunger. He threw the syringe on the floor.

"You better hope you don't get pulled over," Sierra laughed. "Or you'll have some explaining to do!"

◆ ◆ ◆

That summer we registered Aaron for a week-long camp for Type 1 kids known as Camp Kno-Koma. This would be Aaron's first time away from home since being diagnosed, and he and Tammy were both nervous. "There are physicians' assistants and pediatric nurses at the camp," I said. I didn't need to add that he'd be better off at Camp Kno-Koma than spending a golf vacation with me.

We arrived at the 4-H camp early Sunday afternoon. The lodge was filled with kids of all ages carrying fanny packs, and many had pumps attached to their shorts. Many of the parents had worried looks on their faces. The atmosphere served only to elevate our tension.

"When will you be back to pick me up?" Aaron asked after we dropped his sleeping bag and supplies in the cabin.

"Pick up is next Saturday from 10:00 in the morning until noon," Tammy said.

"Be here right at 10:00," Aaron insisted.

The following Saturday we arrived right on schedule.

"Why are you here so early?" Aaron asked. "Can't you go somewhere and come back later?"

We took a seat at a picnic table with other families who had made the mistake of coming too early. The camp staff came over and reported on the week's activities. The discussion was all about diabetes care. "With Aaron, we focused on taking his shots in different parts of his body other than his stomach," the counselor told us.

When we asked Aaron what he learned about diabetes care, he reported that the camp kids had successfully taken miscellaneous undergarments from the counselors' cabin and hung them on the flagpole.

We were thrilled. Aaron had apparently learned some tips on diabetes care while at the same time enjoying a youth camp experience like any other kid.

"I'm coming back again next year!" Aaron declared as we pulled out.

◆ ◆ ◆

For several months, Aaron managed to get by with only the evening Lantus shot since his readings were still below 150. As spring turned to summer, however, he started running consistently over 150. Every meal required a shot and he switched from the needle to a pre-loaded insulin pen. We continued to measure dosage using a chart taped to his kit. At every meal, Aaron studiously checked his sugar and went to his room to administer his insulin shot. We respected his privacy.

"It may be hormones," the doctor told us. The doctor continued to modify the insulin dosage and each time I replaced the chart. This went on for several weeks, and we worried that Aaron was resistant to the insulin.

Later the doctor met with Aaron privately before calling in Tammy. Aaron sat sheepishly in the corner and averted his gaze from Tammy. "It's not uncommon, so don't panic," the doctor said. "Aaron told me he's not been taking all of his shots."

"Yeah," Aaron piped up. "I take the Lantus at night, but that's about all."

"We'll have to readjust his insulin dosage," the doctor instructed. "Keep track of his readings and let me know in a couple of days."

The net effect of Aaron's conscious decision to stop taking insulin was that the dosage was grossly inflated. As a result, when he took his shot according to the current chart, he was overdosing. That led to dangerously low blood sugar.

Hattie, the beagle-Jack Russell terrier mix we adopted after Sam died, somehow sensed when Aaron was low. On more than one occasion, we found Hattie leaning against Aaron on the bed, her ears pulled back and her tail between her legs. We soon learned that this was a telltale sign of low blood sugar.

◆ ◆ ◆

During the early months, Aaron's blood sugar seemed to level off. He'd lost 70 pounds, dropping from a size 38 waist to a size 30. And despite the setback caused by the failure to take shots, Aaron seemed to be doing better again. I held out hope that maybe Aaron had Type 2 diabetes, which could be controlled by pills, diet and exercise. Almost a year after the first hospital visit, the doctor confirmed that Aaron's "honeymoon" period was over. His pancreas was still producing some insulin, but that wouldn't last. Aaron was insulin dependent, no ifs, ands or buts about it.

Hearing the news, Aaron told the doctor that he wanted to start on an insulin pump rather than taking shots. This was Aaron's choice. After all, he's the one with a non-functioning pancreas.

The insulin pump presented pros and cons.

On one hand, Aaron no longer needed to get up by 8:00 a.m. to eat breakfast and take insulin. The pump also allowed him more freedom to eat like a teenager—as long as he remembered to take insulin and didn't binge on a large order of fries.

Proper pump protocol requires checking blood sugar before every meal. If the reading exceeds a stated number, insulin is injected through the pump, a process known as a "correction." After eating, additional insulin is injected based on the carb count, otherwise known as a "bolus."

This turned out to be more complicated with a teenager. "Don't remind me," Aaron told us one day. I convinced Tammy that we needed to allow Aaron to take ownership of the condition and manage it on his own. She agreed, but Aaron questioned her willingness to stop being a helicopter parent.

Not surprisingly, when we sat down for supper, Aaron neglected to check his blood sugar. Instead, he chose to stuff a handful of French fries in his mouth.

"You need to check first," Tammy said.

He looked at me triumphantly and proclaimed, "I told you she wouldn't stop telling me to check."

Later that evening, I privately told Tammy that we needed to give Aaron some room. "He's going to test you," I said. "And you cannot react."

"That's easy to say," she said, choking up, "until you see your son putting his health at risk."

Needless to say, letting Aaron go out on his own was never easy.

When Aaron was a high school freshman, he spent Halloween hanging out with a friend downtown. I chose to make light of the situation.

"He's probably getting high," I texted Tammy.

"What?"

"Yeah, afraid so" I answered. "They were going to Wendy's for a Frosty. His blood sugar is probably running over 300."

On the other hand, Aaron needed to change the infusion site every three days. At first the site change required that he insert a two-inch needle in his leg, stomach, arm or buttocks. This process—which at first took almost 45 minutes to complete—was not pain-free, to say the least. Over time, the technology improved and Aaron grew to accept the pain. The new site came with a shorter needle and a universal device that was placed against the skin and then pushed to insert the site. Eventually he learned to change a site standing in the lobby of a Vegas casino.

◆ ◆ ◆

During middle school, Aaron worked hard to take advantage of his new diagnosis. At lunch he turned administering insulin into a scene worthy of an Oscar. "Does that hurt?" girls would ask.

"Not much," he would say, wincing as the needle pierced the skin.

He also had the benefit of choosing a classmate to accompany him when he needed to go see the nurse. Friends still laugh about it years later.

During seventh grade, he visited the nurse's office when he felt his sugar levels were too low or too high. In eighth grade, it was the main office where some of the eighth-grade girls worked.

"We ask him if he feels like going back to class, and he says 'no, not yet,'" the principal said, explaining why Aaron often missed science class.

"I'm sure he doesn't 'feel' like going to science class, but from now on, have him check his blood sugar in class" I said. Ignoring Tammy's icy glare, I added, "He's not going to die in class, and if he does, I promise I won't sue."

A couple weeks later, I casually asked Aaron about school. "Are they helping you with your diabetes management? How's that going?"

"Yeah," he groused. "I have to check in class. I used to go to the office, but somebody put a stop to that."

By the time he reached high school, Aaron worked to avoid drawing attention to having diabetes. Sometimes he succeeded, but not always. Aaron tells a story of his geometry teacher calling him up to her desk on the first day of class.

"Mr. Owen, I see we have contraband," she said in the stern tone of an old-school high school teacher.

"What?" Aaron asked in the incredulous tone of a high school sophomore.

"You have your cell phone out?"

"What? That's my pump!" He spent the rest of the day answering questions from fellow students about his insulin pump.

◆ ◆ ◆

When the middle school golf team prepared for the season-ending tourney, Tammy made plans for what snacks he could keep in his golf bag.

"I don't know if the rules allow players to take food," the coach said cautiously. "They're not allowed breaks either." A few days later the coach announced that he'd chosen another player, despite Aaron having started all but one match that season.

"I can talk to the coach," I said, trying to keep my brewing anger under wraps. "Under Section 504 you're allowed an accommodation."

"It's okay," Aaron said with a sigh. "Plus the other kid's an eighth grader."

"We'll let it pass," I said. "This time."

When Aaron started high school, he quickly discovered that the band director, Mr. Scott, knew a lot about both teenagers and diabetes. Mr. Scott's granddaughter had Type 1 diabetes and Mr. Scott was Type 2. During band camp Aaron asked to take a break based on his blood sugar.

"Check it," Mr. Scott instructed. Aaron pricked his finger and placed a drop of blood on the test strip. Immediately upon hearing the meter beep, Mr. Scott looked at the reading.

"128! I'd kill for 128," he shouted. "Get back on the field."

◆ ◆ ◆

Tammy and I became well-versed in Section 504, the law governing accommodations for students with disabilities, and advocated on Aaron's behalf with school administrators and teachers. I even applied the law to a restaurant contest. We were in Columbus at Gameworks, a restaurant and video game establishment. A promotion advertised 25 game tokens for anyone who could finish the deluxe triple cheeseburger with a large order of fries.

"I can definitely eat that," Aaron boasted. I had no doubt that he could, but I also knew that a large order of fries contained at least 70 carbs. I applied 504 jurisprudence to solve the dilemma.

"Excuse me," I said as the waiter passed by. "My son is taking your challenge, and I have no doubt he can finish these fries." Seeing a 14-year-old at the table, the waiter nodded in agreement. "But, he's diabetic and he really shouldn't eat all of these fries. Wouldn't want his blood sugar running too high, I'm sure. Can you make an exception based on his disability?"

The poor guy was speechless and left to look for his manager. A few minutes later, the manager came over. Upon seeing Aaron drawing up insulin in his syringe, he handed Aaron 25 tokens.

Aaron also took advantage of his diabetes at Disney World. The theme park had a policy of allowing diabetics to jump to the head of the line when temperatures were above 80 degrees.

"It's so the insulin doesn't get too hot," Aaron explained. As we moved into the priority lane to Space Mountain, I noticed quite a few glares from people who were sweating in the main line that snaked through the concourse. I felt guilty at first, but thinking about all the site changes, I ignored the glares.

Another arena where Aaron needed a break was when he played hockey. I used to sit quietly in the stands during practice. I watched as Aaron broke off from the drills before the others to grab a Gatorade so he wouldn't pass out from low blood sugar. Other parents threw disapproving glances across the ice.

Traveling also presented unique challenges. On more than one occasion Aaron forgot his insulin and pump supplies, and we faced the choice of a making a late-night run out of town to deliver insulin or visit Aaron in an ER the next morning. When Aaron flies, the pump inevitably sets off the metal detector. Aaron regales in telling the story of his first solo flight at age 14. "The alarm sounded and I told them I had an insulin pump. The TSA chick told me to step over for a search. I didn't mind since she was kinda hot," Aaron tells the story. "But then this old guy comes around the corner putting on the rubber gloves."

◆ ◆ ◆

We joined the Charleston chapter of the Juvenile Diabetes Research Foundation (JDRF) and attended the annual fundraising walk and other support activities. The Type 1 kids range from just a few months old through retirement age. Some, who were diagnosed soon after birth, don't know of another way of life. Others, like Aaron, faced the diagnosis later.

For Tammy, JDRF is more about outreach than fundraising. She took a lead in starting a mentor program that connects older Type 1s with newly diagnosed Type 1s. For Type 1 families and friends, the JDRF sneaker symbol is like the fish symbol was to Christians in ancient Rome. All of our cars carry the sneaker magnet with the message, "I love someone with juvenile diabetes."

The summer after Aaron's freshman year, we attended a national conference of "Children With Diabetes." Aaron was attending the teen sessions and I suggested to Tammy that we split up between the parent sessions. "If you want to go to the mother's session at 10:00, I can go to either Emotions of Diabetes or New Developments in MDI."

"Do you even know what MDI stands for?" Tammy asked.

"No." I answered. "Why?"

"It stands for 'multiple daily injection'. Aaron's on a pump."

"I guess I'll go to the psychology session instead."

"Tammy's the one who needs to go to that session," Aaron said as he sulked away.

The Emotions of Diabetes session was presented by a cardiologist everyone called Dr. Bob. "Let's talk about what you want to talk about," Dr. Bob told the group. He started on the front row and listened patiently as parents expressed the many emotional issues that come with being the parent of a diabetic. After about 20 minutes, it was my turn.

"How do you deal with emotions rising and falling with blood sugar readings?" I asked. "In our house, the mood at the dinner table is set by my son's reading." Dr. Bob nodded and I continued. "My son could ace a big test, but if his reading is high, my wife panics."

Sensing some negative vibes from the crowd, I omitted my facetious remark that Aaron could come home with a suspension notice and all would be well if his reading was 101, and straight As would be meaningless if his reading was 218. A guy sitting a few rows behind me pointed at his wife. She didn't notice, as her icy glare remained locked in on me. A few other murmurs confirmed that ours was not the only household facing this issue.

Dr. Bob reminded us that when it comes to blood sugar readings, the operative verb is "check," not "test." "It's not a pass/fail," he told us. "When you say 'test' to a teenager they think grades."

Another rule to remember. Just what I needed.

◆ ◆ ◆

Later I met another father in the bar for a drink. Aaron and the other father's son stopped by. "How was the program?" we asked.

"Great," Aaron said with a grin. "They were preparing us for college."

"And?"

"We learned to count carbs for alcohol."

The presenter happened to be standing at the bar. Overhearing our conversation he smiled and said, "It's true. I'm going to have a gin and tonic and I'll cover with five units." He stopped to check his blood sugar and then explained that diabetes and alcohol is complicated. Beer has carbs and increases blood sugar, hard liquor decreases blood sugar, and mixed drinks with sugars (like margaritas) are a mixed bag.

"And they are supposed to keep track of this when possibly intoxicated?" we asked.

"That's why they need to tell their drinking buddies that they are Type 1 diabetics," the presenter told us. "So if they pass out, their friends know to find out if it's because they've had too much alcohol or too few carbs."

We laughed at the time. The idea of Aaron turning 21 seemed far off, and we had other battles to fight.

"SHE'S THE MAJORETTE!"

"SHE SHOULD TRANSFER TO Capital High. She'd love it." I overheard Aaron saying as I came through the door. He was sitting on the couch talking on his cell phone.

"Hey, who are you talking to?"

Aaron shook his head and waved his hand at me, staying focused on his conversation.

"If she needs a ride, she can stay here during the week and ride with me."

"Aaron, who are you talking to?"

"Oh," he said, paying no attention to me, "We have space. She can stay in Sissy's old room."

That certainly piqued my curiosity.

"And Tammy will make sure she does her homework."

I'd had enough unexpected surprises for a Monday, so I raised my voice.

"Aaron!"

Aaron placed his right hand over the phone and turned to me. "It's Brooke's mom." Returning to his conversation, he said, "Capital's a good school. And Brooke could join the band."

On Tuesday, with a mixed sense of excitement and trepidation, Tammy and I readied Sierra's bedroom for another teenage girl.

◆ ◆ ◆

Tammy fondly remembers the first time we saw Brooke, back in December of 2005. We were standing with other band parents on the corner of Court and Lee Streets, watching the Christmas parade, shuffling our feet to fight the cold. Eventually, the "Pride of Elkview Middle School" turned the corner. The majorettes led the way, wearing Christmas pajamas as part of a holiday motif.

"Look at how pretty that girl is," Tammy said as the lead majorette marched by twirling her baton. She was a tall girl, with her hair piled high and a genuinely bright smile. "Even in seventh grade she's really pretty," Tammy said. "Most girls look awkward at that age."

The following spring, Aaron started hanging out with a friend at the ice rink.

"Does this friend have a name?" I asked.

"Her name's Brooke," Aaron said indignantly.

"Tell me about her."

"She's in band."

"What instrument does she play?"

"Flute," Aaron replied. "Please stop asking me questions."

Two days later we were checking out at a local department store when a woman and two girls walked through the doors. I noticed that Aaron and the older girl glanced at one another awkwardly.

"Hey," Aaron said.

"Hey," the girl replied with a shy grin.

By this time the woman, whom I presumed to be the mother, and I were each standing a step behind our respective middle schoolers, waiting to see if we'd be noticed or introduced.

"Oh," Aaron said. "This is Brooke."

"Nice to meet you," I said with a polite nod, all the while thinking, "She's no flute player. Aaron's hanging out with the majorette!"

◆ ◆ ◆

Aaron and Brooke continued skating and hanging out through middle school, though I'm told they never "dated." We often took Brooke home, dropping her off at the entrance to a modest, middle class subdivision located a few miles north of Charleston. "I can walk from here," she always said.

Several weeks later Tammy quietly alerted me that the drop-off routine had changed. "She doesn't live in the subdivision. She lives in an apartment complex behind the subdivision. She was afraid of what we'd think." We took the change in routine in stride.

After middle school the kids went separate ways, Aaron attending Capital High School and Brooke attending Herbert Hoover High School—that is, until Aaron convinced Brooke's mom to allow Brooke to change schools, offering room and board in the process.

The plan was for Brooke to come over on Sunday night and then go home after school on Friday. Those are the hardest days to parent a teenager, but this time we had experience managing a teenage girl. And Brooke couldn't be as rebellious as Sierra.

Tammy set a curfew. Shortly before 10 o'clock, we closed our bedroom door with confidence that all electronics were off and the kids were in their bedrooms reading.

Years later, when Brooke turned 18, she smiled and told me the rest of the story. "Aaron and I used to go downstairs to watch TV after you and Tammy went to bed," she said. "We crawled across the floor so we wouldn't set off the motion detector."

While Tammy took charge of the curfew, or so she thought, I followed up on homework.

"We both have to read *Fahrenheit 451* for English class," Brooke announced one evening.

I volunteered to go to the bookstore after supper to buy each kid the book.

"I already read it," Tammy said. "Unfortunately I deleted any memory of it to make room for property law."

I remained silent. When I went to the bookstore that night, I picked up three copies.

"I'm just reading it in case they need my help," I said.

"Right," Tammy said, rolling her eyes. "Just try not to 'help' too much."

I limited my "help" to occasionally asking the kids what they thought about a particular scene. Of course, I first described the scene in vivid detail. They would just smile and say they agreed with me. I never asked if they read the book.

◆ ◆ ◆

The other task that fell to me was teaching Brooke to drive.

"OK, not bad," I said calmly as my Toyota slid to a stop two feet from the rear bumper of the car in front of us.

"Oh my God!" Brooke screamed. "I'm sorry!"

"Just try and remember to allow more time to stop when it's raining," I said.

Brooke appreciated my calm demeanor, adding, "Mom always freaks out."

"No worries," I replied.

"Hey, can I see my phone?"

"Not while you're driving."

Enforcing the "no texting while driving" rule with Brooke was critical, given that Brooke took texting to new levels.

During her sophomore year, Brooke was doing a research paper on texting and needed to know how many texts she had during a month. Since the cell phone account was in our name, she asked Tammy to obtain the information.

"You're not going to believe this," Tammy told me.

"What?"

"Do you want to know how many texts Brooke sent last month? 5,000!"

"Good thing we went with the unlimited text option."

Brooke originally had a cell phone that her mom loaned her with limited minutes. This posed a problem because we had become accustomed to constantly communicating with the kids via text, and Brooke seemed to run out of minutes at inopportune times. So we gave her Sierra's old cell phone, with the caveat that she might get some unintended calls for the governor.

I often received text messages from Brooke checking to see when I would pick her up so she could practice driving.

"Where are you?" she asked.

"En route," I texted before pulling out of the parking garage.

Brooke called two minutes later. "Hey. What's 'on rootay' mean?" To this day "on rootay" remains one of my programmed text responses.

In turn, Brooke taught me some new text acronyms.

"She says, 'LMAO,'" I said as I checked her cell phone while she drove. "What does LMAO mean?"

"You don't know?" she exclaimed.

"No, I don't know."

Brooke slapped the steering wheel as she burst out laughing.

"Sound it out," she told me.

"Love? Lots?" I said. "I don't know. I give up."

"Laugh... my..." Brooke said, barely able to contain her laughter.

"Oh my God!" I shouted.

◆ ◆ ◆

The other facet of Brooke having her cell phone on our account was that her mother needed Tammy's assistance to ground Brooke from the phone. She would let Tammy know when to disable the service and when to reactivate it. This seemed like a workable plan. Or so we thought.

"Hey!" Sitting in a standard, business-class motel room outside of Chicago, hearing Brooke's soft voice brought a smile to my face. I didn't think to question why she was calling from a landline.

"What's Tammy's birthdate?" she asked. I provided the information, naively assuming she might be buying birthday cards.

"Thanks," she said sweetly. "I know her social security number, but AT&T needs the date of birth too."

I didn't ask. Nor did I tell.

This wasn't the first time Brooke had put me in a parental quandary. One time she forgot to get a signature for a science class field trip. I feared she might ask Tammy to forge a signature. Instead, Brooke relied on her wit and force of personality.

Everyone who ever passed through the halls of Capital High School knows that there is no cell service in the science lab. Everyone but the science teacher, that is. Brooke offered to call her mom from the classroom. That evening she and Aaron couldn't stop laughing as Brooke told the story.

"I hit some buttons on my phone and said, 'Hey Mom, is it okay if I go on that field trip I asked you about?'"

"Kids were burying their heads in their hands to keep from laughing," Aaron inserted.

"Then I said, 'OK, thanks. I love you, too,'" Brooke said.

Tammy and I shared a look of stunned surprise, then concluded that if the science teacher was that gullible, we were justified in invoking the doctrine of in loco parentis and allowing Brooke to go on the field trip.

Neither of those instances, however, compares to the time I let Brooke bring her boyfriend, Jacob, home from a soccer game.

It happened on a Sunday afternoon. Brooke and I had driven just over an hour from Charleston so she could watch her boyfriend play in a soccer tournament. The game was canceled due to thunderstorms. Seeing the disappointment on the kids' faces, I offered Jacob a ride with us. He walked across the parking lot to check with his parents, then came running back and hopped in the back seat.

We stopped to eat on the way back. Midway through a personal pan pizza, Jacob announced that his parents were stopping to check on him. As we walked outside, Brooke filled me in on the details of their contract.

"OK, his parents think you're my dad," she said. "So I need you to play along." Before I could respond, she added, "They just pulled in."

I walked out apprehensively, undecided how to handle the situation. I wanted to do what I could to let the kids spend time together, but I was not comfortable saying, "Nice to meet you, I'm Brooke's father." As I approached the curb, Jacob moved away from the car door, and I saw his mother leaning out the car window. We'd met years ago when we were both coaching youth soccer.

"Oh!" his mother exclaimed, her face breaking into a broad smile. "We didn't know it was you!"

"Same here!" I said, privately thinking, "There's a lot you don't know."

◆ ◆ ◆

Brooke sometimes found it easier to tell people that I was her dad. I discovered this when we stopped to make an appointment for Brooke to get her hair done.

"What's the name?"

"Brooke Owen."

I stood mute, my emotions swinging between concern that Brooke thought she'd be adopted and laughing out loud. As we left, Brooke explained her reasoning. "It's less confusing, since you pay the bill. And you're like my surrogate father."

"I don't mind," I told her. "They think I have two beautiful daughters."

The staff never asked Brooke about Sierra, but they did mention me.

"So, your dad's a lawyer," the stylist told Brooke in an effort to make conversation. "That must be interesting."

"My dad's a coal miner," Brooke said.

"No," the stylist insisted. "He's a lawyer. Like your mother."

◆ ◆ ◆

Without a doubt, however, the most complicated situation involved Justin. Aaron had been playing matchmaker between Brooke and Justin since middle school. During a camping weekend at the end of eighth grade, Aaron "chaperoned" Brooke and Justin while they fished and played in the river.

"You two should date," he insisted. Brooke smiled nervously and Justin glared at Aaron.

The following year, Brooke confided in me—as her "surrogate father"—that Justin had made overtures toward dating. Since Justin had spent the past two summers living in our house, this situation had all the makings of a sitcom. I imagined Justin calling to ask for advice on how to approach Brooke. Fortunately, Tammy stepped in and suggested a solution.

"You should see if Justin wants to join us for dinner on Saturday night," Tammy suggested. "Maybe we can go to a movie, too."

"Just what a couple of teenagers want," I laughed. "Double-dating with a couple of middle-aged parents."

Then again, we did have keys to the car and a credit card.

We decided that the politically correct way to handle this "double date" was to have Brooke stay at our house for the weekend so we could pick Justin up. The kids seemed to enjoy dinner and we had a nice conversation.

The movie taught Tammy and me a lesson in 21st century dating. As I was watching the movie I felt my phone vibrate. "Is Justin having a good time?" the text read. I looked to my left and saw Justin leaning forward, watching intently, while Brooke slouched back with her phone in her hands, her thumbs moving rapidly over the screen. All I could do was shake my head and wonder, "How are these kids ever going to learn to communicate?"

◆ ◆ ◆

Brooke eventually grew homesick and her mom found transportation to Capital. Brooke still spent many weekends at our house, and we watched with pride when she crossed the stage to receive her diploma. Later she called for advice about college and careers before deciding on nursing school. During the summer following her freshman year in college. Tammy and I ran into Brooke at Panera Bread. She introduced us to Jonathan, a quiet kid who seemed to sense that I played a role somewhere between friend and father.

Brooke and I met for dinner a few weeks later. She explained that WVU had offered too many temptations and she had enrolled in a nursing program in Charleston.

"So," I said. "Tell me about this guy." Brooke's sheepish smile told me what I wanted to know. By the time we got together again, the relationship had reached the point of talking marriage. "We want to get married, but not until I've finished school and he's finished with the police academy."

A couple years later, Tammy and I attended Brooke's nursing school graduation. "You're our first post-high school graduate," Tammy said proudly. Brooke thanked us, then asked if she could list my name as a reference.

Tammy learned from Facebook that Brooke was engaged and pregnant. I sent a couple of nonchalant texts to Brooke, eventually asking, "Is there any news you want to tell me?"

"Maybe," came the reply. Even in a text, I could see Brooke's sheepish smile.

A few months later Tammy and I sat in the Capitol and watched our majorette march down the aisle carrying a bouquet of flowers.

TAR

A ARON SAT ON THE bare ground and tended his fire, wearing only a flannel shirt, jeans and wool socks. Betrayed on Maundy Thursday, delivered to Rowdy on Good Friday, looking to be released on Easter Sunday.

Rowdy sits on a barren patch of ground at Turn-About Ranch in the foothills of the Escalante Mountain Range in Utah. New arrivals spend their first three days at Rowdy. Their shoes are confiscated, and they are directed to a piece of hard ground demarcated by a circle of granite rocks. They keep a fire going to mitigate the cold breeze as the temperature drops to just above freezing. They sit in silence, hearing only the crackling of the fires and animals howling in the distance, while the tracker watches from his perch on the cabin porch.

◆ ◆ ◆

Aaron had grown increasingly defiant. Despite the efforts of teachers and friends, he had missed a third of his freshman year at Capital High School. We had worked with teachers, counselors and diabetes professionals to address the problem. Nothing seemed to work. Sensing that we were nearing the end of our rope, one of my running partners mentioned an educational consultant who had a reputation for helping parents with troubled teens. Tammy and I contacted the consultant. When he asked for any information about our 14-year-old son, we uploaded report cards for the past eight years, medical records and a battery of tests.

Tammy and I, along with the consultant, talked to Aaron one evening. Sitting at the kitchen table, Aaron offered terse answers to the consultant's questions. The possibility of going away to a boarding school or other program was mentioned, but we stressed that we preferred that Aaron just go to school. The next day Aaron refused to go to school. That was when the consultant recommended Turn-About Ranch.

We googled the name and found the official site and numerous blogs. The ranch's website displayed picturesque mountain ranges with horses and smiling teenagers, coupled with glowing narratives boasting of the ranch's success stories. Other web pages claimed that TAR was an apt acronym for Turn-About Ranch. "The isolation, forced labor, antiquated gender roles, and mandatory Baptist instruction are sickening," one blogger wrote.

"You need to trust me on this," the consultant intoned, glaring at us over his reading glasses. "I know one of the counselors at TAR. I'll pull some strings so that he's assigned to Aaron."

After a conference call with the consultant and the TAR director, I worked on completing the program application. Tammy filed the paperwork to borrow $50,000 against our life insurance policies. My mother seriously questioned our decision, but in the end, she offered a monthly stipend to help defer the cost.

◆ ◆ ◆

Parents employ a variety of methods to transport defiant teenagers to TAR, ranging from quiet persuasion to outright deceit. One parent told his son that TAR was a Utah ski resort. As soon as his dad pulled into the gravel lot in front of the wooden lodge, the teen excitedly jumped out of the car, ready to hit the slopes. Instead, his dad drove off with the younger brother, and the teen was told to take off his ski boots and get inside his circle of rocks.

Tammy and I were either too innocent or too honest to employ deceit. The thought of telling Aaron, "It's spring break, let's take a ski vacation in Utah," never crossed either of our minds. And expecting Aaron to make the trip voluntarily seemed out of the question. "I can't get him to school," I said. "There's no way I'm getting him to Utah."

The consultant told us to hire a trained "escort." He offered a recommendation, adding that "Eddie" was waiting for our call. Tammy preferred that Aaron go voluntarily. I mediated a compromise: we would give Aaron the chance to make the trip voluntarily, but if he balked we'd hire Eddie.

On Tuesday, Tammy and I came home after work to make our pass. We found Aaron sitting downstairs in his PJ pants watching a movie.

"Aaron," I began, "we need to talk..."

Tammy calmly leaned on the edge of the couch and spoke softly. "Hey buddy," she began. "We've been talking and we think it's best that you go to the ranch program."

"No!"

"Aaron," I said firmly, "you have to go. If you want, you and I can go to Columbus tonight. We'll go to the game place and then we'll fly out tomorrow."

"No!" he shouted, louder this time. "I'm not going! And I'm not staying here." He stopped the movie, stood up and went to his room. Within minutes he came out, fully clothed with a suitcase. When he started packing insulin and pump supplies, we fully appreciated the gravity of the situation.

"We need to find somewhere for him to stay where he'll be safe," Tammy said.

"What about Brooke's?" I asked.

We felt terrible asking. Brooke lived in a two-bedroom apartment with her mother and younger sister. But we were desperate.

Tammy called Brooke's mom and asked if Aaron could stay with them for a couple of days. Being well aware of our situation, she readily agreed. I told Aaron that rather than running away, he could chill at Brooke's house for a few of days. He accepted the offer and I dropped him off.

Then I put in a call to Eddie.

All we knew about Eddie was that the consultant had recommended him and the staff at TAR had accepted deliveries from him. Eddie explained that he and his wife would come to Charleston, pick up Aaron, drive to Columbus, fly to Las Vegas and then drive to the ranch.

Eddie and his wife took the red-eye to Charleston that Thursday. We met them for the first time on our lunch hour. Eddie looked to be a stout 250 pounds, standing just over six feet. A bald head accentuated his no-nonsense, tough guy image. He displayed a quiet confidence as he reviewed his protocol for convincing teenagers to go peacefully. He prided himself on never having to use force to get a teenager on the plane, but he made a point of showing us the pair of wrist ties that he carried in his back pocket.

The plan was for Eddie to take custody of Aaron shortly after midnight. They would drive to Columbus to catch an early morning flight to Las Vegas, then drive to the ranch. We concluded that having some guy snatch Aaron from the apartment while Brooke and her sister slept was above and beyond the call of duty for Brooke's mom, so we told Eddie we'd have Aaron at our house. He asked for a detailed layout of the house. "I prefer that he be boxed in, with no back door or window to try and escape," Eddie explained.

"When I arrive," he instructed, "take me to the room he's in, say 'Aaron, we love you, this is Eddie,' then leave the room. He'll probably be screaming at you, but don't respond. Just leave. If he's polite, once I have him in the car, I'll let you know and you can tell him goodbye. And if he's still yelling, we're leaving. I'll call you when we get there."

Aaron remained at Brooke's house. Neither Tammy nor I tried to talk to him, both because he probably wouldn't have anything to say and we didn't want to lie to him if he asked about our intentions. We kept the details from Brooke's mom so she wouldn't feel compromised. At the same time, Brooke called me every day to pump me for information.

"I can't tell you what might happen or when," I told her.

"Is he going to the ranch?"

"Like I said, Brooke," I repeated, "I can't tell you."

"You're going to send him away, aren't you?"

"Let's not talk about it," I responded.

Our plan to get Aaron back to the house was, in hindsight, disingenuous, but it was a far cry from a fictitious ski trip. We told Brooke's mom that we needed Aaron back at the house later that evening, preferably as close to midnight as possible. She had been fighting a cold and offered to make a trip to the ER shortly after 11 o'clock, telling Aaron that he needed to stay at our house while she was at the ER. All went according to plan, and Aaron returned home shortly before midnight on Thursday.

Aaron went straight into the library to get on the computer. He didn't seem to notice that we readily allowed him to jump on the computer at midnight, much less that we were both wide awake and fully dressed. I sent a text to Eddie, letting him know that Aaron was at home, awake and in the library, a convenient 10 feet from the front door.

As the appointed hour grew near, the minutes dragged on. Tammy and I stayed back in the master bedroom with the dogs. Both dogs sat upright, their ears up and forward, heads and necks erect. Shortly before 12:30 the dogs stirred and we heard the sound of a car coming up the driveway. We walked to the front hall, exuding whatever calm demeanor we could muster.

As I opened the door, Aaron turned to look over his shoulder. A look of resignation crossed his face and he didn't even get up from his chair.

Following the script, I just said, "Aaron, this is Eddie."

"We love you," Tammy added.

We turned and walked away.

Eddie's soft voice was barely audible, and Aaron's tone was quiet and calm as well. After a few minutes, Eddie's wife came back.

"He'd like to say goodbye to the dogs," she said, adding, "You can come out too."

Aaron bent down and petted Hattie and Dolly.

I gave Aaron a firm handshake. "Good luck," I said.

Tammy fought back tears and gave Aaron a hug.

Once the car pulled away, we called family members to let them know that Aaron was on his way and that, all things considered, the handoff went well. Both of us put up a good front, but keeping our composure wasn't easy. Especially when I placed a call to Brooke.

"He's gone," I said. "We're heading out in the morning. We'll get together when we get back in town."

◆ ◆ ◆

Though the die was cast, Tammy and I wanted to see the ranch. We scheduled a 6:00 a.m. flight to Las Vegas. Final destination: Escalante, Utah. I was too wired for sleep, so I stayed up and watched a movie.

We reached Las Vegas early Friday afternoon, boarded a shuttle to the rental car terminal, and headed north across the desert. The scenery between Las Vegas and Escalante is breathtaking, particularly the deep red hues of the mountains in the Zion National Forest. Dried up gullies run along the road and vegetation is sparse. Snow-capped mountains circle the horizon in an unending ring. But at that point, our hearts were so heavy it was difficult to enjoy the scenery, no matter how breathtaking.

We found the ranch on the outskirts of what passes for the town of Escalante. At the base of the ranch was a small white house and a wood-framed chapel. The parking lot consisted of a smattering of gravel on the hardened dirt. Aaron was already at the ranch, but we were not to see him. Instead, we toured the grounds and reviewed the details of Aaron's diabetes management regimen.

A staff member met us at the office and we delivered additional medical supplies. Three boxes of clothes had been shipped two days earlier. Ironically, being sent away meant new clothes. We had been instructed on the TAR dress code: no-brand jeans, black or blue t-shirts with no slogans, and simple cowboy boots. The signature red hat to be worn outdoors at all times would be provided upon arrival.

One of the ranch directors arrived in a jeep to give us a tour. A couple of kids gave us a tour of the lodge where Aaron would be staying for the next 100 days. Both had been at the ranch for more than 80 days, and they were counting the days. There were no calendars in sight, but I saw notches on the bed posts.

The guys took us out back and showed us how to rope a calf, using a metal frame replica of a calf. "That's a half," the kid said as he swung the rope around one of the metal horns. "We have to be able to do both a half and a full—that's over both horns."

"Aaron will never master that," I said to myself.

We learned that upon arrival at Rowdy, the kids are told to remove their shoes because teenagers are less likely to make a run across the desert if they're going on bare feet. Still, we heard stories about a girl who made it two miles into the desert before the tracker arrived in a jeep to bring her back.

The ranch's tracker fit Hollywood's image of a mountain man. He stood over six feet tall with a 40-inch waistline, a long scruffy beard and unkempt hair. He wore cowboy boots, a Stetson and a leather vest.

Aaron tells a story of a 15-year-old who threatened to make a run. The tracker sat quietly at the table, sipping his soup. "Just remember," he said, "I'll find you. And out in the mountains, it's just you and me. My word against yours." The kid slept in his bunk that night.

Quite honestly, I admired the tracker's technique. I could tell from his soft eyes that he liked those kids, and his goal was to keep the kid in his bunk and out of the desert.

After a couple of hours, we finished the tour and headed back through the mountains toward Las Vegas. Tammy was particularly torn up, knowing that Aaron was on the ranch and she couldn't see him, not even at a distance.

We attended Easter services at the First Presbyterian Church of Las Vegas. The church appeared to be of 1970s vintage based on the architecture, a single floor with large windows in the sanctuary. Looking around at the congregation of retirees, we worried that we might be candidates for the "moments with children" segment. Eventually some grandkids came in as families filled up the pews. Tammy and I set aside the irony and smiled politely as we shook hands with the families seated nearby.

Our Easter dinner was at a patio restaurant along the Strip. We spent the afternoon touring the casinos, where the crowds seemed oblivious to the day of the week, much less Easter. We headed home the next day.

◆ ◆ ◆

Aaron survived his three days sitting outside at Rowdy, confined in silence to the circle of rocks that surrounded his fire. His first post on the ranch's website read: "My activities were writing letters home.... I also cooked over a fire.... I have learned that I miss my parents.... I also learned not to let blind cats near a fire." We received Aaron's letter a few days later. It was brief and to the point. Suffice it to say, he was not a happy camper.

Aaron moved on to the lodge, and we received weekly updates via the ranch website. A new picture was posted each week along with a note from Aaron. The first photograph showed a tired, defiant teenager. Later photographs showed hints of a smile. In his posts he mentioned shearing sheep, fixing a pipe leak, digging fence postholes and stacking hay. Aaron's letters remained terse, except for his story about roping a calf and cutting off the testicles. On that occasion, he offered an animated and detailed depiction of the entire process. Castrating a calf was undoubtedly the highlight of his TAR experience.

He also talked about some of the other kids. "After being here for a few weeks, I was able to meet other kids that were in a lot worse situations than me. We are not bad people, we just need a chance to redeem ourselves."

◆ ◆ ◆

Tammy and I took our second trip to Turn-About Ranch on Mother's Day weekend. The occasion was the midterm visit, a chance to spend two days with Aaron and talk with his personal counselor.

We came alone, saying no to Brooke's continued requests that she accompany us as his surrogate sister. "He's like a brother to me," she pleaded.

Lodging at Escalante consisted of a small bed and breakfast and rental cabins. The innkeeper had not seen us before, so he correctly guessed that we were arriving for midterm. We quickly discovered that Escalante's dining options were likewise few and far between. We chose a pizza place within sight of the motel.

We were seated outside on the deck, and after a few minutes a woman at the next table interrupted our conversation. A plump woman in her early forties, she didn't have the tanned, rugged look of the locals. "Excuse me," she said. "I couldn't help but overhear you talking. Are you here for Turn-About also?" We soon realized that TAR families monopolized four of the five tables. Two were attending for graduation and the other for the midterm visit. We moved the tables around and shared common stories of rebellious teenagers, hanging on any word that provided encouragement or a sign of hope.

The woman who initiated the conversation said that she and her husband had seen signs of improvement in their son during the midterm visit. They were anxious, but optimistic that their son would get back on track once he returned home.

The other graduating family was from Southern California. They assured us that they had seen improvement in their 16-year-old son. Of course, they planned to leave from TAR and take the teen to a six month "step-down" program. The father apparently worked in the investment business and seemed unfazed at spending another $50,000 to board his teenage son until Christmas. They had a daughter who seemed intent on avoiding the fate of her older brother.

A husband and wife, whose only child was at TAR, were attending for the midterm visit. They were from upstate New York and worked together in the real estate business. The wife seemed traumatized by the anticipation of seeing her son for the first time in six weeks and listened intently to the other parents. Her husband spent much of the evening sitting in his rented BMW focused on closing a sale and making dinner reservations for Sunday night in Vegas.

◆ ◆ ◆

The kids were not told in advance that it was time for midterm visits, though their bedpost tally probably gave them some idea. The parents gathered in the classroom building located across a field from the lodge. Shortly after nine o'clock, we saw the kids leaving the lodge. As soon as they saw faces in the window, Aaron and another kid broke into a run.

Aaron was wearing blue jeans, a black t-shirt, boots and a jacket. He held a red baseball cap in his hand. Leather work gloves were sticking out of his back pocket. He'd lost some weight and shed his long hair.

Tears flowed, mostly from the parents, as the kids came upstairs. We hadn't seen or talked to Aaron since that night almost two months earlier when Eddie appeared at the front door. Tammy rushed over to give Aaron a hug. I waited a moment and then gave him a firm handshake.

"Did you bring Brooke?" he asked.

"This time it's just us," Tammy said.

"You should have brought her," Aaron said. "Siblings are allowed to come."

Though we were his only visitors, Aaron still seemed happy to see us.

"I wasn't sure if this was the weekend, but I knew it was soon," he said. "When we didn't go with everyone else this morning, we figured it was our turn."

We walked around the main buildings and then drove over to Rowdy. Aaron introduced us to the resident cat. He picked up the cat, affectionately stroking its fur. Pointing out the cat's charred tail, he told us about the cat's story. "He came over to see me when I first got here," Aaron said. "He's blind and he gets too close to the fires."

A log cabin serves as the staff quarters and storage building. A corrugated metal tub hung on the wall. "That's what we use for hygiene," Aaron explained. "We haul buckets of water from the creek and hold them over the fire for hot water." He added, "They only give you 10 minutes to bathe."

Aaron was excited for us to meet Wayne, one of the two supervisors at Rowdy. Aside from maintaining order, Wayne's job included teaching the kids how to start a fire with two sticks and how to throw a hatchet.

I was dubious about the chances of a kid who played video games 12 hours a day learning to start a fire without a lighter. Wayne insisted that Aaron show us how it's done. Aaron carefully laid out the twigs and dead grass and then methodically started rubbing sticks together. When a spark appeared, he quickly laid the stick near the pile and then softly blew on the spark with measured breaths. The dead grass caught the spark, and within seconds the twigs were on fire.

Next Aaron showed off his prowess with a hatchet, throwing it so that it stuck in a tree about 10 feet away.

"Impressive," I said.

"I can teach you to do that in two throws," Wayne boasted.

"Right," I thought.

Tammy looked at me skeptically with a grin.

I threw once to no avail.

"Look at your release point," Wayne said. It struck me that the key was releasing the hatchet so that the head would be rotating toward the tree when it struck. I focused on the release point and threw it again.

Whump! The ax blade struck the tree and dug in. Both Tammy and Aaron cheered.

We were also required to participate in group activities at Rowdy. One was the trust fall, which entailed each of us falling backward off a five-foot-high platform, much like the old Lipton Tea commercials. Except that instead of falling into a swimming pool, we were falling into the arms of a group of middle-aged parents and rebellious teenagers, "trusting" that they would catch us. Tammy volunteered to go first. She fell straight back with full faith that we would catch her. I admit my legs buckled.

Aaron showed us around the main campus, which consisted of two lodge buildings, the classrooms and the barn. Dotted around the campus were circles of rocks.

"Those are impact circles," Aaron explained. "When you get in trouble you have to go sit in the circle and you can't talk to anyone."

"Have you been sentenced to impact?" I asked.

"Couple of times."

Changing the subject, I asked, "How's the roping?"

"I'll show you," he answered, pulling on his leather gloves and picking up a rope. He lassoed both horns on the first try.

Next we headed to the barn. The place was spotless—as much as a barn can be—and the tack room was immaculate.

"Everything has to be in place," Aaron explained. He selected a bridle and took us out to meet Linus. Taking responsibility for a horse and learning to ride is a key part of the TAR program. Aaron loves horses, and he was clearly showing off in hopes we would buy him a horse.

For the afternoon, we were allowed to take Aaron off campus so long as we stayed within a 20-mile radius. We stopped for ice cream at the local dairy bar. Three-fourths of the customers were families like ours, two parents and a teenager wearing a red ball cap. Later we found a park and walked the few streets of Escalante. On Saturday we were allowed to take him off site for the day and the radius was extended to 50 miles. We drove east into the mountains and ate lunch in what passed for the nearest town.

The scenery was incredible and we stopped a couple of times to get out and walk around. We talked some about Aaron's "self-reflection" and how he might do better, but mostly we just tried to enjoy the time together. We had a 5:30 p.m. deadline to have Aaron back at the ranch. We said our goodbyes, leaving Aaron behind and heading back for our second visit to Las Vegas.

Mother's Day in Vegas was no different than Easter in Vegas. We ventured into the casinos after lunch. One of our law partners had told us to bet $20 on the roulette wheel—5 red. Ten minutes later we left empty-handed and spent the rest of the day walking on the Strip before catching the red-eye.

A few days later, Aaron's update on the site was that his accomplishment for the week was "getting along with my parents." He added, "I miss everyone. It was hard to see my parents leave again."

◆ ◆ ◆

Aaron's graduation from Turn-About Ranch was the fourth week of June, the same week as his birthday. We arrived on Thursday, and Aaron was allowed to leave the ranch and stay with us for the two days before the ceremony.

We met again with Aaron's personal counselor. The meeting was less than productive. The counselor suggested that we send Aaron to boarding school, and he recommended a school in the northeast. We responded that boarding school was not an option, both financially and because we didn't feel that we could send Aaron away again.

Following the meeting, we made the rounds to thank the staff before attending the horsemanship show. Aaron showed his horse along with a girl from Minneapolis who also arrived on Maundy Thursday. Her parents explained that she was heading out to a six week "step-down program."

The graduation ceremony was based on a Native American tribal ceremony. Parents and teens sat in a circle. Everyone, including moms and dads, had to read their own self-reflection statement. Tears flowed and we acted like all would be fine, but privately Tammy and I braced ourselves for the three weeks between coming home and the start of band camp.

As we left Escalante, Aerosmith's "Highway to Hell" blared from the radio. Aaron broke into a wide grin and altered the words, singing "Highway from Hell" at the top of his lungs.

Once again we were flying out of Las Vegas. We showed Aaron the Strip and attended a show, but passed on the casinos.

"Maybe we'll come back when you're 21," I told him.

"SOMETIMES I STILL HEAR YOUR VOICE"

MR. SCOTT HAD A plan.
During summer band camp, director Bob Scott assigned Aaron and Cody as roommates. It was Aaron's sophomore year and Cody's junior year. Tammy and I arrived at Concord College on Saturday to watch the band practice its show and bring Aaron home.

After the show, Mr. Scott darted back and forth between the instrument trailers, stopping to give instructions and answer questions. Despite his small stature (just over five-and-a-half feet) and the gray pony tail extending through the back of his Capital High band ball cap, Mr. Scott had a commanding presence. Having been the band director since the school opened 18 years earlier, when Mr. Scott barked out orders across the parking lot, both students and parents obeyed.

I was standing amid the seeming chaos when I saw Mr. Scott pivot on his left foot and start walking toward me in long strides.

"Those two can use each other," he bellowed, pointing to Aaron and Cody as they pushed a xylophone up the trailer ramp. A few minutes later, I saw the guys throwing backpacks and pillows into the back of Tammy's minivan.

"We're giving Cody a ride home," Tammy said nonchalantly.

◆ ◆ ◆

Cody was a big guy, standing nearly six feet tall and weighing well over 200 pounds, and played the tuba. "Actually, the marching instrument is called a sousaphone," he corrected me, explaining that the tuba had been modified for marching bands by John Philip Sousa. Cody's knowledge of marching band trivia stood in marked contrast to the first impression he created with his shoulder-length hair, scuffed black motorcycle boots and tattered white t-shirt. His given name is Gunner, but he goes by Cody.

Aaron and Cody continued to hang around together. We often gave Cody a ride to and from football games and band festivals. Before long, Cody was coming home with us and sleeping over. We celebrated his birthday with his favorite meal, fried chicken, and added another pair of band bibs to the laundry after each football game and band festival.

Seeing the guys arriving together, Mr. Scott nodded with approval. "They're good for each other," he said. "Cody's a good kid, but he tries too hard to act like the tough guy. Aaron's not afraid to tell him to calm down. Aaron needs somebody to keep him in line, and Cody isn't afraid to do that."

Cody stayed over for Thanksgiving, which turned out to be a blessing. On the Monday before Thanksgiving, Tammy hit a deer at the bottom of the driveway. Cody knew how to field dress a deer. He took charge and showed Aaron how it's done. On Thanksgiving morning, I came down to the garage to find Aaron and Cody standing at a card table cutting up deer meat. The table, floor and both guys' clothes were covered in blood.

"Good morning!" Cody said. "Care for some venison?"

"Mr. Scott likes liver," Aaron said.

"We'll save it for him," Cody said holding up a red glob dripping with blood.

◆ ◆ ◆

Cody and Aaron had the same geometry teacher, though they weren't in the same class. They both complained about the teacher, who was admittedly "old school." Cody's geometry class was scheduled right after the first lunch period, and he started skipping class to have lunch with his girlfriend. With so many kids at lunch, the staff did not notice that Cody was taking an extra lunch period.

But somehow Tammy found out.

"Listen up, young man," Tammy said one night. "If you don't stop skipping geometry, I'm going to come to Capital High School at 12:25 and I'll walk you to class."

"Yeah, right," Cody laughed. "I dare you."

"We'll see," Tammy answered.

Aaron looked at Cody and shook his head.

I sensed that Cody had mixed emotions. He feared the embarrassment of being escorted to class, but at the same time he wanted to see if Tammy truly cared enough to escort him to class.

He got an answer within two days. Tammy left the office shortly after noon and headed to the high school. This continued for several days until Cody agreed that he preferred to go to class on his own.

A few weeks later Tammy sent the teacher an e-mail about Aaron's grades. The reply contained an additional message: "YOS has been skipping again." Tammy quickly interpreted the acronym to mean "your other son."

From that day forward, we referred to Cody as "YOS," and Tammy periodically showed up at the commons to make sure her other son was still going to geometry class. Cody didn't mind the "YOS" moniker, but his mother started grounding him from overnight stays.

"Don't worry," Aaron promised. "When you turn 18 you can move in permanently."

◆ ◆ ◆

By the fall of Cody's senior year, Aaron, due to his contin-ued truancy problems, had been moved to a juvenile facility in Huntington, about an hour away. Still, we made sure Cody had transportation to football games and band festivals, and I stayed on as a member of the team of band parents who handled props for the shows.

On one of our weekly calls, Aaron reminded us of his promise. "Cody turns 18 this month," he said. "Remember, I told him you guys would let him live with us."

"If that's what he wants to do, it's okay with us," I said.

"He's planning on it. You know he doesn't get along with his mother."

We invited Cody to come over for dinner to celebrate his birthday with fried chicken and ice cream. That evening I sent him a text to find out what time I should pick him up. He said he'd be ready close to seven o'clock. When I reached the top of the hill and turned to the left to park, Cody was sitting in the window at the end of the trailer where his room was located. He held out a suitcase.

"Just in time," he said as I got out of the car. "Can you put this in the car while I get more stuff?"

His mother stood at the edge of the trailer and glared at me. I hauled a few loads while listening passively to Cody and his mother debate what belonged to him. Once I knew he had his clothes, computer and television, I suggested that he leave the rest for another day.

"We're not going to solve anything now," I said in a firm lawyer voice. "Let's get going."

◆ ◆ ◆

Cody moved into Aaron's bedroom. We didn't have enough furni-ture for the television and computer, so Cody undertook to build an entertainment center. He carefully selected individual pieces of treated lumber for the project and consulted with his grandfather regarding what gauge screws were best. He finished by staining the wood with a red-toned stain.

Cody brought Tammy and me to the garage to show off the finished product.

"How are we going to get it upstairs to your bedroom?" we asked.

"We can carry it," Cody replied with his typical bravado.

I eyeballed the dimensions and lifted one end about an inch off the ground.

"This weighs a ton," I announced. "No way are we going to be able to carry it."

Seeing the disappointment in Cody's face, I quickly improvised a solution. "We can haul it in Tammy's car to the front door, and from that point we'll use furniture pads."

"My car's not that big," Tammy said.

"We'll make it work," Cody replied.

And make it work we did.

Once inside, we set the center on furniture pads and maneuvered it across the hardwood floor with ease—until we reached the hallway to the bedroom. The hallway runs perpendicular to the family room, thus requiring a sharp turn from the doorway to the hallway. In a scene reminiscent of my parents moving a player piano into three basements, we somehow managed to employ Cody's geometry knowledge to make the turn.

◆ ◆ ◆

December marked one of the coldest winters on record, and a winter storm knocked out the power at the house. In our case, that meant no lights, no heat and no running water. Since we had two dogs, looking for other accommodations was not an option. We took Cody with us to take showers at the office and spent the evenings tending the fire. Everyone slept on the floor near the fireplace.

We ventured to Home Depot one Sunday when a load of generators was scheduled to arrive. We stood in line for over an hour and the crowd grew restless. At one point I thought Cody might assume the role of sergeant-at-arms, but fortunately the truck arrived before the crowd grew out of hand. We loaded a new generator in the back of Tammy's SUV.

Cody drove home without incident—at least until the final turn in our driveway. That's when the tires slipped. Before Cody could right the steering wheel, both wheels on the passenger side were off the pavement. Cody let out a stream of expletives.

"I guess we'll carry the generator from here," I said calmly. It was getting dark by the time we were finished with the generator, which we couldn't get to run because I didn't have enough gasoline, and I didn't want to risk putting a second car in a ditch.

"Let's go sit by the fire, I said. "You can do your homework by candlelight again."

"I can get the car," he insisted.

"Tomorrow."

The next morning we left together in my car. Tammy's SUV remaining stranded.

"I'll call AAA later today," Tammy said.

"If we could get some rope, I could get it out," Cody said. "We'll wrap the rope around the tree and—"

"Cody," I declared. "We're getting the car out by check."

The power remained off for several more days. One night I came home after work and found Cody and Tammy sitting by the fire.

"We're cooking supper," he said. "Grilled cheese and tomato soup." Cody held a cast-iron frying pan over the fire while Tammy heated the soup.

Cody enjoyed cooking. He often helped Tammy in the kitchen, paying close attention to her lessons. At the same time, he offered his own culinary insight: "Everything is better with bacon."

The power came back on in time for Christmas. Aaron got to come home for the holiday and we enjoyed our traditional Christmas Eve dinner together. Afterward, I ran over to a friend's house to pick up the Xbox to be left under the tree for Cody on Christmas morning. In keeping with tradition, Tammy found special ornaments for both guys. We think about Cody every year when we hang the sousaphone ornament.

◆ ◆ ◆

We stayed home for New Year's Eve, planning a simple champagne toast at midnight. However, Aaron had either failed to take enough insulin to cover for supper or significantly underestimated his carb count. He grew sicker and more irritable as the night went on. By midnight he was lying on the couch with the telltale signs of high blood sugar.

"You probably have ketones," Tammy said. "We should get you to the hospital."

"No!" he screamed. "I'll be fine."

"Aaron!" Cody said in a tone that was firm without being bossy. "Let's call an ambulance and get you to the emergency room."

"No!"

I appraised the situation. Tammy looked pale, almost on the verge of tears. Cody's face betrayed his self-imposed "tough guy" facade. Both were clearly worried.

"Look," I said. "If he doesn't want to go, it's his choice. We just have to go to bed. Hopefully he'll be alive in the morning."

We delayed a minute to see if my comment had caused Aaron to change his mind. When it was apparent that he was not budging, we headed to our respective bedrooms, passing on the traditional champagne toast.

Cody noticed how I approached situations more diplomatically than he did.

"I don't know, it's just not in my nature to be calm," he told me. I already knew that, having listened to the fourth quarter of the Super Bowl on the radio as I drove through the East End looking for Cody. Minutes after the Colts sealed their victory, Cody's girlfriend sent Tammy a text that Cody was at the emergency room.

Apparently he'd lost his cool—he couldn't really say why—and he tried to bust out a brick wall.

"You've got to pick your battles," I often said. "Sometimes 'being a man' means having the confidence to stand down."

◆ ◆ ◆

Cody was attending class without need of an escort, but we still kept abreast of his school work. We took him to a performance of *Macbeth* at the Greenbrier Valley Theatre. He was most interested in Act V, Scene viii. That's when Macduff enters stage right carrying Macbeth's head. We also watched the movie *Tuesdays With Morrie*. Cody and Tammy enjoyed the book, though I questioned why Cody wasn't reading *Hamlet*. Having read both *Macbeth* and *Hamlet* during high school, I wouldn't have needed to buy the book.

We continued to encourage Cody to maintain as close to a B average as possible in hopes that he would qualify for a college scholarship. The majors he was considering were culinary management and forensic science. He was interested in a small college in Kentucky, and a recruiter visited Cody at the house. I talked at length with Cody about the pros and cons of a small college versus a large university. Tammy stayed in contact with the recruiter and the admissions office.

In mid-April, Cody brought home his report card for the third nine weeks. "Passing all of my classes," he said, sliding the paper across the table.

"But a D is not all Cs or better," Tammy said, passing the card back. "We want more for you."

"I'm 18 years old. I'm an adult," he said.

"And you live in our house," I replied. "I recognize you're free to make your own choices, but I'm not going to sit back quietly and watch you make bad decisions."

Cody was 18 and when he announced that he was moving back

to his parents', all we could do was help him pack. And even though he wasn't planning to go to college that fall, we still watched with pride as Cody walked across the stage and received his diploma.

◆ ◆ ◆

Cody started working that summer through a temporary service, doing general labor at the Civic Center.

"The supervisor is an idiot," Cody told me one evening.

"You just need to bite your lip and do what he tells you," I said.

"He's wrong," Cody replied.

"He's your supervisor."

"But he's an idiot," Cody persisted.

"And he's your boss," I replied.

Another time, Cody posted his work grievances publicly on Facebook.

"OK, you don't like your supervisor," my private message to him read. "Now the whole world knows. None of this is private, trust me. My advice—don't put this out on FB."

"I meant for him to see it," Cody responded. "He can't fire me over my opinion."

"As a lawyer, I'm not too sure about that."

"Would It make u feel better if I took it down?" he asked.

"Yes."

"OK. There ya go," Cody replied, showing the "edited" post.

The following year Cody became a father. He comes by both the house and the office on occasion with his baby girl. Often he asks for advice, both legal and other. "I knew that's what you'd say" is a common refrain.

On one visit Cody sat at the kitchen table, beaming with pride as his girl bounced on his knee.

"How old is she?" I asked.

"26 months."

"And she already has pierced ears?"

"Not my idea," Cody said, glancing over to make sure his wife was still absorbed in conversation with Tammy. "But I recall what you used to say: 'Pick your battles.'"

"Good call," I said, nodding my head.

"Yeah, sometimes I still hear your voice in the back of my head."

GREEN CAP AND GOWN

FROM THE DAY WE adopted Aaron, we knew he'd go to college. The only question was whether he would attend my alma mater, Michigan State, or my dad's alma mater, the University of Minnesota. We visited both campuses when Aaron was in middle school. When he joined the Capital High School Marching Band, I told Aaron and Justin that one day they might perform at the Rose Bowl.

Aaron marched to "Pomp and Circumstance" wearing a green cap and gown, but when the Spartan Marching Band marched onto the field at the Rose Bowl, Aaron watched as a spectator.

◆ ◆ ◆

In elementary school Aaron was an enigma. He was a below average speller and slow in math, but his vocabulary was off the charts. During one conference, the principal noted his spelling grade and followed by asking about vocabulary.

"Oh my," the teacher said with a wide-eyed look. "He's got a better vocabulary than me."

Aaron was an avid reader, although his grades didn't always show it. One time he read a story at home and talked about the story in detail with Tammy. The next day he brought home a worksheet with all wrong answers. He explained that they had to finish it before they could go out for recess.

"But you knew the answers," Tammy said.

"Yeah, but all we had to do was fill in the blanks and those words were shorter."

During middle school, Aaron's academic issues appeared to stem from a tendency to use his diabetes as a virtual hall pass and an inexplicable failure to turn in assignments. To this day, he persists in pleading his innocence.

"I turned in those assignments," he says indignantly. "The teacher lost them!"

When Aaron entered high school, we anticipated that he would grow out of his sloth-like approach and blossom. He got to know a lot of the upperclassmen during band camp. When classes started, he was anxious to meet up with the rest of the brass section. Tammy and I watched every band performance with pride as Aaron caught on to the band's routines without a hitch. While his classroom performance was not exactly stellar, he managed passing grades. But following the fall band season, Aaron appeared more lackadaisical. At first he just missed the car pool and we raced to school to beat the tardy bell. Then he started to miss most of his first period class.

One day in late January I was driving into work when Tammy called to say that Aaron was refusing to go at all. I blew a gasket as I turned around and stomped into the house yelling "Aaron!" at the top of my lungs. No kid of mine was going to stay home from school.

Within a few days, however, Aaron tested my resolve. Weighing almost 200 pounds and standing a mere two inches shorter than me, physically dragging him out of bed was not an option. Instead, I called his bluff and said to Tammy, "We need to go to work. He's had his chance and he can suffer the consequences."

Aaron discovered the consequences when he found himself on a plane bound for Escalante, Utah, home of the Turn-About Ranch program for troubled teenagers. He finished out the semester at TAR and returned home for his sophomore year.

Once again Aaron managed to stay focused through most of the fall band season and then fell into his old habits. We tried everything to coerce Aaron to get to school. Mr. Scott, the band director, volunteered to come by the house at 6:30 a.m. to offer Aaron a ride. Our younger neighbors came over to rouse Aaron out of bed and take him to school. Justin's grandmother let Aaron stay over on school nights so that Aaron would ride to school with Justin. Nothing seemed to work.

◆ ◆ ◆

In mid-March the school filed truancy charges.

The first stage involved a referral to the state welfare department to investigate why the student was truant—in other words, to find out if it's the parents' fault.

"We're lawyers," we explained. "We value education." Having read about parents being charged in connection with student truancies, I reiterated that we were not the problem. But rules are rules and procedures are procedures. The department assigned a mentor to Aaron, and his first responsibility was to complete the required home study.

"I need to observe the entire family," the mentor informed us. "Is there a time when you are all home?"

"I run on Monday, Wednesday and Friday," I said. "But come any Tuesday or Thursday. We're usually up by 6:00."

On the following Tuesday, I was showered and dressed when Aaron's mentor arrived promptly at 6:00 a.m. I sipped my coffee and read the newspaper under the watchful eye of the West Virginia Department of Health and Human Resources. The mentor, Rami, sat quietly across the room. I tried my best to be a good sport and act as if no one was in my family room, but I was too polite and too curious not to start a conversation.

"Where are you from?" I asked.

"Palestine."

I was taken aback. I'd never before heard anyone refer to Palestine, as opposed to Israel.

"What brings you to West Virginia?" I asked.

"I'm a Christian," Rami explained. "We're persecuted in Palestine."

The irony was overwhelming. Here was a man who had left his parents on the West Bank and fled for religious freedom, and my son was upset because he didn't like his science teacher.

Rami tried, but in the end he failed to get through to Aaron. The DHHR sent another mentor. Bryan visited shortly after we came home from work one evening. Tammy and I walked outside when we saw the compact car pull up. We stood in awe as a figure standing almost seven feet tall worked himself out of the car.

We sat with Aaron at the kitchen table and talked for almost an hour. I listened politely, all the while thinking, "This guy must have been a basketball player." When we were done talking with Aaron, Bryan asked if we had any questions. I was too intimidated to ask.

"Let me tell you about me," he volunteered. "I played basketball for WVU and then for the Globetrotters."

In contrast to Rami, Bryan used a more direct, "in your face," approach with Aaron. "Man," he'd tell Aaron. "You need to get it together. Be a man for crying out loud."

Despite the mentors' best efforts, Aaron continued to miss school. Failing to show up for summer school was the last straw. In July Aaron was placed in state custody at a juvenile detention facility in Huntington just over an hour away. We were allowed one 5-minute telephone call per week and one 30-minute visit per month. I happened to be in Huntington for a meeting on the day of our first call, so I drove by the facility out of curiosity. Promptly at seven o'clock, I found a parking lot and called in on my cell phone.

"Hey," Aaron said when he came on the line.

I struggled to find the right words. Casually saying "How's it going?" seemed out of place. I could offer nothing more than, "Hey, it's good to hear your voice."

Aaron started asking questions about the legal process. "Aaron, it's out of our hands," was all I could say. Before I knew it, Aaron was saying, "I've only got another minute." He asked about Dolly and Hattie and I assured him that both dogs were fine.

The following week I had a major trial. On Sunday, however, I put my trial materials aside and drove to the facility for my first in-person visit. I had to wait a couple of minutes before someone came to open the door, and then I waited in the hallway. Aaron came down the hall, wearing gym shorts and a t-shirt. We exchanged a firm Owen handshake. Aaron showed me his room, which he shared with another resident, and then we looked for a private place to talk.

We found two kitchen chairs, circa 1957, and set them out on the cracked linoleum floor in the dimly lit hallway. I was taken aback by the reality of the situation. My son was detained in a state facility, known to the kids as "juvie," and I had less than an hour.

"Have you talked to the social worker?" Aaron asked.

I bluntly replied, "No, it's out of our hands."

Aaron started to say, "I don't know why," but I cut him off.

"You stopped going to school. This is not what Tammy and I want either," I said. "But there's nothing we can do."

I steered the conversation away from pleas for Tammy and me to somehow use our "connections" to fix the situation. Instead, we talked about the routine at the facility. The food was okay, and once a week they took a trip to the store and the residents were allowed to buy soda. Having only one television without an Xbox met their definition of cruel and unusual punishment.

After awhile we went outside and took turns shooting baskets. The cracked asphalt court and adjacent grass field were surrounded by an eight-foot-high chain-length fence.

"I don't know why they have the fence," Aaron said. "They can't come after you if you leave."

"Seriously?"

"Last week some kid left," Aaron told me. "They just tell your judge."

"Well, I wouldn't advise making a run for it."

◆ ◆ ◆

Later in the fall, Tammy and I were permitted to take Aaron off site for a couple of hours, and eventually he qualified for an overnight trip home once a month. When we dropped Aaron off on Sunday nights, he had to check in with the counselor on duty and empty his pockets to ensure that he wasn't bringing in any electronic devices or other contraband.

Aaron now talks about how he stashed cigarettes in his underwear. "You could sell them for a dollar each," he boasts. When anyone asks how the residents managed not to get caught, Aaron repeats the mantra, "Snitches and bitches end up in ditches with stitches."

At the same time, Aaron did attend class. He completed the fall semester on site and attended Huntington High School for the second semester. At the end of the semester, Aaron discovered that he was just shy of the number of credits necessary to be classified as a senior. Two months later we conceded and asked the judge to release Aaron and allow him to work toward a GED.

◆ ◆ ◆

I knew the ins and outs of the GED process, having shepherded Sierra through the process two years earlier. When Sierra came to live with us, Tammy and I had qualms about whether she could manage the Big Ten social scene, so we encouraged Sierra to consider small colleges dedicated to music. The summer before Sierra's senior year, she attended a two-week intensive music study at Ithaca College. She remained on the college track at the start of her senior year, but within three months of moving out, she quit school.

Except for seeing Sierra for her 19th birthday, I didn't see or hear from her for almost a year. I created a MySpace page in hopes of staying in touch with Sierra, but received scant messages in return and eventually no response whatsoever. I finally reached the breaking point. It was time to give up, delete the MySpace profile, and move on.

That same night I was reading *Facing the Giants*, Max Lucado's book about the biblical story of David. A chapter titled "Tough Promises" tells the story of David and Mephibosheth, the invalid he invited to his table because of a promise he had made long ago to Saul.

Sitting in our living room in a leather chair, I broke down in tears. It was as if the author were speaking to me personally. Prompted by the author's questions, I realized that I was tired, I was angry, I was disappointed. And, like David, I had made a promise. I had to ask myself, "Could I give it another chance?"

The MySpace profile remained open.

A few months later a new message appeared out of the blue. Sierra had broken up with her boyfriend and moved back to Charleston. She asked if there was any chance I could take her to South Carolina to retrieve her belongings. Two days later, we were on our way to Myrtle Beach. On the trip back, I casually mentioned that I had seen an advertisement for GED classes. Sierra's response was to look for another radio station.

Three weeks later she asked, "Did you ever find out about those GED classes?"

I took Sierra to the adult education center, housed in a building downtown that had once served as the high school for African Americans before integration. We strolled the hallways while waiting to meet with the counselor. The students were truly diverse, ranging from kids Sierra's age to adults who looked to be in their mid-30s. Seeing their faces, I admired their resolve. Each had a story, something that had caused them not to finish high school. Rather than quitting, they were getting back up off the mat.

A counselor explained the GED process. Sierra would take a test to determine what subjects she needed to work on most. She could attend classes in those areas and complete self-paced workbooks. Nothing was mandatory. It was all up to Sierra to decide.

When Sierra had attended high school, I "helped" her with homework. But in GED classes she was on her own. Getting a GED required passing the test designed to ensure that one possessed the knowledge expected of a high school graduate. No brownie points, no extra credit, no help from Ky. Just the student and the test.

◆ ◆ ◆

In November, Sierra passed the pre-test and arranged to take the December exam. I checked the website for results every day. Two days before Christmas the results were in. Sierra's math score was a mere 20 points above the required minimum, but she made up the difference in language arts.

Sierra and I celebrated her GED with a trip to New York City. While there, we visited Madame Tussauds wax museum and saw *Phantom of the Opera*, Sierra's favorite musical. We also dined at Rockefeller Center. In other words, we bought hot dogs from a street vendor near the plaza.

The following spring Sierra handed me a packet from the school. "This is for my graduation," she said.

"Are you going?" I asked.

"Yeah. I don't really want to, but I know it's important to you."

Tammy and I attended the ceremony along with my mom and family friends. Hearing "Pomp and Circumstance" brought shivers to my spine, and I almost cried when Sierra marched in wearing a green cap and gown.

"We got to choose our color," she told me. "I knew you'd want me to wear green."

◆ ◆ ◆

Two years later, I brought Aaron to the same adult education center. He attended the GED classes through the fall and early spring and took the pre-test in late March. His math score was marginal, but otherwise his scores were adequate—except for writing. The question called for a 100-word essay, but Aaron's response consisted of a mere 23 words.

"Aaron," I said. "You've got to pay attention to the directions. It's a 100-word essay."

"It's just a practice test," he said. "Why should I waste my time?"

On the actual test, Aaron padded his essay enough to both pass the language arts test and pick up enough points to offset his math score, which was a mere 10 points above the minimum.

In late May, Aaron marched to "Pomp and Circumstance" wearing a green cap and gown.

In keeping with tradition, Aaron celebrated with a trip to New York. He chose to invite two friends in lieu of staying in the middle of Times Square. The kids insisted that we visit Madame Tussauds wax museum. Like Sierra, they wanted to see *Phantom of the Opera*, so I saw the Broadway production for a second time. On our visit to Battery Park, we ate hot dogs from a street vendor.

◆ ◆ ◆

Our mantle still displays pictures of Aaron and Sierra in green caps and gown.

600LBS OF SIN!

SHORTLY AFTER MIDNIGHT ON Thanksgiving Eve, 2010, Tammy was home stuffing a turkey while I hung out at the Boulevard Tavern. One of several bars located along Charleston's riverfront, the Tavern is a narrow building that runs deep, with brick walls, high ceilings and a long bar running down one side. A washboard hangs over the door near the alcove that serves as the stage. The place was packed and the band was feeding off the energy from the crowd.

"Mr. Moon... won't you come and dance with me," Sierra sang out. Mike and Josh dueled with their acoustic and electric guitars in the background. "Take my hand and spin me around... I can barely see the ground..."

I sat at the bar sipping a Miller Lite longneck. Watching Sierra hold the microphone high and belt out the chorus, it hit me. This is Sierra's world. I saw the same glow that I see when Tammy is closing a deal. The jump in my dad's step when the wire service sounded a four-bell alarm. The feeling I get when arguing to a jury.

Music is her life.

◆ ◆ ◆

For nine years I'd listened to Sierra singing in the car, in church and onstage. As a teenager she sang along to the car radio as she constantly changed the station. More than once I sat in the car in the garage, waiting so Sierra could finish listening to her "favorite" song.

The first time she sang in church, she tenuously walked to the front of the sanctuary and clung tightly to the microphone. During the first verse of "Consider the Lilies" the congregation gasped and the minister's jaw dropped. They watched in awe, realizing that something special was transpiring.

After performing in *Honk!* and *Bye Bye Birdie,* Sierra was one of a select few chorus members in *Anything Goes!* to wear a microphone. The next year she led the GW show choir as soloist in competitions.

When our law firm sponsored Goodwin & Goodwin Night at the baseball park, Tammy negotiated for Sierra to sing the national anthem. Sierra's voice teacher devoted lesson time to "The Star Spangled Banner" and helped Sierra develop her signature twist: reaching a high G on "land of the free."

"I thought she started too high," Tom Goodwin told me, "but by God she went higher. She nailed it."

A couple of years later, the ballpark auditioned for singers. They accepted Sierra on the first verse and she performed at several games. I printed off the lyrics, but Sierra told me not to worry. "The words are on the scoreboard." My heart skipped a beat when the music started and "Sierra Ferrell" came across the scoreboard.

Sierra continued to put on random performances while working as a motel housekeeper and later a barmaid. Once she started singing while trying on boots at the mall. Both staff and customers stopped to listen.

"Whether it's Radio City Music Hall or the shoe store at the mall, to her it's an audience," her boyfriend, James Brown, remarked.

James was also a musician. He played guitar and hosted an open mic night at a local bar. After Sierra turned 21, she and James performed as a duet. One Friday Tammy and I went downtown to a small bar on Capitol Street to hear them. It was casual, just

James on the guitar and Sierra singing Johnny Cash's "Folsom Prison Blues." I loved Sierra's rendition so much that I bought the song on iTunes.

"I love Johnny Cash but never play it because you don't like country," Tammy said. "But Sierra sings one song and you're a fan!"

The following March Sierra announced, "I'm joining a band. The leader of the band is Mike Pushkin. He's a cab driver."

Mike had been on the local music scene for many years. Most recently he had been playing acoustic guitar with Josh Thomas, a fellow guitarist. They billed the duo "The Filthy No Counts." The story goes that Mike sent a text message inviting people to come to a show. Sierra replied that she'd be glad to sing. Mike invited her to sit in, and the duet was history.

◆ ◆ ◆

One Friday in April, I met Sierra outside her new abode, a room she sublet in the West Virginia Music Hall of Fame. I asked if she had any gigs coming up.

"Tonight at Bruno's. You should come."

"I'd like to," I began, "but, I'm leaving early tomorrow for Indianapolis. Michigan State is playing in the Final Four."

"It's an acoustic show. We start at 8:00," she said.

"Where's Bruno's?" I asked.

By the time I arrived, the show was in full swing. The trio was set up in the bay window. Sierra sat squeezed tightly in between Mike and Josh, a cowboy hat pulled down to shadow her face. She sounded good, though the show seemed to focus on the dueling guitars.

A few weeks later Sierra suggested I join James at the "World Famous" Empty Glass to hear the full band. As I handed over a $10 bill for the cover charge, the doorman asked to see my ID.

"I'm old enough to be your father," I said, handing over my license.

"Hey man," James said as we shook hands. "Have you ever been here before?"

"About 25 years ago." Seeing the posters celebrating the "25th anniversary of the Glass," I felt like an artifact.

"Has it changed much?"

"Not a bit."

Mike and Josh took the stage, joined by a drummer and a bass player. Mike played lead guitar and sang vocals. Sierra sang vocals and shook the tambourine during the guitar jams. The band often jammed out the last ten minutes of a set. Josh played guitar, banjo, mandolin or just about any other stringed instrument. The best testament to his string skills was when someone shouted "Freebird." Although the song was outside the band's repertoire, he played the opening chords before a seamless transition to Sierra's "Mr. Moon."

"We're 600LBS OF SIN!" Mike announced. Seeing the crowd's skeptical reaction, he added, "It's a line from a Grateful Dead song, not our combined weight."

Sierra had abandoned the cowboy hat in favor or an eclectic mix of a Cache blouse, Charlotte Russe skirt, a scarf and tights, topped off with black leather knee high boots. In contrast, Mike wore a New York Jets ball cap and a mechanic's shirt that once belonged to some guy named Jennings. Josh wore a colorful knit cap around his dreadlocks, baggy jeans and sandals.

On occasion Sierra donned a full-blown Indian headdress that we gave her for Christmas. The day the headdress arrived, I asked if she was going to wear it to the gig.

"What do you think?" she asked Mike.

"That stage is kinda tight," he said. "And the rest of us will be wearing black."

"Is this some Johnny Cash theme?" I inquired.

"No. The fairs and festivals convention is in town, and our promoter is bringing some people to the show," Mike explained. "We don't dress that well, except for Sierra, but if I tell them to wear black at least we might not have holes in our pants."

◆ ◆ ◆

That summer the band performed at Charleston's inaugural Live on the Levee series, which the city hosted on Friday nights during the summer. The crowd filling the outdoor amphitheater dwarfed the audience at Bruno's. The young girl who tenuously clutched the microphone at Bruno's had developed a stage presence.

Sierra sang "Coffee Bean," one of her first original compositions. "You're some cup of coffee/I don't drink not anymore/without cream and sugar you're not so sweet," the song begins. Breaking off relationships became a common thread in Sierra's songs. The most quoted refrain from "Tidal Wave" is, "First you gotta let go of my hand/do you really call yourself a man/I want to hit you with a frying pan." Former boyfriends insist the songs are about one of their brethren.

During the Levee show, someone handed Sierra a Coke bottle.

"I bet that Coke is spiked," my mom joked. Sure enough. The next day Mike posted on Facebook: "Note to self. Never take a drink of Sierra's Coke."

As the sun set across the river, the crowd grew silent when the band performed "29," Mike's ode to the Upper Big Branch mine disaster.

"I wrote this in my cab taking an organ for transplant to Pittsburgh," he said. That explains the line "objects in this mirror are closer than they appear."

"29" became the title track of the band's first CD. Listening to the CD in the car I grew to love the beat of "Severine," the chords of "Strip Mine," and the sheer beauty of "29." The music is a perfect match for Sierra's voice, and the lyrics capture the culture of West Virginia:

> *Montani Semper Liberi, maybe not free, but we*
> *work real cheap.*
> *Our reward's in the by and by*
> *Where the mountain's high and the coal runs*

deep.
'Til then we love the men we work for.
They feed our families, they pay our bills.
In kind, we dig their mines
And build their mansions on our hills.

◆ ◆ ◆

I stopped worrying about being carded by guys half my age and ventured out on the bar scene more often to hear the band, from old haunts like the Glass to Sound Factory (Spanky's back in my day) to the Adelphia Music Hall in Marietta, Ohio.

"What time is the show tonight?"

Sierra rolled her eyes. "What time do bands start?"

"10 o'clock?"

In fairness, show times are tentative. One Saturday at the Boulevard Tavern I brought a client who operates the local Miller Beer distributorship—Sierra calls him the "Miller Guy"—to hear the band. As 10 o'clock came and went I promised that the band would start "any minute now." After about 10 minutes the band took the stage and performed a song that included Sierra and all the other members with vocal and instrumental solos. Jim and I joined the crowd with the most raucous applause that 30 people can generate.

"Thanks," Mike said. "That was our sound check. We'll be back in five minutes."

◆ ◆ ◆

Tammy accompanied me to the occasional early evening shows, but 10 o'clock was too late for her. I often ended up going out by myself.

One Friday night at Bruno's, I sat by myself at a table in front of the stage. Feeling awkward, I was relieved when a guy came over to the table.

"Anyone sitting here?" he asked.

"No, take a seat," I said politely.

"Are you here alone?"

Then I remembered. Bruno's is next door to the local gay club. Perhaps I was being a bit paranoid, but just in case, I fingered my wedding ring and said, "Just for tonight."

When the band played near Parkersburg, my mom came with me. Her only complaints were the limited wine selection—"red, white or Riesling?"—and the guitar refrains.

"Your Maestro is like Tom Conlin," Frieda said, referring to the former conductor of the West Virginia Symphony. "Never met a refrain he didn't like."

I often refer to Mike as the Maestro. When he told his grandfather that he was the leader of a band, his grandfather replied, "So you're a conductor?" He was also manager, bus driver and roadie.

The band played gigs across the state, as well as in Kentucky, Ohio and Pennsylvania, performing at bars, music festivals and fairs. Whenever I asked Sierra where she was playing, she told me to check www.600LbsofSin.com. The band traveled in an old school bus that Mike picked up for a few hundred dollars. He commissioned a local artist to paint 600LBS OF SIN! and Sierra's picture on the side of the bus. Tammy started calling Sierra "Susan Dey," the female vocalist from the Partridge Family. A couple of years later, the bus gave out. Mike replaced it with an old church van, emblazoned with "First Church of Nazarene" in place of "600LBS OF SIN!"

Aaron, Justin and I followed the bus on a couple of road trips. One Friday after work, we picked up the guys' girlfriends and the five of us packed into the car for the trip to the Goal Rush, located somewhere outside of Worthington, West Virginia. Three and a half hours later we came around a curve and saw the Sin bus parked alongside a roadside shanty with a neon sign.

"This must be the place," I announced.

The sign on the front door read: "Dress code enforced. Management reserves the right to deny admittance to any patron not wearing appropriate dress."

"There's a dress code?" Justin said. Looking at his neon green polo shirt, he asked, "Is this OK?" The answer came as soon as we walked in. The entire crowd wore leather biker jackets, including the women. Fortunately Aaron had an extra hoodie in the car. We found Sierra, adorned with the headdress and perched atop the mechanized bull.

◆ ◆ ◆

The band was again slated to play the Tavern on Thanksgiving Eve. The week before Sierra had gone to Nashville to a concert. On Saturday Mike called to ask if I'd heard from Sierra.

"No, but she told me she has a ride," I replied, trying to effect a confident tone. By Tuesday I was beginning to worry that our Thanksgiving Eve tradition was in danger of ending after one year.

That night I checked for texts and Facebook updates before going to dinner at a neighbor's house. The message was short and to the point: "Do you still have that airplane ticket?" I quickly confirmed flight arrangements, and texted Mike. "Just got a message from the diva. Says she has flight back tomorrow. Arrives 1:54." The next night Sierra walked casually over to the bar to greet Frieda while Mike and Josh profusely thanked me.

"Just trying to do my part," I said.

◆ ◆ ◆

Cinco de Mayo looked to be another tradition. Tammy joined me and the guys to celebrate the Mexican holiday listening to "the hippie-tonk sound of 600LBS OF SIN!" The band was playing the biggest Cinco de Mayo show in the area—hundreds of people gathering on a Thursday night to drink Dos Equis beer and eat authentic Mexican food. The six o'clock starting time brought out friends, colleagues and clients. "That's your daughter?" people asked. "Where did she inherit her talent?" I just smiled.

The tradition didn't turn out as expected. The next year Sierra missed the gig. She was stranded in Nashville again, but rather than calling me for a flight home she hopped a train.

The band found another female vocalist, and I attended shows on the levee and Capitol Street. No more road trips, though.

Sierra came home for Christmas and soon rejoined the band for a second tour.

"Maybe she'll stay this time," I said wistfully.

"If she leaves again, we're just going on with four guys," Mike replied.

Sure enough, that summer the band played on as a foursome, joined occasionally by Mike's girlfriend and Josh's 11-year-old son Jakob. Then, in October, the band updated its Facebook status.

"The 1st Annual 600LBS OF SIN! Farewell Party and Bridge Day."

◆ ◆ ◆

"Is there a band tonight?"

The bartender hesitated, sheepishly eyeing the clock before answering.

"I think they're starting 10:30ish," I interjected.

A late start seemed appropriate for the 600LBS OF SIN! reunion show.

In early December I got a call from Mike. "Hey, I wanted to let you know the band's getting back together for a show. It's December 20th at the Boulevard Tavern."

When I arrived at the Tavern, I met Josh at the bar.

"Did you bring Sierra?" Josh asked.

"No, but she came over to the house to get dressed and I dropped her off back at her friend's house," I told him. "So she's downtown."

"That's good to know."

"She took over an hour to pick out clothes."

"Yeah, I figured," Josh replied. "She told me that the condition for this gig was that we get dressed up." He tugged on his black shirt. "This is as good as it gets for me."

Shortly after 10:30 the band took the stage for the sound check.

"Mr. Moon," Sierra sang a cappella, "won't you come and dance with me?"

"She's awesome," I overheard a young woman tell her friend. "Amazing out of such a little person."

Within minutes the band was going full steam, opening with "Don't Go Away." All the band members had a vocal part, allowing for another sound check. Then the Maestro led straight into "Severine"—one of my personal favorites that is on both *four and 29* and *Money House Blessing*.

"Like a starving street urchin hunting for a lost bread crumb..." As I sang along, Sierra caught my eye over the crowd standing and moving to the beat and smiled.

"Comet tails they don't burn forever."

I sat back and enjoyed one last show.

Going on 1:30 in the morning, the band started one of its guitar jams. The remaining crowd stood and moved to the beat while Sierra flashed the other band members and the ceiling with a green light pointer.

After 15 minutes and countless refrains, I saw Mike switch to his acoustic guitar. He looked over to Josh and raised his arms in a circle. Josh seamlessly moved from "Franklin's Tower" to the opening chords of "Mr. Moon."

Sierra leaned into the microphone and belted out her song.

"Mr. Mooooon, won't you come and dance with me?"

"Thanks for coming out tonight," Mike told the crowd. "And for the last five years."

After two encores, the band posed for pictures. Sierra squeezed in between the guitar players with a shy smile.

I gave her a hug as she came off stage, shook hands with Mike and Josh and quickly departed.

Yes, this is where she belongs.

HOSTING THE HIPPIES

T HERE SHE WAS, IN pigtails and a floppy straw hat, wearing hiking boots, tight shorts and a halter top. Sierra, a petite five foot two inches, stood out against her traveling companions—a robust young woman wearing a patchwork calico dress, a thin, gangly guy and a dark-skinned man standing well over six feet tall, both outfitted in patched up cargo pants. The kids loitered around a picnic table at the Cumberland Scenic Rail Station, with two dogs and a puppy resting in the grass, shaded from the early morning sun.

I ran to Sierra and hugged her.

◆ ◆ ◆

Three months earlier, Sierra was making headlines as lead vocalist with 600LBS OF SIN! One Saturday she sang Elvis' "Fools Fall in Love" at a wedding and the national anthem at a roller derby before joining the band for a show. The press lavished praise on her: "Wearing a tight blue dress, lace stockings, roller skates and a big Indian headdress, reading from a folded sheet of paper and singing acapella, Sierra crushed 'The Star Spangled Banner.' It was mind-blowing how good she sounded." A reviewer applauded the band's upcoming CD, *Money House Blessing*, which included the catchy "Mr. Moon" and other of Sierra's original compositions.

Within a month, the band's publicist wrote that the band lost its vocalist to a journey of "whimsy and longing."

Sierra's journey began with an abrupt phone call. I was concentrating on preparing witness cross-examination for an upcoming trial when the call came. Seeing James Brown, Sierra's old boyfriend, appear on the iPhone caught me by surprise. "I wanted to let you know that your daughter called me at four o'clock this morning asking me to pick her up at a bar," he said. "In St. Louis."

"What?"

"Yeah. She and some girl named Emily are hitchhiking."

Setting aside obvious questions of safety, we both expressed concern about Sierra's upcoming gig two days later in Athens, Ohio. Sierra called James later that afternoon, and when he asked about the gig she responded, "I'm going to a museum."

We heard nothing more until noon Saturday when Sierra reported that she and Emily were "thumbs out" on the I-70 entrance ramp. The next text came at 9:42 p.m. "20 minutes from Athens, Ohio. Booyah!" James said it best, paraphrasing the lyrics of "Baby Girl"—"Please don't worry cause I'm alright, you see I'm playing with the band tonight."

A couple of weeks later I went to see the band play at a roadside bar in rural West Virginia.

"I've been traveling," Sierra smiled.

"So I hear." I told her that I'd see her at the Charleston Cinco de Mayo party headlined by 600LBS OF SIN!

About two hours before the Cinco de Mayo show, I got a text from Mike. Sierra had just called from Nashville to ask what time the band played. I'm sure Sierra had no idea that Nashville is six hours away—and that's with a car. The band improvised the set list, aided by lead guitarist Josh's son taking the stage. On a set break I apologized to the rest of the band and congratulated the budding musician.

"Where's Sierra?" Jakob asked.

"We'll tell you when you're older," I said.

Money House Blessing arrived the following Tuesday. When I met Mike to pick up the CD, he told me, "Sierra asked for directions to Terra Alta for the festival on Saturday. Maybe she'll be back."

"I hope so," I said, though I sensed that both of us were putting up a front.

On Saturday, Tammy and I went to Pittsburgh to shop for my first convertible, a Mini Cooper. A call from James doused the moment. "Have you heard from Sierra? Emily called. She's hasn't seen Sierra since Thursday... outside of Memphis on the Arkansas border."

While Tammy and my mom looked in the boutique stores, I stood on the street corner and googled the Memphis newspapers to see if any young girls had shown up dead.

An hour later Mike called to say that Sierra had reached the state line, but too late for the show. She repeated her promise to return in time for Friday's CD release party. Late in the afternoon on the day of the gig, Sierra checked in from Asheville, North Carolina, three hours away, give or take. She told Mike she was en route, but a few hours later came a terse text saying she wouldn't make it.

I went to the show, both to support the band and for my own therapy. Sitting on a bench in the back, just in front of the sound guy, I sipped my beer and tried to enjoy the music.

"Our lead singer isn't here," the Maestro told the crowd, "and that's all I have to say about that. Auditions start tomorrow."

After the gig, Josh stood on the sidewalk and vented about "playing a CD release party when you can't do half the tracks on the CD." His hands shaking as he lit one cigarette after another, he talked about how much he and his wife cared for Sierra, as well as how badly they wanted to shake her. Having once been truly homeless, Josh became more agitated talking about "these middle class kids who 'play homeless' to get back at their parents."

The next day I cleaned out the room Sierra sublet from Mike. His emotions ran the gamut from anger over losing his lead vocalist to concern for a 23-year-old girl. Meanwhile, I loaded a multitude of dress boots, cowboy boots, antique boots and seven years of shopping memories into my FJ Cruiser, recalling how Sierra christened it "The Skunkmobile" because of its black body and white roof.

◆ ◆ ◆

I left Sierra a message on her cell phone. "I hope you're doing okay. I'm here if needed." Each night I put my iPhone on the nightstand, praying for a call or text, checking for Facebook updates in the middle of the night. Nothing came.

Later I realized that Sierra had lost her cell phone and no one had shared Emily's cell number. I recalled Sierra taking a call from Emily one night when we'd been out to dinner the last time she had been in town. I went online and pulled up the archived cell phone bill, then found the call. I created a new contact for "Emily."

"Have you seen or heard from Sierra?" my text read. "People here are getting worried. This is Ky, btw."

Two days later I followed up. "Any word from Sierra?" Five minutes later Emily's name flashed on the screen.

"Hey, what's up? It's me, Sierra."

Sierra and Emily were "walking toward downtown Philly," with no future plans to speak of. She promised to stay in touch.

Twelve days later a different number came across the screen.

"Hey, what's up? It's me, Sierra."

This time from New Jersey. She and Emily had parted ways and she'd joined up with a girl named Kitty. She added that they might head through Charleston to switch out her wardrobe.

I added "cheese peas" to Tammy's shopping list. "It's the fatted calf."

On the Saturday before Father's Day Sierra appeared on Facebook. I offered 48 hours of sanctuary.

"Great, can my friends come too?"

"That's three of you, right?"

"No, just two friends. And three dogs." They planned to reach Pittsburgh that afternoon. I offered to pick them up there.

With hippies, I discovered, all plans are tentative.

The ride fell through and I spent Father's Day watching 600LBS OF SIN! perform on the Levee, listening to another young woman sing Sierra's "Tidal Wave."

I spent the next few days preparing for a trial, all the while keeping a close watch on my iPhone.

On Wednesday, the phone rang with a Maryland exchange.

"Hey, what's up? It's me, Sierra. We're headed to Baltimore. But we're trying to make it to Cumberland." I googled the location before offering a ride.

The next day I was on the office phone closing out settlement negotiations when a Delaware number came across the iPhone screen three times in quick succession. Three minutes later I called back and asked for Sierra.

"Who? I don't know any Sierra.... Oh, some chick just used my phone.... No, she's gone."

"OK, that chick's my daughter, so thanks. By the way, where are you?" I asked.

"Aberdeen. Just outside of Baltimore."

A couple of hours later, another call, this time a Maryland number.

"Hey, what's up? It's me, Sierra."

"Where are you guys?"

"We're at this cool swimming hole."

"Where?"

"Aberdeen."

"Call me tomorrow night," I instructed.

She called on Friday.

"We're hopping a train to Cumberland," she said. "Can you come get us?"

"What time might you arrive?"

"He's checking the train schedule. We're an hour from the friggin' train hop." I surmised that they might reach Cumberland by 5 o'clock, but it might be as late as 10 o'clock.

"Let me know when you reach Cumberland, whatever time it is."

The call came at 7:57 a.m. Saturday.

"Hey, it's Sierra. Where are you?"

"Where are you?" I asked.

"Cumberland."

"About an hour away."

"OK, well hurry up. We're at the rail station." At the station I met the group, which had grown to four.

"Can he come too? We rescued him from a crazy guy," Sierra said, pointing to the taller man.

I introduced myself, shaking hands with the kids and lowering a hand for the dogs to sniff. Sierra picked up a hiking backpack that was almost as tall as she, and I picked up her guitar. We filled up the back of my SUV with an array of backpacks and guitars, topped off by a violin. Sierra grabbed the front seat while the others crowded into the back seat. The puppy jumped on top of the luggage and the dogs hopped up on their owners' laps. Fortunately I have no sense of smell.

When the ignition key turned, "Mr. Moon" came through the CD speakers. Sierra turned to me and smiled, saying "You've got the CD!" She told the kids that "Mr. Moon" was her song. Then she changed CD tracks to "Severine," one of the Maestro's songs. "Singing this onstage with Mike was awesome!" Having abandoned the band, however, she was left to settle for me on lead vocals and an audience consisting of three dirty hippies—their term, not mine—and three dogs.

◆ ◆ ◆

Kitty, an army brat, attended high school in England and most recently lived in Kentucky. "When I was a kid I wanted to be a Navy SEAL," she recalled, adding with a smile, "I was a lot skinnier back then." After studying art at Western Kentucky University for a semester, she started hopping trains and is still going 18 months later. She travels with Chicken Nugget, an eight-month-old Australian Shepherd.

Dean is also in his early 20s, a veteran vagabond from Florida who now calls Kalamazoo home. He's been on the rails for a couple of years. Dean relies on others to buy beer and cigarettes because he never carries an ID. He's accompanied by Shira, a golden brown chow, and her two-month-old puppy, Wizard.

Miguel is 26, a native of Puerto Rico who immigrated to the Bronx in 2005. When he's not "traveling," he works as an ethnic cook in boutique Manhattan restaurants. "I don't need a resume, I just tell them give me an hour and I'll show you what I can do. They always hire me," he explained. He joined the group in Philadelphia.

◆ ◆ ◆

We reached Charleston shortly after noon. As I drove up the hill, I called and told Aaron's friend Justin, who was staying at the house, to bring our dogs out. Hattie and Dolly do better meeting canine guests outside. Justin stood on the front porch wearing a freshly-ironed polo shirt and deck shoes, holding the dogs. Seeing his mouth hanging wide open, I could read his mind: "Who are these people? Dogs? What's that smell? What's Tammy going to say?"

We unloaded the backpacks and instruments, and I invited everyone inside. Apparently Dean expected bellhop service. Justin revels in describing Kitty's etiquette lecture when Dean looked around the basement for his bags. "Oh my God! They're letting us stay in their house and it's your bag!"

I showed Miguel the shower, hooked Dean up with the Xbox, logged Kitty onto the laptop, and found Sierra an iPad. My concierge duties completed, I became short order cook, grilling burgers and spreading out cheese, sliced tomato, onion, chips, dip—the works.

No one came.

Eventually Justin and I helped ourselves, and shortly thereafter the hippies began to break away from the electronics in search of food. Sierra stayed glued to Facebook for at least two hours before heating up a burger in the microwave.

Their plan was to head to the annual Fourth of July Rainbow Gathering in the Cherokee National Forest in Tennessee. Kitty had no clue as to the nearest town, but she had the longitude and latitude. The "gathering" is really not an organized gathering, or so they tell the National Park Service. It's just a group of "kids" who happen upon the Cherokee National Forest for 10 days. This coincidental "gathering" also operates a rideshare, although Kitty told me the drivers tended to not show up.

With hippies, all plans are tentative.

◆ ◆ ◆

"Will your godmother be home tonight?" Kitty asked. Sierra had told her friends that I was her godfather, a title bestowed by James years ago. The look on Sierra's face confirmed she had no idea what Kitty was talking about.

"Your godmother! His wife?"

Later Tammy arrived armed with a feast from Bob Evans. We cleared the kitchen counter and prepared a spread of biblical proportions.

No one came.

They eventually trickled in, and as is our custom, we invited the hippies to join us in the formal dining room for Bob Evans take-out on paper plate service.

Miguel stayed and talked for almost an hour. I'm a lot like my dad, a lifelong journalist. Even in the face of seeing Sierra join the hippies, he would have started interviews. I did the same.

I learned about "trainology" and the ways of the road. Apparently Miguel possesses the Crew Change Guide—a handwritten list of nationwide crew changes that's been passed on and updated by word of mouth. Crew change provides the best opportunity to hop a train because (a) the train is stopped and (b) no one's watching. Still, Miguel cautioned, "You have to be ninja to avoid the 'bull,'" as the security guard is known.

The best trains are the modern grainers, because there are walls on the front and back end to provide protection from the elements. (I think he means the 'bull.') Boxcars are more difficult. "You have to find an old railroad spike—these are laying all over the yard—and jam it in the door to keep the doors open," he explained. He added that some cargo owners require that the boxcar doors remain closed when the train is moving, in which case, the rail workers politely ask that the kids exit the boxcar.

"I'm guessing they just look the other way while you find another car," I said. Miguel just nodded. Another option is to ride an empty grainer, "but it's hard to get the dogs in and out." Someone always stays awake and relies on the sun as a clock so that the group can hop off when they reach their destination. Rides vary from two hours to eight hours. Miguel talks about the railroad companies like I talk about airlines. "In this area we ride CSX and Norfolk & Southern, they go east-west, and in the Northeast we ride the Penn Central and New York railroads."

The alternative is hitchhiking. It turns out folks are pretty generous and rides are relatively easy to come by. A common strategy seems to be to put the girls on the entrance ramp. When a car stops, the guys come out of the woods and the girls plead, "Can my friend come too?" In return, the male presence offers a sense of protection.

Tammy asked, "What do you do for food?"

"Oh, we cook," Kitty said. I recalled seeing a Teflon frying pan attached to her bag. She explained that people give them food, as do some grocery stores. "Trader Joe's is the best."

The hippies seem to have as good a hand on the pulse of the political landscape as Karl Rove. California is "great," but folks in the Midwest aren't too fond of the hippies. Cities in the Northeast are a tough sell "because they're so used to beggars."

After dinner, Tammy and I packed up the leftovers—enough for a family of five. "Don't worry," I told her, "between Aaron and the hippies it will be eaten." The fridge was clean by Sunday night.

Later that evening Sierra tried to explain the dirty hippies' concept of hygiene to Tammy. "I stay out in the sun and the hair turns white, so no one can tell I don't shave my legs." Tammy just shook her head.

In that instant I saw the Sierra that so many others see—defiant, rebellious, wasting her talents. I felt like Don Quixote facing the Knight of the Mirrors in the *Man of La Mancha*. I saw my Dulcinea as Aldonza and heard Aldonza scream, "Look at me— see me as who I really am!"

◆ ◆ ◆

Tammy left early Sunday for a weeklong business trip and Justin headed out to visit a friend in Ohio. I fixed a grand breakfast, complete with eggs, sausage, bacon and hash browns.

No one came.

After a few minutes, the feral hippies appeared like stray animals tentatively sniffing out food. They finished it within an hour.

On Sunday afternoon, Dean and Miguel—despite priding themselves on being hardened vagabonds—sat in the air-conditioned comfort of our basement and played Xbox. Kitty found the laptop. Sierra and I went shopping.

Over the years, I've taken Sierra shopping for clothes, ranging from school and work attire to a devil's costume for the band's Halloween gig. Taking her shopping for a water bottle, multi-tool and camping cutlery was a first. Always the savvy shopper, she spent 45 minutes going back and forth to find the best deals.

We cruised around in the Mini Cooper with the top down and stopped to visit a couple of her friends. We talked about her "traveling plans," which I lectured were "bizarre, not to mention dangerous." She told me she planned to head out West after

Rainbow, perhaps to Colorado. Then maybe she'd return and put together a band.

◆ ◆ ◆

The kids planned to leave on Monday afternoon. Aaron left that morning to join a friend at the river. He got up early and cooked eggs, bacon and sausage for his sister and her friends.

With hippies, all plans are tentative.

Not surprisingly, as the clock passed the 48 hour "sanctuary" mark, no plans seemed to be underway. I woke Sierra up and told her that the hiking boots, an early birthday present, would not arrive until Tuesday. Using what Sierra calls my "lawyer voice" I outlined her options.

"You can go today and if you spend even a couple days with someone who has a mailing address, I can forward the boots."

"But we'll be in the woods."

Foregoing a lecture about the consequences of the vagabond lifestyle, I simply said, "OK, then I guess that won't work." Next I offered that the rest of the group, who despite the Xbox and wi-fi seemed to be getting cabin fever, could go ahead and I'd put Sierra on a bus to the nearest town.

"But we'll be in the woods."

"OK, then I guess that won't work."

The remaining options were to go without the boots or everyone could stay another day.

"I need to talk about it with them," she said. I listened in from upstairs as the group convened. Like the bureaucracies they distain, everyone looked for someone else to make the decision.

They finally decided to wait a day.

◆ ◆ ◆

Lacking a supper plan and with no one wanting to go out—although Kitty had showered—I offered to order pizza. I suspected the two beer runs had been exhausted. My gypsy guests consumed so much alcohol that at one point Justin feared they had uncorked the Dom Perignon. He rushed to the pantry, relieved to find the bottle nestled safely behind a bottle of non-alcoholic sparkling grape juice

Tammy often says I'm too subtle for my own good. Instead of simply asking, "Do you need beer?" I asked, "Should I pick up beverages or will a nice Malbec suffice?" The name of this fine red wine shares a close resemblance to some cheap whiskey that Sierra spelled "melbic." "$12 a half gallon," she texted.

"So you want whiskey and wine," I joked. "Sounds like a good name for a song."

"Bring it and maybe we'll write one."

Everyone came.

Later that evening I joined Dean on the patio during a smoke break.

"Did you ever see *Chorus Line*? There's a scene where a kid is performing in a drag show. His parents come to the final show before the kid is leaving with the troupe for the road tour," I said. Dean listened intently as he inhaled on his cigarette. "And after the show the father tells his son goodbye, then turns to the manager and says, 'Take care of my son.'"

"We'll take good care of her," Dean promised.

I nodded and bid the kids goodnight.

◆ ◆ ◆

On Tuesday, two days after the 48-hour "sanctuary," I concentrated on editing a brief to fend off the reality of Sierra leaving for a Rainbow Gathering and then hopping trains to Colorado. At 11:30 a.m., I took an early lunch.

The boots were on the porch. It was time to say goodbye.

Sierra tried on the boots while I ate a sandwich. Then I went down for handshakes and hugs. Miguel and Kitty were most sincere in their thanks, and Miguel promised to pick up before they left. Sierra walked upstairs with me for one last hug before I left for the office.

An hour later my phone rang. The ride Sierra had secured for that evening fell through when her friend discovered that the designated coordinates were in the middle of the Cherokee National Forest. I stopped on the way home to pick up Chinese. I spread out sweet and sour chicken, beef lo mein and General Tso's chicken along with rice and fortune cookies.

No one came.

I helped myself and sat down by Sierra on the couch. Kitty sat in the chair across from us and asked Sierra if she was OK. We shared the same wavelength. There was no ride, the visit had gone on too long, and we both could tell Sierra was unhappy.

"Damnit," Kitty said, "I wanted to be at Rainbow by the Fourth of July.

"You have eight days—" I started.

"You don't understand," came the chorus.

A series of phone calls ensued and eventually Sierra managed to talk someone from Charleston into driving if they could contribute gas money.

"I'll call my mom and tell her we're heading to the on-ramp," Kitty said. "That always gets them!" Sure enough, $25 was on the way. "She hates me hitchhiking," Kitty said with a sly grin.

They are persistent.

◆ ◆ ◆

Suffering from cabin fever, the girls decided to earn some money by flying a sign—standing in the road holding a sign. But it's not that simple. This requires planning, and this is one plan the hippies take seriously. Nothing is left to chance.

"Location, location, location" is not just for realtors. When flying a sign, location is critical. Dean, who apparently had been here before, offered his insights. He seemed to know the best locations around town, and I realized I see a lot of people with signs at these spots. Walmart is a good target, they said.

Next, props and a dog. They decided on two backpacks and one dog. Chicken Nugget drew the assignment.

Finally, they needed a sign. "I've got some in my pack," Kitty said. Like a Hallmark store for vagabonds, the kids carry a variety of signs with slogans like "traveling broke" and "need food."

The irony of being driven to the site in a Mini Cooper convertible was not lost on Kitty. And, in another first, I dropped off my girl to fly a sign.

An hour and six dollars later, the girls called for a ride. When we got home they made a plan. Group A—Dean and Kitty, along with two dogs—would ride downtown with me when I went to work and fly a sign if and until the ride arrived. Group B—Sierra and Miguel—would hitch a ride downtown with Aaron.

◆ ◆ ◆

When I got ready to leave for the office Wednesday, everyone was sound asleep. I gave Sierra one last kiss and headed out.

Later Sierra texted, "Aaron will take us." All I could think was, "Aaron's going to Rainbow? I'll never explain this to Tammy."

I came home to find that Aaron and Justin had reclaimed the Xbox.

"I dropped them off," Aaron said. "Sierra's friend is supposed to pick them up."

"How did you get everyone in the jeep?"

"Don't ask. It wasn't exactly legal. Or safe."

I pulled a quick *Cat in the Hat* clean up in anticipation of Tammy's return on Friday and took the guys to dinner.

"Aren't you going to call and see if they made it out?" they asked.

"Hell no! What if they're still on the entrance ramp?"

With hippies, all plans are tentative.

HOME FOR THE HOLIDAYS

WITH 12 SHOPPING DAYS left until Christmas, Sierra's name appeared on my iPhone.

"Hey, can you get me that plane ticket?"

"As long as I have a location."

"Sacramento."

"When?"

"The day after tomorrow."

A few weeks earlier Sierra said she wanted to come home for Christmas, and I told her she could fly—unless she wanted to hop a train. Needless to say I jumped when Sierra accepted the offer of an airplane ticket. There were seats on a flight leaving Sacramento at noon Friday. Tammy called to confirm the reservation.

We had last seen Sierra in June, when she stopped in with a few friends and dogs on their way to Tennessee for a Rainbow Gathering. Since then I'd caught up with her on a hippie bus crossing Illinois, on the streets of Bozeman, Montana, and my personal favorite: "I can't talk now. I'm on a train."

I have learned to laugh at taking calls from the back of a moving train. Rather than asking, "Are you all right?" I ask if she's riding "dirty face," slang for the front end of a grainer. This explains my co-counsel's surprise when I seemed unfazed about an upcoming trial. "It's because I'm wondering whether my girl will be coming home for Christmas on a Union Pacific grainer," I said to myself.

The evening before Sierra's flight, Tammy and I washed four loads of her clothes, which were still in bins and boxes from when Sierra abruptly left with little more than the clothes on her back, embarking on her "journey of whimsy and longing." I also cleaned up the downstairs bedroom and moved in the dresser that I had left in the garage following last May's impromptu move. I carefully placed Sierra's Native American headdress on a mannequin and hung a couple of her things on the wall.

Friday afternoon and evening were spent checking the iPhone flight tracker app on the assumption that she made her flight. About 10 o'clock I got a text: "Sitting on an airplane in Charlotte. Be there in an hour."

Three planes arrive in Charleston at 11:34 p.m., so Tammy and I joined two dozen other families waiting to greet their loved ones—quite a contrast to last June, when I was the only one picking up passengers arriving at the Cumberland Scenic Rail Station on a CSX freight train. When I saw Sierra, dwarfed by the guitar she carried, I rushed to give her a hug. As I stepped back, she sheepishly apologized for the odor. "I ate a taco for lunch."

As we waited at the baggage claim, she talked about the flight. "I had a middle seat from Phoenix and couldn't sleep at all." Tammy and I wondered if her aisle mates appreciated that she'd spent the last month in an RV with no plumbing. Locating her baggage wasn't a problem. I didn't see any other soiled hiking backpacks on the luggage carousel.

On the ride home, we told Sierra that we'd done her laundry. "Awesome, I can't wait to roll around in my clothes!" I bragged that we matched nearly 20 pairs of socks—a testament to my thorough moving services—and Tammy joked about finding panties that Sierra had brought with her when she came to live with us eight years earlier.

"Oh cool," she said. "'Cause I don't have any on me."

Aaron met us at the door to introduce Boogie, the 65-pound Staffordshire bull terrier mix Aaron rescued from the shelter the week after Hattie died. Boogie sniffed intently. "He probably smells all the dogs," Sierra explained. I thought of all the dogs Sierra has traveled with over the past several months: Marley (Emily), Chicken Nugget (Kitty) and Reptar (Matt, her most recent boyfriend).

Within minutes we were treated to an impromptu concert featuring "Gentle on My Mind," which Sierra stressed was written by John Hartford, not Glen Campbell. Aaron interrupted, bluntly asking the question on everyone's mind. "So, Sis, how long are you here for?"

"Until it gets warm," she replied. "I want to get a job and save some money. Traveling's fun, but it's easier if you've got money."

Shortly after one o'clock in the morning, I carried the backpack to Sierra's room.

I showed Sierra the clothes bins and left her to "roll around in her clothes."

Over the weekend Sierra caught some much needed rest and a long shower, and on Sunday night headed out to renew acquaintances on the Charleston bar scene. "Just don't drink and drive," I told her. "Stay downtown if you need to and don't worry about coming home." At three o'clock she sent a text saying, "I'm staying at a friend's."

She came home on Monday just in time for a Christmas get-together with friends. As soon as our company left, Sierra announced that she needed to get changed for open mic night at the Glass. "Just don't drink and drive," I repeated. The rejoinder came at 3:12 a.m. "I'll be staying here at my friend's house."

In the interim, I experienced a phenomenon only parents can truly comprehend. You don't worry about your kids when they're away, but when they're home you worry all the time. Case in point: at 11:00 p.m. I was awakened by a call from Sierra. "How do you get the car into four-wheel drive?"

I lost the call before I could answer, so I texted the instructions and anxiously waited for a reply. Eventually I drifted back to sleep, having decided that if there had been an accident I'd have received a call from a deputy sheriff. Sierra's reply came at 1:00 a.m. "I'm getting ready to go on stage. Wish me luck."

On Tuesday evening Sierra couldn't find her driver's license. "I can't believe, this," she screamed. "I go all across the country riding trains and hitchhiking without losing my ID and I'm not here 48 hours before I lose it!"

She wasn't too concerned, though. While the Parrot had a new bartender, all the local doormen know her. Plus, "I never liked that picture. And it's only five bucks."

Wednesday we went on a father-daughter date, beginning at the DMV. Remarkably, we had a zero minute wait and were out with an improved picture in 18 minutes. And it only cost me five bucks.

We went to dinner at an upscale Japanese restaurant. Sitting at the bar, Sierra drinking sake and I sipping a martini, we produced a piquant picture: a pretty young girl wearing fancy pants, high boots and a colorful blouse, and me, with my graying hair and black velvet smoking jacket. I boasted to Sierra that I'd once sat at the same bar with Tammy, back in the days of "Cheers." Then I listened to stories of Sierra's journey.

She first visited the Rainbow Gathering, which she enjoyed as it seemed to be a group of carefree people doing their own thing. They left on buses and RVs, most heading West. I interjected, "I can only imagine how the bus smelled." She told me that she had "come to appreciate the smell of the human body."

They also traveled by train, a practice frowned upon by the railroads. Sierra laughs when she tells about the time they almost got caught.

"We got spotted by someone in a tower, and the workers told us to get off," she recounted. "Emily and Henry were riding dirty face and they took off ahead. Kitty and I were running through this cornfield. You should have seen us. I was yelling and beating the corn stalks with my guitar to make a path. Then I looked and saw Chicken Nugget standing on a trail, just looking at us like 'what's wrong with you people?'"

They eventually reached Wyoming, where Sierra stopped to visit Yellowstone. She loved it.

"We should go there. Make it a father-daughter trip."

"I'd love to, but let's get reservations. I hear they're not too keen on overnight camping without a permit," I said, recalling a phone call that came last August.

"Hey, it's me, Sierra. What's our address?"

I gave her the address and she repeated it, adding, "Thanks, we got a ticket for camping without a permit." After a couple of days, I followed up. "Hey, we're going to fly a sign. We need money to pay that ticket so they won't put us in jail." Turns out it's a federal offense.

"The cop was really cool though. He could have ticketed us for having the dogs too," Sierra reminisced.

Sierra also earned money playing music on a street corner in Bozeman. "Matt and I got into an argument, so I went downtown and played my guitar. I made like 40 bucks."

After leaving Montana, the group hitchhiked Highway 10 to Portland, Oregon, where Sierra hooked up with an old friend from Charleston. She asked me to send clothes and talked about staying, though she complained that "I can't make any money here. There's too many homeless people." The week before I planned to visit, she called to say that plans had changed. They were headed to Northern California.

Sierra glows when she describes the redwoods. "They're really awesome." But the lure of northern California was not the scenery; it was the promise of work in the fields—the marijuana fields.

Growing marijuana is legal in California, although legitimate sales are limited to medical dispensaries. Unlike the kids I knew who tried to grow weed in their dorm rooms, these growers actually trim the plants on a regular basis. And that's where the hippies come in handy.

As Sierra explained it, the kids hang out in the bars at night and hook up with farmers looking for help. The work starts at daybreak. They get paid by the pound—I assume the trimmings are measured.

"You can make a lot of money. You get like $200 a pound; you can make like $400 in a day."

I asked if they worked scantily clothed to protect against theft. Sierra rolled her eyes. "They know if you're cool." In my defense, though, all friends of my generation who've seen *American Gangster* have asked the same question.

The October edition of *Newsweek* talked of the "suits" taking over the business of growing marijuana, but that's not the case in Northern California. The payment method reminds me of my aunt who gave money for Christmas with the adage, "If cash embarrasses you, take a check." I inferred that some growers follow a similar mantra: "If cash embarrasses you, take weed."

We finished our date with a beer at Sam's, where Sierra once worked as a barmaid. One of her friends showed up and I took my leave.

I unexpectedly got a second date the following Saturday. 600LBS OF SIN! was playing the Christmas party at the Glass. I wasn't sure whether Sierra would want to see the band or not. My last trip to the Glass had been for the CD release party Sierra had deserted, and here I was waltzing in with her like she was the prodigal one.

"I feel like I'm bringing the perpetrator to the scene of the crime," I told the drummer.

"Oh," he laughed, "it's just like a family reunion."

Sierra ran off to find Josh, the lead guitarist, and then talked to Mike. He took Sierra to the front of the stage and introduced her to Libby, the new female vocalist who sang some of Sierra's songs. The divas smiled politely as they shook hands. The scene reminded me of watching two coaches shaking hands after a hard-fought contest, leaving me to wonder what they were saying and thinking. Sierra offered no clues when she joined me back at the bar.

During the first set we listened to the music, singing along to Mike's "Severine" just like the time we sang for a carload of dirty hippies and their dogs. As the second set got underway, Sierra got up and danced with the same hippie tonk bounce she used to exhibit on stage.

"And now," Mike announced, "we'd like to welcome our archenemy and good friend Sierra Ferrell." The band broke into "Tidal Wave" and the two vocalists, past and present, harmonized. After the song finished, Libby left the stage and Josh strummed the opening chords to "Mr. Moon." Sierra sounded fantastic, with no one but Mike and me realizing she missed an intro. "That's your Christmas present," Mike pronounced.

Later Sierra joined the band for an encore, and at 2:30 the Maestro announced they were done. When Sierra saw me with my coat on she frowned. "Are you wanting to leave? I want to jam with Josh. Only for a half hour."

"Where?"

"In the parking lot."

"Sure." It sounded entertaining until I walked outside and faced the 17-degree wind chill. It turned out that Sierra forgot that Josh and the others had to take down the set and load the Sin van, so the impromptu jam was canceled.

On Sunday I was at the office operating on three hours' sleep when Sierra called to ask if she could take the car to "pick up a friend on the East End." She added "I'll be home all day working in my room."

When I got came home, Sierra rushed to the top of the stairs to greet me.

"Hey, be careful letting the dogs out," she warned. "There's a dog downstairs."

Before I had time to process the situation, she added, "Don't worry, he's a nice dog."

"His name is Reptar."

I immediately recognized the name of the dog that belonged to Sierra's most recent traveling companion, a guy named Matt. My first thought was how to tell Tammy. I took a cue from my kids: I sent her a text. One of Tammy's friends softened the blow by responding, "Another chapter!"

I went downstairs to introduce myself to Matt. As we shook hands, I took a long look—tall, thin but not emaciated, scraggly hair and a beard, appearing to be in his mid-to-late 20s.

"So," I asked politely, "when did you get in?"

"Just today," he said. "I hitched a ride in Little Rock and they were coming here. How lucky is that!"

When Tammy got home, she unloaded the groceries and offered a snack. Sierra declined, but when Tammy reiterated the offer, Matt said, "I wouldn't mind a sandwich." As Sierra made his sandwich, he saw the cans of Spam, which Tammy uses to make gourmet roll-ups.

"Spam," he said with a smile, "the dinner of hobos."

My grandfather promoted Spam for the Hormel Company. I wondered whether he would have taken offense at the comment or recruited Matt for an ad campaign.

Tammy started on supper and I worked out to burn off my growing adrenaline. Meanwhile, Sierra pointed out the shower and offered to wash Matt's clothes. She succeeded on getting him in the shower.

At supper I inquired about Matt's story. He's originally from Florida, where his father, two brothers and sister still live. He's been traveling for about two years. In addition to being a musician (as most traveling kids seem to be), he also keeps a journal and likes to cook.

Matt often travels as chief cook with the Kraken Kitchen, a ragtag group that drives around the country on a bus, serving food to the homeless. They obtain supplies from food banks. "When we explain what we're doing, they're glad to help. We each get one bag of food." And, he added, "Since there's so many of us, we get a lot of food." I had seen a post on Sierra's Facebook page at one of the feedings. I couldn't help wondering if the folks donating to the food banks know how traveling hippies or, as Josh described them to me, "middle-class kids playing homeless," benefit from their generosity.

Before going to bed, Tammy offered the kids a wakeup call, adding "I thought you might want to allow time for showers."

The next morning Sierra took Matt downtown to fly a sign. She had mentioned that he needed to earn some money. Seeing the rain, I thought "Christmas eve, rain, should be a good day." For the record, he made $464.

I told Sierra that Matt was welcome to join us for dinner, a significant concession since one of the few rules Tammy and I established 24 years ago was that Christmas Eve is for us.

"But," I began, "and don't take offense—"

"I know," she interjected, "he smells. I've been trying to get him to let me wash his clothes. I don't know. These kids like to be dirty. I think it's a trend kind of thing."

Matt returned with an armload of food that he had picked up at a local food bank—a can of yams, two cans of beans, dinner rolls and breakfast rolls. He laid the hostess gift on the counter and handed Aaron a box of Milk-Bone. "Somebody gave me these, but Reptar won't eat them," he explained. "I thought maybe your dog could use them."

Tammy took me aside in the pantry. "What do we do with the food?"

"We serve the dinner rolls tonight, put out the breakfast rolls in the morning, and take the cans to the church food bank."

I set the dinner table with the red dishes Tammy inherited from her mother and the Owen family silver. As I've been taught, the salad forks went on the far left. When Sierra asked which fork to use, Matt told her, "You use the outside fork for the first course and move in." Even hippies know etiquette.

After dinner we opened presents. Sierra couldn't wait to find out what I'd bought for Matt. She was relieved to find it was a book by Lao Tzu, his favorite philosopher. Aaron gave Matt one of his beanies. Matt genuinely appreciated the gestures.

The next morning Tammy and I dropped Matt off downtown before we headed to my mom's house for Christmas dinner. I didn't know if this was goodbye or not, and Matt gave no hint as he walked off with Reptar in tow. I watched more with interest than guilt as Matt and Reptar headed down the street. It's the path he's chosen.

Aaron and Sierra drove separately. When we arrived, they were already overlooking the tree and presents, acting like young grandchildren again. They took pictures galore—"Take one by the fire, get one with Bubby and me with the wreath, one by the Christmas tree"—and then posted their holiday photos on Facebook.

We sat down at the dining room table, adorned with red tablecloth and a pine cone centerpiece, just like we were on the Hallmark channel rather than MTV. As Sierra joked about our Christmas Eve dinner—"I can't believe he was telling me what fork to use!"—my mom reminded us, "We aren't the Ovaltine family I once imagined, but that's OK."

When we got home, I inquired about Matt. Sierra reported that he made $450. She added that he had met two Japanese traveling kids looking for a way to Florida and he was thinking of buying a car. I pursued the primary questions: "Where's he staying? Does he have any plans?"

"I don't know," she said, "but I've got to find somewhere else for him to stay."

Matt slept under a bridge Tuesday night. The next day Sierra mentioned the forecast for freezing rain.

"They can stay," I said. "I don't want to leave them out on a night like this." Tammy concurred, perhaps more out of concern for Reptar. "He didn't chose that lifestyle," she said.

The next day I came home from work to find that Sierra and Matt were no longer on speaking terms. It was time for Matt to go. "There's a bus scheduled to leave at 8:00 tomorrow morning," I told him. "I think it's best if you find somewhere else to stay tonight." He said a motel was out of the question. Matt doesn't carry an ID, although Reptar carries his service animal tags, so I dropped them off at the transit mall.

Sierra got all gussied up—the dreadlocks replaced with curls—and left to perform at the Cellar. "Just don't drink and drive," I told her. Shortly after three o'clock she sent a text. "I'm staying at a friend's."

After my early Friday morning run, I took a loop through downtown. I saw a lanky figure, hunched to balance a backpack, walking toward the bus station with a dog in tow.

I drove home to wait for the next chapter.

THE NEXT CHAPTER

"**G**OT THE JOB. DOLLARS flowing soon."

I smiled as I read Sierra's Facebook status. Shortly after returning from her infamous journey of whimsy and longing, Sierra announced, "Tomorrow I'm going to get up early and look for a job."

A week or so later Sierra got up one morning to go job hunting. But first she joined Tammy and me for lunch. Sitting across from her at the Mexican restaurant, I was taken aback by her attire. A sleeveless dress in mid-January? More importantly, I realized that she had found the extra razor Tammy left in the shower.

Tammy volunteered to help on the job search. "I talked to a friend of mine who knows a lot of people in Charleston. She says they're hiring at Embassy Suites." Tammy also preached persistence. "I'd go to every retail store in the mall," she advised, "then talk to the people at Embassy Suites."

I focused on how Sierra might explain her recent absence from the workforce. "You were in a band—you know, doing the music thing—and they got so busy with out-of-town festivals that you had trouble scheduling a day job. And the money was good," I explained. "Then you decided to take some time off to travel."

No sooner had I returned to the office than the texts began.

"Street address?" Tempting as it was to say, "Look at your new driver's license," I forwarded our home address.

"What should I put down as jobs? D:"

"Deliah's, Macy's and the place in Fayetteville."

"What was the place in Fayetteville?" Fortunately I recalled a Mexican restaurant with a canine theme. I googled Mexican restaurants in Fayetteville and replied: "Diogi's."

That evening Sierra reported that she thought she would get a job at Charlotte Russe. "So I didn't go to Embassy Suites. I'd really like to work at Charlotte Russe, and I don't want to take a job at Embassy if I'm going to get the other job," she explained.

Finding it hard to argue with her logic, I probed for details on what exactly they said.

"They took me back and interviewed me."

"What do they ask? I'm assuming it's not, 'Where do you want to be in five years?'"

"If I was an animal, what would I be?" Sierra said, rolling her eyes.

"Well?"

"A cheetah." She finished by telling us that the manager told her they were busy with inventory but would be in touch by the end of the month.

To her credit, Sierra stopped in on the following Monday.

"I got the job. They're going to call me this weekend and put me on the schedule."

Now if I could just get her to tell me the schedule. One morning I was sitting in pajama pants at 7:40 when Sierra yelled from the basement, "Hey, can you take me to work? I have to be there at 8:00. I'll put on my makeup in the car." In a reprise of high school, I drove while Sierra did her makeup. We made it with four minutes to spare. "Out doing open mic and still at work on time," Sierra boasted. "Is that awesome or what!"

We met at the food court for lunch on her first day. "So," I asked, "are you excited about your first day at work?"

"Yeah," Sierra replied. "Hey, did I tell you Mike called? I'm rehearsing with the band Thursday night."

Sierra returning to 600LBS OF SIN!? I was flabbergasted.

"I'm singing with them on Friday night," she said as she headed back to Charlotte Russe, albeit walking toward the opposite end of the mall.

Ironically, Sierra's first gig was at the Empty Glass. The last time she was set to play the Glass she called it off from a moving freight train. The Saturday show was at the Adelphia Music Hall in Marietta, Ohio. The Adelphia is housed in an old factory building, and despite the brick walls and high ceilings, musicians like the sound. My mom and I went up for dinner and the show. It was fantastic. We stayed well past midnight, earning praise from other members of the audience.

"I didn't think you two would make it," one patron said as we walked past. Frieda smiled as she boasted, "That's my granddaughter!"

◆ ◆ ◆

A few days after the night I dropped off Matt and Reptar at the transit mall, Sierra strutted through the front door, followed by a young man.

"I'm borrowing his guitar," she said, pointing over her shoulder as she started down the stairs. "We call him Monk," she yelled from the basement.

Monk looked ready for the country and western scene, outfitted in cowboy boots and a black pearl-buttoned shirt embroidered with red roses. He's about my height, maybe six feet tall, with a soul patch. He works at a local pharmacy compounding prescriptions. He stopped to shake hands with me and formally introduce himself, looking me in the eye and saying, "Hi, I'm Chris."

"I was hitchhiking around the country and had gone off the grid when I stopped in South Carolina for a prescription," he told us. "And the pharmacist had to call Charleston to confirm it. My sister tells him they haven't been able to reach me and asks him to give me a job to keep me there. That's how I got into the pharmacy business."

One night Monk sat down with me to watch the Broncos-Ravens playoff game. Sierra was torn. She had zero interest in football, but she wanted to be with Monk. And, quite frankly, she was nervous about Monk and me "male bonding."

She decided to stay and watch. "Who are you rooting for?"

"Nobody," we said in chorus, "We're just watching. It's the playoffs!"

"Oh," she replied, "I'm for the team with the horsies on their helmets."

Before long, Sierra was expressing opinions on an instant replay. "Look, he's got his arm under the ball. That's a catch!" Monk and I looked at each other, stunned.

"Oh my God! I'm starting to pay attention to this," she screamed. "I'm leaving."

Some evenings Monk came by before Sierra got home. He often joined us at the dinner table, always helping with the dishes.

◆ ◆ ◆

On the Sunday morning after the Adelphia gig, Tammy planned to sleep in, but at 6:35 a.m. she heard a knock at the front door. It was Monk. He was returning from his own gig in Huntington and planned to pick up Sierra, who was coming back from Marietta on the Sin bus. Apparently she had fallen asleep and wasn't answering her cell phone.

Monk had decided to come by the house to wait for Sierra. Since he'd apparently been out all night, Tammy assumed he'd go downstairs and crash. Instead, he said, "Sierra's been bragging about those smoothies you make." Ten minutes later Monk and Tammy were sitting in the breakfast nook enjoying her famous smoothies.

One day Monk was having dinner with us while Sierra was at a rehearsal. "We should give you a key," Aaron joked.

"I like him," Aaron said during dinner one night.

"Is that a good thing?" Monk asked cautiously when I told him what Aaron said.

"I don't know," Aaron replied. "Don't tell Sis. The last time I told her I liked her boyfriend she dumped him."

The dogs liked Monk too. Boogie always ran to greet Monk. One night Dolly was resting comfortably in her kennel when Monk came in. Her arthritis was bothering her and she whimpered until Monk came to pet her.

Aside from Monk, we never knew how many to expect for dinner and I often called ahead to get a head count.

"Yeah, I'm home," Sierra reported one day. "And Zac's here too."

"Zac?"

"Yes," she laughed. "We're just friends now."

◆ ◆ ◆

Sierra had been driving the Skunkmobile. Matt's last words to Sierra before I took him to the transmit mall were, "I hope you wreck the car." She swears he put a curse on her. That weekend she had a fender bender. I probably wouldn't have noticed the scratched taillight if she hadn't told me. But, a few days later, I couldn't help but notice that the entire taillight was gone.

"I backed into a tree," Sierra said when she saw me in the driveway.

"Don't worry," I said, "Aaron backed into a tree once. And I backed into a garage door." Lesson learned—or so I thought.

Sierra's Valentine's Day greeting came in text spurts. "The car's still driveable.... I swerved to hit a deer.... Monk says he might be able to fix up the front bumper.... Oh, and the taillight is completely gone now."

Tammy said, "At least no one was hurt."

In contrast, my immediate concern was how Sierra and I were going to drive to New York the next day.

The previous Sunday night, Sierra had announced that she would be going to New York.

"Emily's dad died," she said. "The funeral is Saturday in New York. She wants me to come." I vividly recalled the day Sierra's friend James called to tell me that Sierra and "some chick named Emily" had hitchhiked to St. Louis.

"How..." I began.

"It's OK. David is coming through on his way to New Hampshire and he'll give me a ride. I need a map.

"Don't worry," she added, "He'll only spend one night."

"How do you plan to get back?"

"I'll take the China bus," she said.

"The China bus?"

"It's a bunch of Chinese people who drive a bus," she explained.

I wanted to ask if there was something more than a tentative schedule for this bus, but Sierra interrupted. "It costs 50 bucks and I don't have any money."

"Where's Interstate 70?" she asked. "David is coming across on Interstate 70."

"It's north of here," I pointed out. "Don't you have gigs this weekend?"

"I can miss the one in Beckley, but I want to go to PJ Kelly's in Clarksburg."

While Sierra looked for I-70, I swiped the iPad to locate the obituary and get directions.

"The funeral is at 11:15 Saturday," I reported. "It's about nine hours away. You can go on Friday night. If you leave right after the service, you'll make it back to Clarksburg in time for the PJ Kelly's gig. I may be able to drive, but I need to talk with Tammy."

Before I had a chance to mention this whimsical plan to Tammy, Sierra came home from work and announced, "I'm off Monday. I go in at 8:00 tomorrow. I mean, I wasn't supposed to work tomorrow, but I switched from Saturday so we can go to New York."

I alerted Tammy and Sierra texted Emily and Mike. Needless to say, they had different reactions. Emily's text read, "Be sure to tell your godfather thank you." Mike's read, "Are you seriously taking Sierra to Long Island this weekend? You think you can make it back on time?"

Sierra was scheduled to work from 5:00 to 9:00 that Friday, followed by a solo gig at Sam's. "Don't worry," she said. "I'm just opening for another band. I play at 10:00."

I was on the road both Thursday and Friday and reached Charleston at four o'clock that afternoon. Rather than going to the office, I decided to go home and take a nap.

"Hey," Aaron greeted me. "Are we still going to the new *Die Hard* movie tonight? We have to go this weekend before Justin leaves." The best line in the movie was when Bruce Willis backed a truck out of a helicopter to keep the gunner from shooting his son: "The things we do for our kids."

After the movie I had the guys drop me off at Enterprise.

"Why are you renting a car?" they asked.

"Have you seen the FJ? And Tammy's battery is dying and I don't want to risk being stranded," I explained.

As I was leaving for Sam's I got a text from Sierra. "Sound guy late. It will be later than 11:00. Sorry."

At 12:02 a.m. Sierra got in the car. "I'm starved."

"Can we at least get on the interstate?"

For the next nine and a half hours I enjoyed Sierra's undivided attention. Rather than lecturing or offering advice on relationships and careers, I told stories about how Tammy and I met and came to be husband and wife nearly 25 years ago.

"I really like listening to you talk," Sierra said as we cruised up Interstate 79.

◆ ◆ ◆

Sierra relieved me at the wheel after three hours, but I didn't get any rest until after Sierra navigated the mountains in driving snow. When I did finally get to rest, I was reminded of Tammy's warning: "Does she know the route?"

"We're making great time," Sierra informed me. "We're on 70 East at that place you mentioned, Hagerstown." I checked the map and politely suggested we take a bathroom break. As we returned to the car I offered to drive, saying, "Hey, I found a short cut to I-81."

Back on course, Sierra told me that she needed to learn "Ave Maria." Turns out she was on the program for the funeral. Sierra picked up my iPhone, downloaded the song on iTunes, and looked up the lyrics. She practiced as we passed through Harrisburg. When we reached Bethlehem, she pronounced herself ready.

We arrived at the church about two hours early. I had to try three entrances before finding an open door. Once inside, I met a man in his mid 50s, whom I later surmised was Emily's uncle.

"We're early," I said apologetically. "Sierra and I just got in from West Virginia."

"Oh! Thanks for coming," he said. "Come this way. Emily's in the back."

I took my cue and followed him back to an antechamber behind the pulpit. I'd never met Emily. She was taller than Sierra with short, dirty blonde hair. Her eyes appeared bloodshot from crying. She wore a black dress.

I set aside any feelings I may have harbored toward Emily for initiating Sierra on her journey of whimsy and longing and offered my condolences.

"Thanks for bringing Sierra," she said as we shook hands.

"My pleasure," I said.

"Yes, thank you so much," her mother added.

I nodded, went to bring in Sierra, then found a place to change into my gray suit. I sat down on the steps in the choir loft—napping on a pew seemed rude—and closed my eyes for 15 minutes.

As the crowd started to come in, I found a seat in the middle of the church and watched the people coming in. Emily's father was 57 when he died, recently retired after 35 years as a Con Edison lineman. The crowd came straight from central casting. Sitting behind me were four men in their late 50s or early 60s. The leader wore a NYFD jacket with "captain" embroidered on the front. Before the service I looked over and saw he had his cell phone to his ear. The man next to him was looking down at the iPhone in his hand.

"It's supposed to be on vibrate," he said. "But I don't think it's working."

"I'll try again," the captain said. "What's your number again?"

Sierra did a fantastic job singing "Ave Maria." The older generation got a kick out of Sierra's using the iPhone for the lyrics. I just held my breath, hoping she remembered that the phone screen goes black after two minutes.

I continued to study the crowd during the reception, leaving Sierra to spend time with Emily and Sean, Emily's current traveling companion. They served beer at the reception, and Sean came over with beer cans in every suit pocket of his three-piece suit.

"It's blue, not black," he said apologetically.

The kids went to check on the dogs—Marley, Diesel and Torino. The church custodian lived across the street and gave the dogs the run of his fenced-in yard.

We left about 25 minutes after 2:00 p.m. I texted Mike that we were on schedule, though barely. When we hit traffic in the Bronx, I wondered if I had spoken too soon. Sierra took the opportunity to get a picture of me at the wheel with the Bronx skyline in the background. She posted it on Facebook with the caption, "If it wasn't for him, I wouldn't be here for her." We eventually made it out of New York and retraced our steps from earlier in the day.

Once we were out of New Jersey and the traffic thinned out, Sierra offered to drive. As I pulled into a Pilot truck stop I noted a flash out of the corner of my eye. A small, dark-skinned woman was standing next to the car with a young boy in tow.

"She wants money," Sierra laughed.

"Dollars? Any money? We need dollars," is all I could make out.

"Should I give her money?"

"Yeah, give her two dollars," Sierra replied. "She's got a gold tooth." I wondered if Sierra was feeling sympathy for the woman and child or admiration for the gold tooth.

As we were leaving, the child was standing with a man pumping gas while the woman roamed the lot. "I don't know why they don't just gas jug" Sierra said as she rolled her eyes. "It'd be a lot easier."

"Gas jugging" is a panhandling technique utilized when someone has a vehicle. The kids hang around gas pumps with a gas can asking for a gallon of gas, presumably weaving a tale of how they ran out of gas. "You just hang around until they kick you out," Sierra explained.

Mike texted to ask, "How's it going?"

"Sierra's at the wheel," I replied. "In other words, we're making good time."

"Look out," was the Maestro's response.

When we reached the Maryland line, Sierra asked for food. We hit a Taco Bell drive-thru. As she pulled out from the drive-thru window, I set her chicken chalupa on the console. Just then she yelled, "How do you get out of here?" and cut the wheel to avoid a curb. The chalupa landed by my feet.

"Oh great," I yelled. I gathered up the chalupa as best I could and handed the remains to Sierra. "Sorry, the rest of it's on the floor."

"If there's any chicken, just pick it up," she responded. "Chill out, I've eaten trash."

We reached Clarksburg with half an hour to spare. Mike and Josh were glad to see Sierra, though from what I overheard, it seems one of them lost a bet.

"Looks like it'll be Coors Light tonight!" Josh exclaimed with a smile.

I managed to stay for a few songs before heading to a motel for the night.

When I got home Sunday, Tammy asked about Sierra. "She's riding with Mike," I said. Still, to be sure, I sent a "good morning" text.

She called right back.

"Hey, what's up?"

"Just check—" I began.

"We ran out of gas. We're still sitting here. At Big Otter."

"Do you need me to bring you gas?"

"Will you?"

So I grabbed a gas can and headed back up I-79. After passing Big Otter, about 40 miles up the road, I started to look for cars across the way. Unfortunately, it's one of the few places on I-79 where you can't see across the road. As I neared the Servia Road exit, Sierra called.

"We're at Big Otter."

"I know, but which side of the exit?"

"We're headed to Charleston."

"I passed the exit," I said. "I'm coming back."

"OK, we're in a silver Nissan."

As I pulled off the Servia Road exit to turn around, I noted a car on the side of the road on the southbound side. It was a Nissan, but it looked more white than silver and, quite frankly, too nice to belong to a bass player. So I just drove on by.

The phone rang.

"I'm coming," I said. "Where exactly are you?"

"We're on the interstate! We're out of gas!"

"Tell him we're near Servia Road," I hear in the background.

I gunned the engine—having been down this road once already I knew the police were not out—and turned back.

John, the new bass player, offered to pay for the gas.

Refusing the offer I said, "If you stay in a band with Sierra long enough, you'll more than repay me."

"I think he might be right about that," Josh said.

Driving Sierra home, I started to ask how long they'd been sitting on the road, but I'd feel embarrassed if I'd passed them twice in one day.

Tammy had food ready when we arrived. Sierra gobbled down her sandwiches and took a quick shower. I grabbed the keys, Sierra grabbed her makeup kit, and I drove her to Charlotte Russe.

With six minutes to spare.

ON THE ROAD WITH SPARTY

"WHY AREN'T YOU AT the office?"

Aaron had emerged from his room at half past noon and was halfway to the refrigerator before he noticed me sitting on the couch.

"I'm taking a long lunch," I said, keeping my eyes focused on the opening round of the NCAA basketball tournament, aka March Madness, and screaming at the television screen. "Come on, you've got to make those shots!"

"Do they know why you're not in the office?"

Aaron heated up leftover pizza and sat down to watch the game. "Who are we versing?"

"Valparaiso."

Midway through the second half, the Spartans appeared to be in control. "If we hold on, I may go to the game on Saturday with Ed and Gary, you know, my college roommates. Depends on the time."

"Can I come too?"

"I'd enjoy that," I said. "But let's get through this game first."

"Oh, we're going to win."

With under 30 seconds to go, Coach Izzo let in the walk-ons and an updated bracket showing a 2:45 p.m. start flashed on the screen. I picked up my iPad and tapped the StubHub app.

I instructed the StubHub search engine to find four tickets and within two minutes I texted Ed and Gary: "Tickets secured." I set down the iPad, put my suit jacket back on and told Aaron, "We leave at noon tomorrow."

◆ ◆ ◆

Despite Aaron's inauspicious beginning with my Michigan State Spartans on their journey to the 2000 national title, I'd come to enjoy watching games with him. He rarely misses the chance for a road trip with Sparty Nation.

We took our first trip to the 2012 Big Ten Tournament in Indianapolis. We left late Thursday after his evening welding class, stopped in Dayton for the night and reached Bankers Life Fieldhouse in time to grab hotdogs before the noon tipoff.

Our seats were located on the 200 level in the corner across from the MSU bench. The crowd displayed a menagerie of colors representing the Big Ten schools, including my dad's maroon and gold. Needless to say, Aaron and I were decked out in green Michigan State sweatshirts.

The band was located directly below our seats and we joined with Sparty Nation when the band played the fight song.

Aaron had learned the music years ago when he joined middle school band in sixth grade and started to play trombone. "They wanted me to play trombone because I was tall and my arms could reach the F note," Aaron recalls. I became concerned that the trombone sat neglected in the corner of Aaron's bedroom. To encourage more practice, I offered $25 if Aaron learned the Michigan State fight song by the day of the football game between the Spartans and the University of Michigan, our arch rival. Aaron accepted the challenge but never asked about getting the sheet music. Rather than chastising him for failing to practice, on the night before the game I mentioned that I'd saved $25. The next morning Aaron found my Spartan Marching Band CD and listened to the song a couple of times. Then he marched into the bedroom and played the fight song. "I play better by ear," he told me. He quickly assimilated the lyrics and the timing of the fist pump.

◆ ◆ ◆

"Are we staying for the next game?" Aaron asked midway through the opening game.

"It depends on whether we win the first one," I answered.

"Oh, we'll win," he replied.

The thrill of the Spartan victory was sweetened by the opportunity to chant "Go Green, Go White" standing side by side with my son. As the final seconds ticked off, we exchanged high fives. Then I found tickets and lodging.

Tammy called later to check in. "How are things?" she asked.

"Let me put it this way," I said. "I'm not ready to die, but if this was my last day on earth I'd go out on a high note."

On Saturday morning we checked out of the motel. Aaron understood my fear of jinxing the team by looking ahead. As he tells it, "One time I went to the bathroom when we were ahead by like six points, and I get a text saying, 'we're down by four, get back here!' Ky wouldn't let me leave my seat the rest of the game."

By the end of the day Saturday, I was back on the StubHub app looking for tickets to Sunday's championship game. The Spartans held off the Buckeyes to win the title. As we watched the confetti fall, Aaron said, "Are you crying?"

He never lets me forget that moment. As if I could ever forget my son's first Big Ten tournament. Much less the Spartans being crowned Big Ten tourney champions.

◆ ◆ ◆

When the NCAA tournament arrived the following year, Aaron told me he wanted to enter the office bracket pool. I offered to help Aaron fill out his bracket, with the understanding that I always pick MSU to go all the way.

"A 12 seed has upset a 5 seed in 24 of the last 27 tournaments," I lectured, "and a 1 seed has never lost to a 16 seed." Aaron took it upon himself to augment my tutoring by comparing statistics for each matchup. The 8-9 matchup between Pitt and Wichita State stumped him. "Look at this, they're really close," he said. "What do you think?"

"Of course they're close. It's an 8-9 game," I reminded him. "Justin's girlfriend goes to Pitt. So I'd take Pitt."

"What about Harvard versus New Mexico?"

"Is it a math or science contest?"

"No."

"Then take New Mexico."

When it came time to pick UCLA versus the University of Minnesota, I put my foot down. "Your grandfather went to Minnesota. Take the Golden Gophers." Aaron clicked Minnesota, then asked, "How about Minnesota versus Florida?"

"The Gophers can't score enough to beat Florida, so take Florida," I said. "Loyalty stops in the second round."

We listened for the scores while on the road to Detroit on Friday afternoon. Aaron asked me how his bracket fared; three of the 5-12 match-ups were won by the 12 seed, the Gophers prevailed and Harvard won its first tournament game.

"I wanted to pick the underdogs," Aaron said with feigned anger, "and you talked me out of it!"

"Give me a break. It's Harvard's first win. Ever," I retorted. "By the way, Wichita beat Pitt. Tell Justin to get a new girlfriend."

Aaron took the wheel north of Columbus. The Mini's "signature" feature is a large speedometer in the middle of the dashboard, so I couldn't help notice that the needle hovered around 80.

"Oh my God," Aaron said, rolling his eyes. "Chill out."

"Spring break rules," I calmly intoned.

Aaron looked over with a rather perplexed look on his face.

"Spring break rules," I explained. "Any ticket up to 10 miles over the speed limit, we split; if over 10 miles per hour, driver pays."

"Seriously?"

"When we were on spring break back in '78 I got pulled over just outside of Charleston," I reminisced. "I got in the cop car and the radar read 67. I was about to ask him to write it up for 65, but he just gave me a warning."

"By the way," I added. "The speed limit in Ohio is 65."

The speedometer needle fell to 75.

◆ ◆ ◆

We met up with Ed and Gary, my college roommates, the next morning for breakfast. We hadn't seen each other for almost 10 years and had a lot of catching up to do.

"I'm kind of worried about Memphis," Ed said. "They've got some athletes."

We spent nearly 10 minutes comparing game notes before talk turned to family. Aaron talked about his apprenticeship training with the International Union of Painters and Allied Trades and I provided an update on Sierra. After summarizing what I referred to as the "Hippies Trilogy," I said that Sierra was back home, working at a retail store in the mall and singing with the band.

"It's like the season on *Dallas* when Bobby had died, then the next season it turned out to be a dream," I said. Ed and I were such devoted *Dallas* fans during college that we skipped a speech by the president of NBC News to find out who shot J.R. "She's back where she was before. It's like the journey was just a bad dream."

Ed mentioned that his oldest son attended the University of Michigan. They watched the MSU-Michigan football game together. "We lost, and I think he feels responsible," Ed said. "I don't know, but we don't watch the U of M games together anymore."

U of M was playing in the first game at the Palace. When we pulled in to pick up the tickets, Gary commented on a couple of guys walking out together—one in Wolverine maize and blue, the other in Spartan green and white. "Look at that," he laughed. "A mixed couple."

We sat quietly through the U of M game, standing only for the national anthem and applauding only for the walk-ons. U of M admittedly looked good. "I hate to admit this," I told Aaron, "but you're watching three future NBA players."

We ate $7 hotdogs for lunch. "There's just something about hot dogs at a game," Aaron said.

"I know, you just have to eat one," Ed answered.

The crowd was a mix of alumni, students and local basketball fans. Some alums, like Gary, were subdued, wearing light green sweaters and turtlenecks bearing small Spartan logos. In contrast, Ed and I went all-out with official NCAA Spartan garb. That morning I had changed outfits more than Sierra did in high school. I left the final decision to Aaron. "Wear the white with the green lettering. It stands out more. And wear the green jacket over it." Aaron wore a freshly-minted NCAA March Madness shirt emblazoned with the Spartan logo.

MSU came out strong in the first half, but due to a combination of misguided turnovers and Memphis athleticism the lead was only 3 at the half.

"We'll be OK," I said with some degree of false bravado. "We've been behind at halftime for most of the year."

"Yeah, I know," Ed responded. "But, man, we're only in this game because Harris is unconscious, hitting on those threes."

Back in college Ed served as sports editor for the *State News*, so I welcomed his insights. "Appling needs to take charge. Trice is too small, not strong enough to run the point. Dawson's got amazing athletic talent, but not an ounce of basketball skills. Byrd's never recovered from that injury and it's all in his head."

"I think Valentine's got loads of potential," I inserted.

"Yeah, but he's not fast enough or quick enough to play point guard in the Big 10," Ed instructed me.

Ever the optimist, I asked about next year.

"If we keep everybody, we're a top five team," Ed explained. "But Payne is playing like an NBA center right now."

Aaron offered his two cents, suggesting that Coach Izzo needed to play more zone defense. The topic of zone versus man-to-man defense has been a point of contention since I coached Aaron's youth league teams. Aaron and I both realized that I was incapable of teaching kids man-to-man defense, and ever since Aaron has been a disciple of zone defense.

The Spartans built a double-digit lead during the second half and seemed content to slow the game down. "I don't know, I don't like this," Gary said. "Someone needs to take a shot." Aaron agreed, "It's like no one wants the ball." Ed just clutched his program and muttered, "Oh man." Nerves tightened even more when Harris and Trice each picked up a fourth foul and Appling left the game holding his shoulder.

Valentine came to the rescue. Proving Ed wrong, he took over the point and made perfectly timed passes inside, where Nix and Payne dominated the paint. The lead reached 20.

With 22 seconds left, Izzo put in Byrd along with the walk-ons. Byrd promptly dropped in a layup. "Oh yeah," Ed yelled, "Byrd needed that." Memphis came down the floor with 16 seconds to go and the crowd headed for the exits. As Gary stood up to leave, Ed got excited. "Memphis averages 70 point a game," he said. "I want to keep them under 50." I stood next to Gary but screamed with Ed, "Go D! Come on!" The ball went out of bounds with 2.1 seconds left, and by then Aaron was ready to go too. Ed and I remained fixated on the court as Memphis inbounded the ball. "No shot!"

As the final buzzer sounded, Ed summed it up: "Oh man, that's the most nerve-wracking 70–48 win I've ever witnessed."

After the game, Aaron and I headed to East Lansing in search of a jersey for the next road trip. I ended up buying a jersey and hat for Aaron, a workout shirt for Tammy and an embroidered MSU dress for Sierra. I warned the student cashier not to laugh. "In 30 years you'll be back here buying this stuff."

We arrived home shortly before the Duke-Creighton game. "Maybe we should watch," I said. "We play the winner Friday in Indy."

"If it's Duke, I'm going with you," Aaron said.

DÉJÀ VU

SIERRA FINISHED DOING HER makeup as I pulled into the mall garage, hopping out as soon as I stopped the car.

"I gotta go or I'll be late. Love you."

Before I could say, "See you tonight," she was off and running.

600LBS OF SIN! played the Polo Club in Parkersburg that evening. The name and accompanying Ralph Lauren-like logo are a misnomer. The specialty of the house is a rack of 24 barbecued ribs and the club doubles as a video lottery establishment. My mom and I certainly looked out of place in our business attire. Ignoring the hostess's double take, my mom asked, "Have you got a table with a good view of the band?"

As soon as we sat down, some of the band members came over. The bass player bragged to my mom about the time I drove 40 miles back up the interstate with a gas can. "He's more reliable than AAA," he joked. "We call him the courtesy patrol." Mike came by to offer condolences on Michigan State's loss to Duke in the NCAA basketball tourney. "I hate Duke," he added. That the Maestro was not a fan of an elite private university came as no surprise. His ode to the financial crisis goes, "The Lord Is My Banker, He's Too Big to Fail."

Sierra stopped by between sets, and late in the show she motioned for Frieda to come up. They danced as Mike and Josh jammed. Shortly after the dance we headed out, and Sierra stopped to give us hugs.

"See you tomorrow."

◆ ◆ ◆

The spring music festival season started that weekend with Hoopla in the Hills outside Athens, Ohio. Sierra and Monk were going a day ahead. I got home early and came out front to see them off. Sierra looked like she'd seen a ghost.

"What are you doing here?"

"I live here," I replied with a touch of sarcasm.

Sierra's soiled hiking backpack was no longer an objet d'art in her room, but instead rested on her back, causing her to slump ever so slightly.

"Going away?"

"We're going to the festival," she stammered. "We'll be camping...."

"I know," I said. "I'm just giving you grief. You are coming back?"

"Yes," she sighed with exasperation. "Oh my God."

Monk came out to finish loading the car. When he opened the rear hatch, he proudly pointed out the new tent and air mattress.

"We'll get a lot of hippies in that," Sierra said.

"No hippies," Monk shouted, pushing away imaginary hippies.

◆ ◆ ◆

A couple of weeks earlier, Monk had asked Tammy if she thought Sierra was going to stay.

"I think it's 50-50," she replied. "Emily shows up in the van on a nice spring day, Sierra's gone."

Tammy had met Emily a few weeks earlier. Not too long after our New York trip, Boogie began barking wildly at three o'clock in the morning. Rushing outside to see what caused the commotion, Tammy screamed. "There's a van out there! With three dogs!"

I immediately thought, "That would be Marley, Torino and Diesel."

As Tammy struggled to pull Boogie back in the house, we heard footsteps coming from downstairs.

"Hey Sean," I said.

"Hey, how's it going? Sorry about the dogs," he said as he moved the gate blocking the stairs to the basement.

"I'm Sean," he said, extending his hand to Tammy.

Tammy managed a polite smile as she shook his hand. "I'm Tammy."

Boogie kept us up the rest of night, defiantly pacing around the bedroom. He'd done the same when Reptar and Matt visited for Christmas.

Sierra joined us at breakfast, clearly unaware that anything was out of the ordinary. Then again, "ordinary" had become a relative term. Sierra often had friends visit, and we were never quite sure who might come up the stairs. The kids generally hung out downstairs around Sierra's bedroom. And the refrigerator with the beer is located down in the laundry room.

That evening Tammy was sorting laundry when she bumped into a young woman grabbing a beer from the fridge.

"I'm Emily. Thanks so much for letting us stay."

Later that evening Tammy reminded me that "a little communication helps." I'd neglected to tell Tammy that in addition to Sean and three dogs we were also hosting Emily.

After a couple of days, Sierra found another place for the traveling kids to stay.

"What about the dogs?" Tammy asked. "I hope they're not stuck in the van."

After a few days Emily and Sean hit the road, and Sierra returned to her day job at Charlotte Russe and performing with 600LBS OF SIN!

◆ ◆ ◆

Sierra was still wary of driving after her encounter with a deer that nearly totaled the Skunkmobile. (That's her story and she's sticking to it.) Tammy and I remained on standby to provide transportation for Sierra's job at the mall, sometimes on a day's notice if we were lucky. We left the Maestro in charge of getting Sierra to gigs.

Tammy overheard Mike and Sierra going over the upcoming schedule: the Hideaway Saloon in Louisville on March 12, the Glass on the 17th, Hoopla on April 6. Sierra repeated the dates as she wrote them on her calendar.

"Oh," Mike added, "we're at Los Agaves again this year for Cinco de Mayo."

"OK," Sierra said, "what's the date?"

Both Mike and Tammy burst out laughing.

Sierra was not amused.

The manager at Charlotte Russe helped Sierra work her schedule so that she could make the shows. One Saturday, however, Sierra was scheduled to work until 8:00 and the Sin Van was scheduled to leave at 7:00. I dropped Sierra off at the mall, confirming that I would pick her up at 8:00, prepared to run up the road.

I arrived at the mall shortly after 7:30, stopping to wait at Starbucks. A few minutes after 8:00, I ambled past the store. No sign of Sierra. I sent a text. No response. I called Sierra's phone. No answer.

After a few more tries, I got a text from Mike. "Are you trying to reach Sierra? She's asleep in the back of the van."

Musicians.

◆ ◆ ◆

Three weeks later, on the Sunday night Sierra was supposed to return from the Hoopla festival in Athens, I once again found my calls and texts going unanswered. Late that night Tammy texted Monk to see where they were.

"Oh, I meant to tell you," he replied, "Sierra stayed with the guitarist from the Rumpke Brothers to write music. She's coming back tomorrow."

"I hope that's the case," Tammy said as she told me what Monk had said.

"Me too," I said as I turned off the lamp by the bed.

The following morning, after a sleepless night, I left Sierra a voicemail. "I hope you told the manager you'd be gone."

"I'll call soon," she texted.

Two days later I followed up with a text. "Hey you! I'm getting a lot of questions. Are you coming home?"

The answer came within a matter of seconds. "No, but I'm fine."

I stared momentarily at the iPhone screen, then broke the news to Tammy.

"I'm sorry," she said, clutching my arm.

Next I called Monk to let him know.

"Really," he said with a hint of surprise. "She said she was just going for the day to write music."

"She's not writing music. She's traveling."

I alerted Mike that the band would once again be playing Cinco de Mayo without a female vocalist. "Better teach Jakob the chords to 'Severine,'" I added, recalling how the band relied on Josh's son to fill the void when Sierra ditched last year's show.

The band decided to go on without a female vocalist. "This is the title track of our CD," Mike would tell the crowd when signing "29." "That's not me singing on the CD, but I've got to sing it now."

◆ ◆ ◆

Tammy and I decided to maintain Sierra's cell phone and iPad data plan so she could get in touch with us if she needed, like the previous summer when she called to say the Yellowstone Park police needed the home address for a camping citation.

No calls or messages came, but eventually Sierra updated her Facebook status from the Union Pacific railroad station in northern California: "Sunburned but in the Roseville pines." In the weeks that followed, Sierra maintained a picturesque journal under the heading, "Going Going Strong." One photo showed Sierra standing by a railroad trestle with snow-capped mountains on the horizon: "in the Sierras." I particularly admired the composition of another shot, a CSX container stacked on a flatbed train car standing out against the mountains, but I thought it best not to "like" a photograph taken while trespassing on a train. Other traveling kids commented on the pictures, adding snippets of their own visits to various swimming holes and other hop-off points.

Sierra traveled as far north as Seattle ("guess I'm in the wrong place to wish for no more rain"), then back through Portland ("it's a black hole") and back to Oroville, California, to hang out with Kitty.

The posts from Utah were less enthusiastic. "It's hard when you've got a broken collarbone and you have to carry your worldly belongings on your back." Apparently alcohol and backpacking over Utah's rocky terrain don't mix.

More news from Utah arrived in our mailbox: eight envelopes and a postcard addressed to Sierra Ferrell. I don't open Sierra's mail without permission, but this time I didn't have to. The envelopes bore the legend "Attorney Advertising Material." One was emblazoned with a bull dog and the slogan, "kick ass criminal defense attorneys." Though taken aback at what my profession has become, if Sierra needs a lawyer, I'm hiring the bull dog.

"Official correspondence" from the Circuit Court of Umatilla County, Oregon, came later. At least Sierra learned her home address.

◆ ◆ ◆

Sierra called in mid-July.

"Hey," she said cheerfully.

"Well, it's nice to hear from you. So where are you?"

"Back in California, but I'm coming home for a few weeks."

"Any idea when? You do realize that your driver's license expires on your birthday?"

"I know, August 3. I'll be back before then."

"Any plans after that?"

"I'll stay a few weeks," she said. "I'll find somewhere to stay—he's got a dog. Then we're going to visit his family in Kentucky."

"Does 'he' have a name?"

"Noah."

"I look forward to meeting him."

"Yeah," she replied sheepishly.

"And?"

"Polly's almost seven and she doesn't travel so well anymore," Sierra explained. "We want to find a good home for her. She's a good dog."

"Sierra, we have two dogs already.... No promises."

I changed the subject and asked about the itinerary following Kentucky.

"Hawaii. He's got family there."

It's also Sierra's birthplace.

These plans led to numerous jokes around the office.

"Does she know there's no train service?"

"I don't know," I replied. "Maybe she plans to stowaway on a freighter."

"I wouldn't mention that—she might try it."

◆ ◆ ◆

Two weeks before her birthday, Sierra announced on Facebook that she was "on rootay—WV bound. Gotta ways to go. Looking forward to the ride. Take me home freight train, take me home."

Aaron and Justin were curious about when Sierra might arrive.

"I have no idea." As sophisticated as Apple has become, the map application doesn't calculate travel time via freight train.

"I guess there's not a train schedule," Justin said with a laugh.

"Actually there is," I replied, "but I'm not sure it's legal, so I don't keep one."

We were left to rely on Facebook for status updates.

Within a day Sierra posted from Wyoming, having successfully gone through Utah without needing the services of
a kick-ass criminal defense attorney. She enjoyed a bottle of
champagne while sitting in the shade on a "skirted pig." A trailer
with side skirts loaded on a flatbed rail car leaves enough head-
room for a petite young hippie to rest on her backpack. Later
she posted a picture of a locomotive, adding "made it just in
time to catch this bad boy." Gives new meaning to "making your
connection."

Sierra got waylaid in Cheyenne, Wyoming. By a street fair.
"Can I get like $50 to buy people presents?" she asked. "And I need
a guitar or I am going to die." I blamed my inability to move cash
from my wallet to Wyoming on the "@#%$ bankers." "I know,"
she responded. "It's okay."

No news came for a few days. I held my breath, wondering if
I'd come home to find Sierra, Noah and Polly taking up residence
in the treehouse. I seriously thought of this as a lodging compromise. After all, Sierra does say she loves sleeping outside.

In California she lived under a bridge. One night when I tried to
call her, Sierra texted that she couldn't hear the phone because
"where I'm at is kinda loud." I naively assumed she was playing an
open mic. Wrong. The next day I called and again seemed to have
a poor connection. "I'm under a bridge!" Sierra screamed.

She even posted a picture of her home away from home on
Facebook. It looked neater than the way she left her room. I sent
my mom a copy with the re: line "your granddaughter, the troll."

"What?" Frieda exclaimed. "I just googled troll. Why is she
doing that?"

"Because the role of 'urchin,'" a reference to Mike's line in
"Severine," "was so confining, so Elizabethan."

"Touche," Frieda retorted.

Being a parent of a gypsy—they prefer the term "traveling
kids"—leads to many odd habits. When running in the morning,
my partners look at people sleeping under the bridge with idle
curiosity.

"Doesn't look like an L.L. Bean backpack," one of my part-ners joked.

"I'm just glad it's not the one from Cabela's," I thought.

◆ ◆ ◆

Sierra's birthday came and went with no news. The next morning she posted pictures from downtown Chicago.

Later Aaron told me, "Hey, Sissy's going to be in town next week." I left a message asking Sierra to confirm.

"Calm down," came the reply. "Soon enough. I really don't know when I'm going to be there."

"Also I have short hair now," she added.

I winced, recalling Sierra's response when I invited her to dinner on her 19th birthday: "I have a Mohawk."

Sierra stayed in Indianapolis for a friend's Saturday night gig and then went to Louisville, where she enjoyed a day at the zoo with Noah's mother and sister. I half-expected to get a call asking for a ride. But then I saw Sierra's RSVP for the Sin's show at the Hideaway Saloon in Louisville.

"You have to admire her," I told Tammy. "She leaves the band—twice—and now she's going to ask to catch a ride home on the bus. Maybe I should warn them she comes with a dirty hippie and a dog."

"She'll end up on stage with them," Tammy said, rolling her eyes. "Those guys will melt."

"Thank you for the real good time Louisville," the band's Facebook page read. "Those who were there were treated to an impromptu reunion set with Sierra Ferrell... and she was in rare form!"

Mike called me the next day. "I thought you'd want to know. We gave Sierra a ride back in the van. But," he added, "no hippie boyfriend and no dog."

"WORK SMARTER, NOT HARDER"

"YOU SHOULD GO TO culinary school," I told Aaron when he asked what he should do for a career.

"Why?"

"Because you like to cook, you're a good cook, and you've got charisma," I said. "I can see you owning your own restaurant someday."

"I know, but I don't need to learn how to cook."

"Listen, if you don't want to hear my advice," I said. "Don't ask."

◆ ◆ ◆

Having an 18-year-old sleeping all day and playing Xbox all night was getting old. Fast.

One morning I came back from my six o'clock run to find Aaron sitting on the couch watching television.

"What's up?" I said.

"Not much," he replied. "I'm tired. I'm going to get some sleep."

"Aaron," I said. "It's 7:30 in the morning."

"I've been up all night," he said as he headed down the hall.

A few minutes later I updated Tammy on Aaron's status. She just sighed and shook her head. "I don't know what to do about him," she said.

"Me neither," I said, feeling my heart rate rising like I was still running. "But we've got to do something."

Part of my problem was finding an opportunity to talk with Aaron. He'd fallen into a routine of getting up in the early evening—my supper was his breakfast—and going to bed when I was headed to the office.

The stress was building. Fortunately, Aaron was already up and searching for food one night when I arrived home from work. I capitalized on the opportunity by casually asking about his future plans.

"I don't want you to think we're trying to get rid of you," I said.

"Don't lie. Yes you are."

"OK, so I am," I admitted. "But that's the natural order of things. You turn 18, you move out of your parents' house. Obamacare means you can stay on our health insurance until you're 26, not that you have to live with us until you're 26."

"Oh, I don't mind," Aaron said with a grin.

When we did talk seriously about career plans, the discussions usually turned out to sound like a broken record. But for Aaron's diabetes, I'd probably have insisted he join the military.

◆ ◆ ◆

I'm sure Aaron took a career test in school. When I took the Kuder preference test in eighth grade, I followed my father's advice. "Choose the answer that involves writing whenever possible," Dad told me. "And never choose to work alone." I recall the smile on Dad's face when I told him the preference test pegged me as a journalist.

When I got wind that Aaron was taking this test, I passed on his grandfather's advice. I'm also confident that he rigged the test to suggest he be a ranch hand.

◆ ◆ ◆

Aaron didn't seem to mind celebrating his 18th birthday living at home that summer. But as the autumn leaves began to fall, both the boredom and the tension intensified. That's when Aaron told us that he wanted to go to school to learn welding.

Tammy grimaced and shook her head when she heard this idea. I once more suggested culinary school. Aaron insisted that he wanted to become a welder. Eventually I relented, telling Tammy, "He likes to work with his hands, and the job market for welders is good. Plus, I don't see any other options." At the same time, I knew absolutely nothing about how one becomes a welder.

A breakthrough came in October, ironically after finding my way out of a corn maze. I was attending a diabetes family support group outing and found myself talking to the father of his recently diagnosed 15-year-old son. I listened to his story and let him know that he was not alone.

"I still can't count carbs correctly," I confessed. After a few minutes we both grew tired of talking diabetes. I asked, "What do you do for a living?"

"I'm a welder," he said.

I swung my leg over the picnic table bench and turned directly toward him. "My son is interested in welding," I said. "Any suggestion for schools?"

He told me that one of the best programs was located in Marietta, Ohio, about 15 miles from my mom's house. A plan began to come together. That evening I broached the subject with Tammy. We reviewed the pros and cons. As usual I tended to look at the pros and she reminded me of the cons. In the end we saw no other options. The next day I mentioned the idea to Aaron.

"Hey, you should have come to the corn maze yesterday," I told him.

"Why?"

"One of the other fathers is a welder," I said. "He told me about a good program."

Aaron instantly sensed my positive vibe. He pointed the remote at the television, punched the off button, and turned to look me in the eye. "What did he say?"

By the end of the week, I joined Aaron on a tour of the welding school. The instructor met us as we entered the shop area. He looked to be in his 50s, judging by the gray hair that protruded from under his bandana. Like the students, he wore a leather apron, heavy work boots and dirty jeans. Metallic dust covered the floor.

"We pride ourselves on keeping the shop clean and organized," the instructor boasted.

He showed us the stations, various welding tools and the classroom area. It wasn't the lecture hall I'd envisioned years ago, but I sensed that Aaron seemed at home.

"Do you want to enroll?" I asked.

"I really don't have a choice," he answered. "I've got to do something."

"Is this what you want?"

"That's what I've been trying to tell you," he said.

◆ ◆ ◆

Aaron enrolled for the January semester. On Christmas day he found a welding helmet under the tree along with a tool chest. On New Year's Day we moved his bed, television and Xbox to my mom's house, where Aaron took up residence in my old bedroom. Since my mom worked three days a week and Aaron attended evening classes, he didn't seem to mind rooming with Frieda. Both Aaron and Sierra brag that they've got the coolest grandmother: "She drinks wine and eats chocolate. And drives a convertible."

The first weekend, Aaron came home filled with stories about the school, his classmates and instructors.

"There's this one guy," Aaron said, starting to laugh. "He's a nice guy, but his grammar is awful. I don't think he ever learned about double negatives."

Another weekend Aaron came home with a metal plate that he had welded together. I listened politely as he described the work product, with absolutely no idea what he meant. On more than one occasion he tried to explain stick and MIG welding, but I still don't understand the difference.

As far as Tammy and I could tell, Aaron was progressing from stick to MIG welding without any problems. We no longer changed the subject when friends and colleagues asked the inevitable question, "What's Aaron doing these days?"

"He's taking welding classes" sounded so much better than euphemisms like "He's considering his options."

A rude awakening came in June. Aaron had thrown his jeans down the laundry chute, so I picked them up to throw in with a load of dark clothes. Out of habit, I checked his pockets. Pulling out a movie ticket was nothing out of the ordinary. Out of curiosity, I looked at the movie title: *The Avengers*. No surprise. Then, in a revival of the time I uncovered cigarette butts in Sierra's garbage, I read the rest of the ticket stub.

"Wednesday, 5:35 p.m. Grand Central Cinemas."

A burning sensation arose in my stomach.

Later that evening I confronted Aaron. He couldn't credibly deny that he'd skipped class to go to a movie. Having lived with two lawyers, I expected that he might raise some due process or search and seizure objection. I outflanked him, however, saying, "Why did you leave the ticket in your pocket? If you had thrown it out, I wouldn't be in this position."

We contacted the school's attendance officer and learned that Aaron's "movie night" was not the first time he'd missed class. We talked with Aaron and reached the consensus that maybe he would do better going to the day classes. At the same time, we stayed in touch with the instructor.

A few weeks later the instructor called. Clearly, Aaron's heart was not in welding. I asked if Aaron could obtain any certification based on what he had completed. The instructor acknowledged that Aaron had mastered MIG welding and could pass the test.

"I wish he'd finish," Tammy said, clearly exasperated.

"I know," I replied. "But let's face it, he's not going to finish. And, if he doesn't want to work as a welder, it doesn't make any sense for him to take another three months in welding school."

Tammy sighed, shook her head and nodded in resignation.

When Aaron came home that week I told him to meet me at my office.

"Let's go in the conference room," I said. The change of venue clearly disturbed him. He sat down and swung around in the chair nervously as I shut the door.

"Why are we meeting here?" he asked.

"I want you to be focused," I said. "This is serious and we need to find a solution."

He just nodded, making eye contact while waiting for me to continue.

"You don't like welding, do you?"

"I don't know, it's just that..." he began.

"Be honest," I said. "You don't want to work as a welder."

"It's just..." he began to say before I cut him off again.

"It's hot, it's dirty, and it's hard work," I said. "And if that's not what you want to do, then let's stop paying tuition for it."

Aaron's shoulders relaxed and a smile came across his face. "Are you serious?"

"Yes," I said. "But, I want you to finish out the MIG. Your instructor thinks if you practice you can pass the test. At least you'll have one certification."

"Oh, I can pass the test right now," Aaron replied. By this point he was sitting upright with his hands on the conference table.

"Then do it," I said.

Afterwards, we met Tammy for dinner and discussed plans going forward.

"You need to find a job," we told him. "Soon."

◆ ◆ ◆

That fall Aaron told us he was interested in construction, specifically drywalling and painting. We talked to a friend who had contacts in the local union, and he arranged for Aaron to apply for the apprenticeship program of the International Union of Painters and Allied Trades.

Aaron was accepted into the program, but the training program didn't start until January. That meant another couple months of hanging out, because the prospect of finding a short-term job seemed dismal.

In mid-January, Aaron left for several days to attend the first training session. He returned with a combination of "war stories" and safety instructions. To this day Aaron will look for the best way to manage a project, whether it's moving a king size mattress or putting furniture together. Inevitably he'll remind me to "work smarter, not harder." He also bragged about sandblasting a tank while standing on a plank hanging thirty feet in the air.

Another time he came home with t-shirts emblazoned with "IUPAT Families for Obama" and "Buy Union" bumper stickers on his truck. "I got one for you too, Tammy," he said as he passed over a shirt. Tammy's grandfather, a diehard union man until the day he died, would have enjoyed seeing his Republican granddaughter wearing an AFL-CIO t-shirt.

Aaron attended training once a week each month. The weeks in between training were spent texting his union rep to see if any jobs were available and waiting for the phone to ring. Unfortunately, the only jobs were out of state, some as far away as Indiana, and the per diem offered to apprentices was minimal.

By early June, Aaron decided that a career as an industrial painter was not in the cards. I told him that if he wasn't going to continue, then he at least needed to call the business agent and tell him.

"Always try to leave on good terms," I said. "West Virginia's a small state and you never know when you'll cross paths again."

By that point, Tammy and I quit trying. "Eventually he'll get bored playing Xbox," I said.

"We can only hope," Tammy replied.

◆ ◆ ◆

Aaron worked for a brief period as a short order cook at a barbe-cue joint and then as a general laborer for a company that sold and installed commercial office furniture. That gave him the opportunity to get a Class D license, which led to gainful employ-ment with a rural ambulance company in Doddrige County as an ambulance driver. I've often been reminded that the politically correct term is "Emergency Vehicle Operator."

The station was located just over two hours away, so Aaron stayed at the station three to four nights a week. Which meant he was finally able to put his culinary skills to good use—as the station chef.

WASABI

OUTSIDE OF ABE LINCOLN'S birthplace, the hub of activity on Saturday night in Bardstown, Kentucky, was the local Chili's Grill & Bar. The bar patrons included a husband and wife decked out in UK apparel, a couple of guys in their early 30s still carrying their golf ball markers on their caps, and a petite girl in her mid-20s wearing torn black lace stockings and a Hermes knockoff green silk scarf, sitting with a gray-haired gentleman decked out in Michigan State apparel.

"Hey, are you with Sierra?" came a text. "Has she got her pup yet?"

"Not yet. Eating supper. Then 25 minutes to Elizabethtown."

Sierra proudly placed her now current ID on the bar and told the bartender to make whatever margarita he chose—as long as he used the biggest glass.

Sierra had returned to Charleston a few weeks earlier, arriving with little more notice than when she departed in early April. Her plan was to stay a few weeks, renew her driver's license and earn a few dollars.

Her final task was to get her dog. While I was less then enthralled with the idea of Sierra taking responsibility for a dog, it was a fait accompli.

The lineage of Sierra's puppy goes back to Sierra's first summer of traveling. Riding out of Asheville, North Carolina, Sierra hooked up with Kitty, already a seasoned traveler at 21, and Chicken Nugget, Kitty's Australian shepherd puppy.

The year before, Kitty met a traveler named Jake, who was riding the rails with Tuna, a German shepherd/Catahoula leopard mix. Kitty and Jake were married—by an Eagle Scout—in the woods outside Biloxi, Mississippi on February 11. (211 is the moniker of their favorite whiskey.) Tuna and Chicken Nugget consummated their relationship. The kids kept one of the litter, Bacon, and headed back out on the road. Feeling the love after the Rainbow Gathering in Montana, Tuna and Chicken Nugget repeated the cycle. Kitty and Jake came back to Kentucky to live in her parents' basement while they waited for Chicken Nugget to have her litter.

Kitty gave traveling kids first dibs provided they met her adoption criteria: (1) willingness to keep the dog and take care of it, (2) name the dog after a food, and (3) travel to Elizabethtown to pick up the dog. Sierra insisted that she could take good care of a puppy, and she had a name in mind: Wasabi.

I didn't need to ask how Sierra planned to get to Kentucky.

After our Saturday night supper in Chili's Grill & Bar, we drove to Elizabethtown, where we met Kitty to pick up the puppy. Kitty apologized for not meeting us halfway. "Jake starts work tomorrow at the Ford plant," she explained.

Sierra and Kitty spent a few minutes trading traveling stories, and then we headed back to Charleston. Wasabi was restless at first, but eventually snuggled onto my jacket. Sierra sang "Mr. Moon" for a lullaby. Sierra was staying with a friend in Charleston and I dropped her and Wasabi off shortly after one o'clock in the morning. Despite the hour, when I arrived home I set my alarm. Wasabi would need puppy chow.

◆ ◆ ◆

Sierra had returned to Charleston several weeks earlier, catching a ride on the Sin bus following her impromptu reunion with the band in Louisville. The evening after I received Mike's text that she was on the bus, Tammy answered the doorbell to find Monk standing on the front porch.

"I brought you something," he said with a smirk.

On cue, Sierra stepped from behind the porch column.

"I'm back in town," Sierra announced. "I need some clothes for tonight. We're going to the Glass."

I was pulling into the driveway when I received a stoic text. "Sierra and Monk are at the house." I went straight to Sierra's room and gave her a hug. Clothes were strewn across her bedroom floor.

"I've got so much stuff!" I bit my tongue as I recalled replacing the closet rod that gave way under the weight of Sierra's "stuff." An hour later she came upstairs to say goodbye.

Two days later, I pulled in the driveway to find a young man in his late 20s standing near the front porch, taking a relaxed drag on a cigarette. He stood about six feet, stocky, with short brown hair and a neatly trimmed beard.

"I'm Noah," he said, holding out his hand.

"Nice to meet you."

"Hey!" Sierra came walking over from the treehouse.

Next I heard Boogie barking loudly, standing in the library window looking out. Sure enough, he had spotted Polly, a seven-year-old black lab. I went inside and hooked Boogie up. "Best he meets Polly outside," I explained.

Though almost as big as Boogie, Polly cast a wary eye and started toward Noah before meeting Boogie nose to nose. They carefully sniffed each other out, and then Polly headed to the grass. Boogie turned his attention to Sierra and wagged his tail excitedly.

Once inside, Sierra took Noah downstairs to gather clothes. I politely waited a few minutes before going down to remind her that I needed to get back to work.

Sierra was laid out across the Tempur-Pedic mattress reading her book of birthdays. This is a book that purports to identify whether people are compatible based on their birth dates. "I'm telling him why Emily and I are soul sisters," she explained.

◆ ◆ ◆

A few days later I took Sierra out for a father-daughter date night. The bartender smiled brightly as we sat down. "Sierra! Haven't seen you for a while. I've missed your singing." Then the waitress came over. "Sierra! Did you cut your hair?" We toasted Sierra's safe return over sake and a gin martini.

"You know," I began, setting down my drink, "how you live your life is up to you. You are 25 years old. But, I will tell you that if you want to earn a living singing, riding trains and sleeping under bridges is not the best way to get there."

"I know," she said, her eyes staying focused on her second cup of sake. "Hey! I made $60 flying at Walmart this afternoon."

"So," I asked in a stealth effort to discover what led to the plethora of Utah attorney solicitations that had come that summer, "what was the best part of the summer and what was the worst?"

"The festival in Seattle," she said with a twinkle in her eye. "Of course we had to sleep under a bridge because it rained all week."

"I take it Utah was the low point?"

"I broke my collarbone!"

"So I heard," I said in an omnipotent tone, adding with a smile, "I'll never forget going to the mailbox that day and seeing those attorney letters."

"Oh, that was just a citation for trespassing on railroad property," she said.

"I thought that was in Oregon," I replied. "You're getting 'official mail' from some circuit court there. Now, getting back to Utah…"

"It's nothing."

"Sierra, every criminal defense lawyer in Utah was asking you to hire them."

"That's because I rode that ambulance," she said. "I wish I had never taken the ambulance. But I had a broken collarbone and was carrying my backpack."

"I know. I've seen the bills."

"I'd really rather not talk about Utah."
I didn't say any more.

◆ ◆ ◆

Sierra and I made plans for her to come over on Saturday to go through clothes and celebrate her birthday. I invited Noah and Polly as well.

"We'll come early," she promised.

Saturday I received a Facebook message shortly before one o'clock. "Be there soon. Just woke up." I rushed to the store for burgers and Boston cream pie.

They arrived 45 minutes later.

"Hey, you've got hamburgers ready. And Boston cream pie," she said, looking up with a smile. "I'm not hungry."

Tammy came home and we gave Sierra her presents. I'd already replaced the boots from last year, and Tammy added a book about "the soul of a woman" and a locket with ruby slippers (with a $50 bill and our cell numbers enclosed). "In case you ever want to come home, just click the ruby slippers," Tammy explained. And, of course, a new cell phone.

"Hey," Sierra said, "What's Ferguson's number?"

"It's in the phone."

"Ky, Ferguson, Tammy," she read as she thumbed through the contact list.

"Mike P," she added, rolling her eyes.

"Never know when you'll need a cab."

◆ ◆ ◆

I put the Boston cream pie back in the fridge, wondering if Sierra would be back before the filling spoiled. She called on Wednesday.

"Hey, we're taking Ferguson home and we're coming over for Boston cream pie. See you in 20." Forty-three minutes later we heard a car in the driveway.

We served Boston cream pie and gourmet coffee to Sierra, Noah and Ferguson. Polly just tried to stay close to Noah.

"She's seven," Sierra said. "She's nervous about Boogie. And Dolly's too grouchy." Turning to Noah, she added, "Dolly's 13 years old!"

Polly didn't seem to know where she fit—almost as big as Boogie but a few years older—but a good six years younger than Dolly. Eventually the three dogs worked out their pecking order. Boogie was a true gentleman, letting Polly eat from his food dish.

Polly has been traveling with Noah since she was a puppy. Sierra told us that when they were in Chicago they made Polly "service tags" at a local Kinko's so that they could take her into the movie.

They left a few minutes after 10:00. Sierra was driving her mom's car and she had promised to have the car back by nine o'clock.

My cell phone vibrated just before one o'clock the next morning. I ignored it. Two minutes later I got a text. "We need you. Car overheated on the hill."

"Our hill?"

"Yeah."

I debated whether to wake up Tammy and decided against it. I got up quietly and found a pair of shorts.

The screen illuminated again. "We're coming up the hill."

I met them outside.

"You can hear it," Sierra said, as if I didn't believe her.

I mentally took stock of the situation. Sierra and her hippie boyfriend, plus a dog, and an overheated car with malfunctioning power steering evoked memories of driving a '71 Mustang to Michigan State. But for the kindness of strangers and the willingness of my parents to travel, I might still be outside Athens, Ohio, with a leaking radiator hose or in Columbus with a broken fan belt.

"Come on in and we'll deal with it tomorrow," I said. "Just try to be quiet."

"This will be great," Sierra told Noah. "We can watch a movie on the big screen."

Sierra rummaged through the fridge, Boogie paced behind the bedroom door, and I pondered whether my marriage of 25 years would survive the night.

◆ ◆ ◆

When I got home from work the following afternoon, I found Sierra stretched out on the couch. Turns out she had slept all day. Noah and Polly were waiting patiently for Sierra to wake up.

"Hey, what are you doing?"

"I've got a soccer game at 7:00," I replied. "What are you doing?"

"I've got a job interview at 5:00."

"I take it you need a ride?"

"Do you mind?"

I waited patiently while Sierra changed clothes and did her makeup before loading everyone into the Mini. Polly seemed relaxed sitting in the backseat, resting her head on the side of the car and enjoying the breeze. She seemed to prefer the convertible to a freight train.

I dropped the kids off at Buffalo Wild Wings and left for my soccer game. I felt a pang of guilt, abandoning Sierra without a ride. "She'll be fine," I told myself. "After all, she made it to Seattle for crying out loud."

Not to worry. Aaron happened to be at Lowe's. He picked up two traveling kids and a dog.

◆ ◆ ◆

"You'll find me in St Albans/sleeping under bridges & toasting your subs at the way," read the Facebook update. Sierra indeed had joined the Subway team while Noah worked the "taco line" at a nearby Taco Bell.

"They want me to train for assistant manager," Noah told me. "But I don't want to deal with being in charge."

Two weeks later Sierra called to see if I wanted to "chill." After I accepted, she added, "but no talking about jobs or careers." I fed the dogs and let Tammy know that she'd be on her own for dinner.

Sierra came down the street carrying a purse, a backpack and of course a guitar.

"I guess Noah's working tonight," I said as we started down Capitol Street.

"He's back in California."

"What?"

"Yeah, he left a week ago," Sierra told me. "I'm going in a couple of weeks."

"Where to?"

"The fields," she answered with an impish grin. "We're going to earn some money so we can go to Hawaii."

Sierra added that she might work for a couple more weeks to earn some money to buy Carhartt overalls and a backpack. When our burgers arrived, Sierra broached the balance of her plans.

"I'm getting a puppy," she announced.

I took a long sip on my beer while I pondered my response. I chose to inquire how she and the puppy planned to travel out west.

"Are you hitchhiking or riding a train?"

"Train," she replied.

Seeing that I was speechless, Sierra changed the subject.

The next morning I received a text inquiring whether dogs are allowed on the Amtrak.

"Maybe you should go to Kinko's and get her a card," I replied in jest.

"Service animals have to be six months old," came the response.

Finding that animals can't travel on passenger trains, I researched which airlines flew between Louisville and Sacramento and their policies on traveling with pets. I reported the results of my research to Sierra and confirmed plans for the trip to Kentucky on Saturday. I also reminded Sierra of her promise to clean her room before she left for California.

"Why? I'm coming back with you."

◆ ◆ ◆

On the Sunday evening after we came back with Wasabi, Sierra brought her puppy over to meet Dolly and Boogie, Wasabi's "cousins." "She's going to travel with other dogs," Sierra said. "So she needs to get used to being around other dogs."

Boogie first paid more attention to my jacket, which Wasabi had used as a blanket on the ride home, than he did the puppy, but eventually he carefully sniffed her out. Dolly surprisingly trotted over and wagged her tail as she and Wasabi rubbed noses.

After a few minutes with the other dogs, Wasabi flopped down next to Sierra's fringed boots and went to sleep. Sierra played the guitar and sang, joined by Aaron playing the spoons. I threw two dollar bills down in a canister sitting on the coffee table between the brother and sister musicians.

"Split it 50–50," Sierra shouted.

"Yes!" Aaron exclaimed as they exchanged a high five.

◆ ◆ ◆

The following Friday night, Sierra found a puppy sitter for Wasabi and invited me out for a drink. An acoustic quartet was performing at a local bar downtown. As they started their second set, the band leader announced that the bar owner had "suggested" that "we invite Sierra Ferrell to join us."

Without further prompting, Sierra picked up a guitar and adjusted the microphone. She performed a couple of songs, including one of her originals. Both earned generous applause.

"You should sing for a living," I told her when she returned to the table.

"I know" she replied. "I want to start a band."

"How many musicians would be in the band?" Facing a cold glare in response, I added, "Sorry, I'm just curious."

"So am I!"

LUBE IDOL

"**H**EY," SIERRA SAID WHEN I picked up the phone. "A friend of mine told me about a karaoke competition at Quaker Steak," she said. "First prize is like $500."

"I take it you need a ride?"

"I'll be at Brandon's." Sensing my hesitation, she added, "Don't worry, he's just a good friend. I'm not ready for another relationship."

Relations with Noah had broken off a few weeks earlier. He had headed west in early October on the assumption that once Sierra secured Wasabi she would follow suit. Those plans turned out to be tentative.

On Thursday, I arrived early at Brandon's and walked Wasabi while Sierra debated which scarf to wear. Once a decision was made, we piled in the Skunkmobile and drove to the restaurant. I watched with trepidation as Sierra spread out a blanket in the back seat and handed Wasabi a toy. "We'll be back, baby," she said. I cracked the windows to let in the cool night air and made a mental note of the time.

Once inside I ran into James Brown, who has had an on again, off again relationship with Sierra. "The Godfather!" he shouted as we shook hands, adding, "I told her she should do this."

At the same time a young guy, maybe 27, strutted into the restaurant. He was nattily dressed in all black and his hair was tousled just enough to look grungy without passing as a traveling kid. "That's Hoover," was all the kids told me.

Hoover handed Sierra an entry form. I jokingly asked Sierra if she remembered her address. She scowled as she handed me the paperwork.

"Oh my God," she said when she read the rules. "You can do either karaoke or use an instrument! I should have brought a guitar." I checked my watch and then offered to go back after a guitar.

"I'll go with you," she said. "You won't know which one." Earnestly seeking to avoid a wardrobe change, I reiterated my offer.

"OK," she sighed. "It's the black one. Make sure to get a pick."

Hoover didn't seem to run a tight schedule. When I rushed back in carrying a guitar, people were still hanging around the registration table.

"So, you decided on the guitar," Hoover said as he handed Sierra a name tag with the number 10. "What are you singing?"

"I don't know, maybe one of my originals," Sierra replied, turning to me to add, "Let's get a drink."

The tables near the stage were taken, so we went across the restaurant and took seats at the end of the bar. As we sat down, some guy who looked to be 40 put down his beer and asked Sierra "to watch my beer while I go out for a cigarette." He returned in less time than it takes for a full cigarette.

"Thanks," he said to Sierra, oblivious to my presence.

"No problem," she said.

"You come here often?"

"No," she said. "I'm singing in the competition."

"So you like to sing?"

"Yeah," she replied casually.

I took a drink and smiled.

"So, what do you do?" he asked.

I thought to myself, "I ride freight trains and fly signs. How about you?"

Sierra was more diplomatic. "Right now I just want to work on my music." This banal dialogue lasted for several minutes, by which time contestant number two had taken the stage.

"Well," Sierra said as she stood up, "I need to go listen to the competition." She turned to me and smiled. I offered a slight nod and stayed put. The guy took Sierra's bar stool and watched her walk across the room, oblivious to my presence until she left the room.

"You from around here?"

"Mink Shoals," I said.

"That's a ways away," he said, slurring the last two words.

Tempted as I was to mention it's only a 15 minute drive, I just asked, "How about you?"

"Alum Creek. Just down the road."

"You must come here often," I said.

"Oh yeah, I like to come and talk to the pretty girls." He smiled. "Like that cute little thing that was just here."

I took a swig of my beer and smiled.

Then the small talk turned to professions. He volunteered that he rents mobile home properties in southern West Virginia and knows several real estate lawyers, as well as the former prosecutor.

"We only use him to get us out of jail," he laughed. He told me that he was married, had a 25-year-old girlfriend and was in love with the bartender. "Ain't she pretty?" he slurred as she set down another beer. I raised my beer in acknowledgement.

"So how about you? You got kids?" he asked.

I put down my beer and looked over at the guy. "Two kids."

The blood drained from his face. "Is that your daughter?"

"Yes."

He sat speechless for a few minutes and then slurred profuse apologies before leaving to smoke a cigarette. I paid my tab, exchanging a knowing smile with the bartender, and went out to walk Wasabi before going back to watch the competition.

◆ ◆ ◆

Sierra took the stage and Hoover graciously adjusted the microphone and plugged in Sierra's guitar. She sang "Ramble On" by Led Zeppelin. The crowd seemed to pay little attention, perhaps because most of the crowd had come to support one of the other 19 contestants.

After the last contestant, the judges retired to their respective restrooms and then returned to tally scores and announce the finalists. "Should we take 8? Or 10, maybe?" Hoover asked. "Let's go with 10," one of the judges chimed in. The seventh number announced was Sierra's number 10.

Sierra and I went out for a late supper and talked about what song she would sing for the finals the following week. "I'd be glad to help you decide," I said, "but since I don't listen to the radio, I have no idea what's popular."

On the ride home Sierra sang along with the radio and then she announced that she might sing the song that was playing. I grabbed my phone and used the Shazam app to find out the name of the song. I texted the link to Sierra. "Feel free to buy it on iTunes," I offered. The next day my e-mail inbox had receipts for two Autolux albums.

◆ ◆ ◆

On the day of the competition I asked James if he knew the schedule.

"7:00 p.m.," he texted. "What's she singing?"

"No idea," I responded. "And whatever it is will change five times between now and seven o'clock."

When I arrived to pick up Sierra, I was surprised to see that she had butterflies. She was anxiously throwing garments aside on the couch in search of a scarf while Wasabi chewed up the remnants of a sock.

"Wasabi!" she yelled.

"She's just being a puppy," I said.

"Wasabi! I wish you'd grow bigger!"

I just took a deep breath, then volunteered to take Wasabi outside and load her in the backseat.

We pulled into the parking lot right at seven o'clock. Hoover was standing out front smoking a cigarette.

"You were supposed to be here at 7:00," he said with a grin, glancing at his watch.

"Hey, I got her here within five minutes," I replied. "For Sierra, that's on time."

A few minutes later Hoover came over with Sierra's form and asked about her song. "What's that say? F-L-E-T?"

"It's Fleetwood Mac."

"'Magic Man' is by Heart."

"My bad," Sierra said. "Maybe I should do a Heart song."

"How about 'How Do I Get You Alone?'" James interjected.

"Sure."

A few minutes later the event got underway with a teen-ager playing an original song on the guitar, followed by an older woman singing karaoke. Sierra was number 10.

"How's it going?" came a text from Tammy.

"Nervous," I replied.

One of the other competitors came and sat down near us. She was a young African American woman who had dressed up for the occasion. She and Sierra exchanged nervous smiles, and they were then joined by a friend holding the singer's baby. The songs seemed to take forever, but finally the girl handed over the baby and took the stage. Eight down, two to go.

Sierra took the stage and it took a few seconds for the sound system to be adjusted for her voice. Once she got going, she nailed it.

I joined the crowd in loud applause.

Counting the scores took less than two minutes and Hoover was back at the mic.

"Beginning with third place," he bellowed, "Number seven."

The crowd applauded as the young man made his way to the stage.

"And for second place... " Hoover hesitated as my heart pounded faster. "Number three!"

"And finally, the 2013 Lube Idol," Hoover once again hesitated for effect, "with a perfect score of 100, number 10!"

"YES!" I shouted as I pumped my fist.

Sierra was halfway to the stage when I sat back down. I couldn't see her petite frame on the stage, and for a split second wondered if I had heard correctly.

Then I found Sierra on the stage accepting the Budweiser electric guitar and $500 cash.

"How about the bank?" I heard James say. Sierra stuffed the wad of cash in her purse.

"Congratulations," I said, giving her a hug. "Nice guitar."

Hoover sensed my sarcasm.

"My dad represents the Miller Lite guy," Sierra explained.

"I guess you can replace the skin on it."

I offered to buy Sierra dinner to celebrate.

"No," she said quietly, "that's OK."

"You want me to drop you off to at Brandon's?"

"Actually," she said, "he's picking me up here."

Sierra reached over to hug me and gave me a peck on the cheek.

"Thanks. I love you."

"I love you too," I said, "but you can't leave the Budweiser guitar in my car."

THE GRETSCH

THANKSGIVING PLANS WERE TENTATIVE.

In early November, Sierra decided to move in with a friend in Huntington. I loaded a dog kennel, two suitcases and a guitar into the Skunkmobile and drove Sierra and Wasabi to their newest abode, a dilapidated white structure located on the main drag toward downtown. The building was of some historic significance, having served as a prominent funeral home in the 1920s. The stained glass windows, Doric columns and high ceilings offered testament to its better days. Black and white photographs adorned the walls, standing in sharp contrast to the crumbling plaster and exposed wall studs. Pieces of artwork were carefully placed throughout the main room, topped off by a skeleton skull in a corner.

Sierra's friend Chris served as the building's caretaker. He appeared to be in his early 40s, with long hair, a leather jacket, and a cigarette in hand. He worked as a freelance photographer and his place was a magnet for the arts community. Sierra mentioned jamming with a musician who stopped over after performing at Mountain Stage. On other nights poets and artists hung out on the bare furniture in the former parlor room.

"Be careful where you step," Sierra told me when I came to visit. "People were painting last night." She was too late. Wasabi had already run through the paint before jumping to greet me.

"Wasabi!" I yelled. "Your girl is getting my dry cleaning bill."

"You can wash it off in the bathtub," Sierra said. "Don't use the sink. It's got a hole in it." Despite the broken sink and chipped plaster, before we left Sierra made the bed with the same care as she used when visiting my mom's house. I left after lunch with no further idea as to Sierra's plans for Thanksgiving the following week.

◆ ◆ ◆

Sierra's Thanksgiving greeting clarified our holiday plans. "When you bring dress look at shoes and bring ones you'd think I'd wear with it black jacket if you grab black shoes happy gobble gobble." I informed Tammy that once we finished Thanksgiving dinner we would be leaving for Huntington. As the last leftovers were put away, Tammy asked if I'd talked to Sierra.

"She's not answering," I said.

"Will she be there?"

"Let's hope so."

We headed out for the hour-long trip, armed with two dresses, three pairs of shoes, and two pieces of pumpkin pie, but no idea as to whether Sierra would be around. When we arrived, Sierra was out walking Wasabi.

"Sorry I missed your call," she said. "We went over to his parents' house for dinner and I didn't have my phone." All we could do is laugh and share the pie. Sierra loves pumpkin pie, and it's tradition that I won't eat it without her. Afterwards, we took Wasabi to the dog park.

A few days later, Boogie ran to the door and started barking. I opened the door to find Wasabi standing on the front porch, a German shepherd at her side.

"He's nice. His name is Barker," Sierra shouted as she and the dogs walked by. "I'm always wearing the same clothes, so I'm bringing my stuff back to keep at one place." A tall guy with long hair and a thick beard waited politely on the porch until I waved him in.

"Oh," she added, "This is Keith."

Sierra proceeded directly to the kitchen, opened the refrigerator and started pulling out lunch meat for sandwiches while Wasabi looked for Boogie's food bowl.

Barker marked the edge of the fireplace.

"Don't worry," I said with a smile. "Happens all the time."

I chatted politely while Sierra served cold cuts. After several minutes, Sierra casually announced that she and Keith were going to Amy's after she changed out her clothes. I helped Sierra carry her luggage—two Samsonite suitcases, one red like my grandmother's, the other maroon like my grandfather's—to her bedroom. I had cleaned up the room the week before so my mom could use it over Thanksgiving.

"Wow," Sierra exclaimed. "This room looks like $40."

I sat down while Sierra sorted clothes across the floor.

"I met a guy," she said. "And I really like him. It's kind of scary."

Before I could ask, she added, "It's not Keith."

"This sounds serious."

"No... I don't know," she replied. "I feel like a teenager."

Sierra glowed like a teenager when talking about "the guy." Naturally, he's a musician. He plays bass guitar and stand-up bass in a touring band called the Hackensaw Boys.

"So you love this guy," I surmised.

"I wouldn't go there yet," she smiled.

"By the way, while we're on the topic of guys," I said. "Who's the guy with the German shepherd?"

"He's leaving tomorrow on his way to New York."

In the meantime, Sierra planned to stay at Amy's house and perform on open mic nights.

Amy is a personal trainer. She lives in the east end of Charleston on the fringes of a neighborhood best known for drug deals and prostitution. When a local lawyer was arrested for solicitation in the neighborhood, everyone scoffed when he argued that he "just happened to be in the area." But on Saturday morning I myself "just happened to be in the area." Earlier that morning Sierra had asked me to stop by.

"Amy's having an art show," she said. I accepted the invitation.

Having dropped Sierra off, I recognized Amy's house and with luck found room to park. As I crossed the sidewalk, a couple came out of the house next door in the midst of a heated argument, both screaming that the other should leave. I headed straight up the steps. Suddenly I realized there were two doors, and I had never waited long enough to see which Sierra entered. Fortunately, the door on the right opened. A woman in her early 40s, standing nearly six feet tall with short bobbed hair, extended a hand.

"I'm Amy," she said. The interior was neat and well-kept, a string of lights on one wall and a branch I had cut from my Christmas tree sat on the table with small bulbs hanging on it.

"This is nice. It's got a bohemian feel," I said. Amy took my compliment as intended. Paintings hung discriminately throughout the hall and the front room. Ironically, just a week before I had visited the Metropolitan Museum of Art.

"There's art through the whole house," Amy explained. "We're having a show today. Everything with a price tag is for sale." I settled on a piece that appeared to have French Impressionist influences.

"It's spray paint on canvas," Amy explained. At the Met I saw oil on canvas, but no spray paint.

"These are Queen Anne's lace along a river," she continued. "I painted this at the Greenbrier River."

"They have a place at the river!" Sierra joined the conversation. "You can hang it there. You can give it to Tammy for Christmas!"

I stayed for a few minutes and noted the plethora of musical instruments, including guitars, a keyboard and a mandolin.

"There will be all kinds of musicians here today," Sierra said.

As I left, I noticed that the couple next door were still out on the stoop, although this time they were asking each other to stay.

That evening I chauffeured Sierra to an open mic event. Surprisingly, we arrived early. Since Wasabi was sleeping calmly in the back seat, we thought it best to drive around rather than disturb the pup. The neighborhood was decorated for Christmas. Seeing a house with an elaborate manger set, Sierra remarked on how "everyone wants their lives to be like the movies, but that's not the way life is."

"Our family story sure isn't like the movies," I laughed. "But it would make a pretty good movie."

◆ ◆ ◆

The following Monday I was back in my normal routine, waiting outside a courtroom with a group of attorneys. All of us were looking for some topic of conversation other than the impending argument.

"Are you ready for Christmas?" one asked.

"When your kids are 20 and 25, it's easy," I responded. "One wants a laptop and the other wants a guitar. Since I don't know a lot about computers and even less about guitars, I'm letting them pick out their presents. It's easy, but it kind of takes away the magic."

Aaron picked out his laptop online, but I was informed that online shopping wasn't a viable option for a guitar. "I have to play it and see how it sounds with my voice," Sierra said firmly.

"OK," I said. "Where does one go to find out how a guitar sounds with your voice?"

"Fret 'n Fiddle," she answered. "And John Lilly says there's some place in Barboursville."

"What's the name of the place?" I asked.

"I don't know," Sierra said. "Can't you figure it out?"

The top search result for "guitars in Barboursville" referred to the Route 60 Music Company.

"Both are open this Saturday," I told Sierra. "Given the magnitude of the purchase, you should go both places."

That Saturday I arrived in the Mini to pick up Sierra. As I waited for Sierra to get ready, I discerned that her friend Nick was joining us. Then, as I hooked up Wasabi, out of the other bedroom came a tall guy with a medium build, early 30s with dreadlocks.

"He lives!" Sierra joked.

"Ha ha," the guy groused. "What's up?"

"We're going to look for my guitar. Come with us." Mike introduced himself to me and asked if he could join us.

"Sure," I said. "But I'll warn you my car's a tight fit."

"We can do it!" Sierra said, pumping her fist.

Mike grabbed some coffee and we crammed into the Mini. Fortunately, the drive to Fret 'n Fiddle was only 20 minutes. Guys and dog alike were happy to get out of the back seat.

Sierra walked Wasabi down the street before we went to the shop.

"What's the price range?"

"We'll see," I said, "but it's substantial."

"OK, but if you see me looking at something that's too high, tell me. I don't want to get my hopes up."

"It's a deal."

Always the savvy shopper, Sierra started out by looking in the $300 range. She found a refurbished acoustic and started to play. Mike, who I discovered had played in various bands over the years, brought over another guitar and Sierra continued to perform, her audience consisting of me, the guys, the shop owner and two patrons.

"I really like this one," Sierra said.

Noting the price, I told her to keep her options open.

Sierra started looking over guitars along with Nick and Mike. The sight of three kids in their mid-twenties, two with long hair and beards, didn't impress the shop owner. But then he took a second look at me.

"Are you financing this?"

"You got it," I said, patting my rear pocket.

He suggested to Sierra that she try the Fender.

"I really like this one, but I'm not sure," she said after trying out the Fender.

"Let's do this," I suggested. "We can go to Barboursville and see what they have. If nothing strikes your fancy, we can come back."

"OK."

The weather was unseasonably warm, so we put the top down and allowed Wasabi and the guys to breathe in the back seat on the 45-minute drive.

While Fret 'n Fiddle was a small shop with two rooms, the Route 60 store looked like a performance hall. Guitars lined the walls, surrounding drum sets and other instruments. I randomly headed over to one corner. I was eyeing prices when I heard Mike tell Sierra, "This is where you want to be."

Across the store I saw a small studio lodged in the corner. "It's her Christmas present," I reminded myself.

I walked in the studio and saw it, a white maple, off-white colored electric/acoustic Gretsch. At the time, I didn't know that George Harrison played a Gretsch on *The Ed Sullivan Show*. It just looked like Sierra.

I checked the price tag: $2,122.

Sierra walked back in the studio. "This looks nice," I said, handing her a red maple model with a price of just over a thousand dollars. "Gentle On My Mind" never sounded so good. Mike smiled and nodded.

"Let me see that one," Sierra said, pointing to another guitar.

The guitar sounded good, but it didn't quite measure up to the red maple.

Hearing Sierra's melodic voice and seeing my gray hair, the manager saw opportunity and came right over. Rather than ignoring Mike and Nick like vagabond hippies, he enlisted their support.

"How you all doing today?" he said. "Nice sound, isn't it?"

"Pretty sweet."

"Let me know if you have any questions."

As the manager stepped out, Sierra saw the white maple Gretsch.

"It's a little out of my price range," I said.

"Can I at least hold it?"

Sierra handed the red maple to Mike. I handed down the white maple. Mike strummed the red maple and Sierra joined in with the white maple.

Even I could hear the difference. The sound emanating from the white maple guitar matched Sierra's voice. Needing to buy time, I told Sierra to play a few chords and then let Mike play the other guitar.

"To compare, just of out curiosity," I added.

"You like that one, do you?" The store manager appeared out of nowhere.

"Yes!" Sierra gushed. "But I guess it's above my dad's price range," she added with a frown.

"I can give you a good deal on it," the manager said. "It's near the end of the year and I don't want to pay tax on inventory."

"Really? How much?"

"Maybe I can take off $500. Let me see what I've got in it."

Sierra looked back at me with wishful eyes.

"Hey, do you think Frieda would want to contribute?" I headed out in the store and dialed my mom's number. I quickly explained the situation, finishing by saying, "This is the real thing." My mom offered to contribute $500.

Upon returning to the studio, Sierra was still playing the white maple Gretsch. The look on Mike's face confirmed what I had told my mom. This guitar was the real thing.

"How much did he tell you?"

"$1,500. I think. Go ask him."

I found the store manager, who was beaming almost as brightly as Sierra.

He quoted the final price, tax included.

"Does that come with the case?"

"Of course. Hardshell case."

"Then I guess my girl has a Gretsch," I said.

"This is the best Christmas ever," Sierra said.

On the ride home Sierra casually mentioned that she had a gig the next night at the Empty Glass.

"Yes, you can take it now," I said. "I'm sure you'll need to practice."

The Gretsch played the Glass two Sundays in a row, then headed for a gig in Asheville, North Carolina, and on to Nashville.

"WE'RE GOING TO THE ROSE BOWL"

I STARED AT THE tickets in my hand, then looked up at the Rose Bowl. That's when it hit me. "Ky, Michigan State is playing in the Rose Bowl, and you're going to the game."

A month earlier friends and colleagues had been asking, "Are you going to the Big Ten championship?" "No," I would answer, launching into what had become a prepared statement. "Earlier this fall I agreed to accompany my mom to *The Glass Menagerie* on Broadway. At the time we didn't seem to have a quarterback."

I wore a green MSU tie to the play, and as Act I came to a close I hurried out to check the score. MSU 10, Ohio State 0. I avoided all temptation to sneak a peek at my iPhone during Act II, but as soon as we left the theater I was back online. At that point OSU had taken a 24–17 lead midway through the third quarter. We walked briskly back to the hotel. Every few steps I hit the refresh button on my iPhone.

We found a table at the hotel bar, Times Square to my right and a bank of television screens to my left. Michigan State kicked a field goal, making the score 24–20.

Minutes later the Spartans took possession again. The bar crowd cheered as the team moved into Ohio State territory. Two plays later the cheers grew louder as MSU scored a touchdown to take the lead with minutes remaining.

The defense held Ohio State on fourth down, and the offense cautiously stuck to the running game before punting. With the clock running down and Ohio State facing a critical fourth down, some guy randomly walked over to our table, impeding my view. Seeing his green shirt, I assumed he was a fan.

"Quite a view," he said in a quaint British accent, looking over Times Square.

"Yes it is," I said politely as I craned my neck to see the TV screens. The visitor moved on just as a Michigan State defensive back stopped the quarterback short of the first down marker. The crowd roared.

Three plays later, a Michigan State running back broke loose for a 30-yard touchdown run, making the score 34–24 with less than three minutes remaining. The defense held, and with 1:21 left, the Spartan offense took the field. I prepared a text to Aaron, waiting for the final gun to hit the send button.

"We're going to the Rose Bowl!"

◆ ◆ ◆

"Can Justin come too?" Aaron asked.

"If he can get off work," I replied. "Tell him I need to know ASAP."

Justin traded shifts and called in favors, going so far as to plead with his mom to work his New Year's Day assignment. All shifts were covered.

A client once told me the priority for major sporting events is tickets, transportation and lodging. So I began surfing Stubhub, pulling the trigger when prices jumped. I also logged on to the alumni page and ordered tickets to the tailgate party.

"We have game tickets and tailgate tickets," I reported to the guys. "Next step is transportation and lodging, but no worries. We can borrow Sierra's 'traveling broke' signs, and it will be warm enough that we can sleep under a bridge."

"Only one problem," Aaron responded. "We'd have to take Sierra so she can flag down the drivers and then say, 'Hey, can my friends come too?'"

Since Sierra had a gig scheduled the day before the game, I booked a flight out of Columbus, relied on Tammy's Marriott Platinum status for lodging, and found a rental car.

Each time the "your credit card will be charged" message appeared on the screen, I repeated MasterCard's advertising slogan: "Going to Michigan State's first Rose Bowl in 25 years with your sons, priceless."

◆ ◆ ◆

The flight out of Columbus left at 10:50 a.m. Saturday. Given that Aaron is not a morning person, I suggested that it was better to leave Friday night rather than worrying about getting Aaron awake at 5:00 a.m.

Having a 20-year-old driver in a C-Class Mercedes alleviated any concern over timing. We arrived at the airport seven hours ahead of our flight.

I suggested we check out the nearby Waffle House. As we pulled into the parking lot, we noted that ours was the only Mercedes in sight and an armed police officer was standing guard.

Shortly after 3:00 a.m., we located a Steak 'n Shake. "Now this looks like a parking lot," Justin said. "Recent vintage Hondas and Toyotas." We ordered burgers and shakes. The waiter delivered our food with his standard routine. "Stay as long as you like."

"Be careful what you offer," Justin said.

We stayed almost two hours.

Once at the airport, we checked in and looked for an outlet to recharge our plethora of Apple devices.

When we boarded, I let the guys pick our seats. They picked the row adjacent to the wing. "Less turbulence," Justin said. Aaron allowed Justin to take the window seat. As the plane took off, Justin blasted the theme from *Top Gun* through his earbuds.

We flew to Chicago, but stayed on the plane since the lay-over was less than 30 minutes. Meanwhile, the flight attendant warned us that we had a full flight. "Every seat will be taken," she reiterated.

The first arrival was an elderly couple. The gentleman sat across in the row behind me and pointed to the seat behind me.

"Take your purse and sit down," he growled loudly. "Need a cough drop?"

"No," the wife replied. "I'm fine."

Justin looked at me, his eyes bulging and his mouth hanging open, his non-verbal way of saying, "What is happening here?"

Then a baby moved in two rows behind. She drowned out the *Top Gun* theme on both takeoff and landing.

We had a two hour layover in Phoenix, most of which was spent sitting on the floor around the one pillar in the C con-course with an electrical outlet. When we boarded the plane, Justin looked out the window at the luggage conveyor nervously. "Do you think our bags made it? My luggage isn't going to make it. They're going to lose it."

At 4:35 p.m. PST, 16 hours after leaving Charleston, we stepped off the plane into the sunshine. Aaron started to put on the winter coat he got for Christmas. "Aaron," I said, "you don't need a coat. It's 70 degrees out here."

When we reached the baggage claim, Justin panicked. "It's going to be lost," he repeated. "I know it."

Justin's bag was the next to the last bag to come down the carousel. "Thank God!" Justin screamed. "I worked 20 hours of overtime to pay for those clothes."

A couple of days before the trip, Justin went to the mall in search of clothes for LA. He told the clerk at Pac Sun, "I want to look hip. I'm tired of looking like a 34-year-old guy with a job who's got it together."

When we checked into the motel at Manhattan Beach, Justin asked Aaron and me for fashion advice.

"Does this clash?"

"Yes," Aaron answered.

"Which shoes—blue or gray?"

"Gray," I said. "Is there food in our future?"

◆ ◆ ◆

On Sunday morning I got up early—my body still operating on Eastern time—and went for a run on the beach. By sunrise the surfers were paddling out to meet the waves. After I got back and showered, the guys started moving about. "Get moving," I badgered them. "You've got to see that beach."

We drove down toward the beach. As we crested a hill, the ocean came into full view. Basking in the sunshine and seeing the crashing waves, Justin was overwhelmed.

"I'd give up my guns to live here!" Coming from a guy who owns an arsenal, that meant something. The sight of a vintage sports car removed any lingering doubts.

"We need to move here," Aaron shouted.

"Seeing this makes life worth living," Justin added, "as long as it's here."

We walked just over a mile down the beach, rubbernecking and gawking at the beachfront homes. After another mile in the fashionable Pac Sun shoes, Justin realized he was "definitely not a skateboarder." He added, "I need to get inserts."

Aaron noted that most of the dogs were big. "This would be perfect for Boogie," he said. I had to admit Aaron's dog would fit right in on the beach, especially with the bright-colored doggie polo shirts he wears to protect against his skin allergy.

Justin focused on the "beautiful people." "I've only seen five unattractive people," he quipped. "And I'm with two of them."

That afternoon Aaron found a place that rented surf boards. At 32 bucks, it seemed like a steal.

"Do you want a wetsuit?" the clerk asked.

"No," Aaron replied.

"I can cover it," I said.

"No, I'm okay," he insisted. "But I need sunglasses."

"That's another 30 bucks!"

"Is my eyesight not worth $30?"

I bought sunscreen, too.

Aaron handed me his insulin pump and carried the board down to the beach. He snapped a picture and updated his Facebook status: "This where ima be the rest of the day."

He was back in two minutes.

"I need to get the wetsuit," he said. "That water's freezing!"

A few minutes later, Aaron came strutting across the beach in a black wetsuit.

"It was free," he told me. "I guess they know you need one."

Aaron paddled out about 400 yards to meet the surf. I lost sight of him after a high wave crashed in, and for a split second wondered how I would explain this to Tammy.

Aaron returned, but without sunglasses.

"Those sunglasses got lost in the first wave."

"You're done?" Justin asked.

"That's hard work!"

"You were out there for less than an hour!"

"Those waves are huge!"

We walked back up the street to return the surfboard and headed for the motel. I neglected to hand back the insulin pump. By the time he got out of the shower, Aaron had been off the pump for over two hours.

"You should check," I said.

"You don't want to know my blood sugar reading," Aaron told us. "I should probably be in the hospital." Eventually the readings became more palatable, though Aaron didn't feel like eating.

"Looks like he's going to live," I told Justin. "Let's go to dinner without him."

Justin enjoyed his first cheese board appetizer followed by spare ribs that were as good as advertised. "You really can eat them with a spoon," Justin said.

Sipping a glass of wine, I decided it was time to offer some parental advice.

"You know," I began, "It's times like this—taking your kids to dinner and not worrying about ordering the cheese board—that make those years spent in college worthwhile."

Justin nodded and said, "That's what I've been realizing."

◆ ◆ ◆

The next day we conducted our own tour of Hollywood and Beverly Hills. Sites included the Hollywood Walk of Fame, the Chinese Theatre, Rodeo Drive, and—the guys' favorite—LA Tattoo. The guys insisted on lunch at In-N-Out Burger. Justin seemed to enjoy the greasy burger at the famed drive-in as much as the *les trois fromages* the night before.

"Who can afford to shop here?" Aaron asked as we drove down Rodeo Drive.

"I don't know, probably movie executives. Maybe lawyers."

"Then why don't you and Tammy move here?"

"Tell Mr. Goodwin that the firm would benefit from a Western presence," Justin suggested with a grin.

Driving around Los Angeles is no easy task. The guys' sudden outbursts didn't help, but eventually I watched traffic to anticipate the cries of "Oh my God! Did you see that car?" Bentleys, Rolls, Porsches and vintage muscle cars are common in Southern California.

It seemed like everything is more elegant in Southern California, even the traveling kids. We saw one girl standing off the I-405 exit ramp.

"I think that's the most beautiful body I've ever seen," Justin remarked.

"Yeah," Aaron interjected, "but she needs to stop wearing such nice clothes if she wants to get any money."

"Her parents are probably plastic surgeons," Justin said, adding with a smile, "Damn middle class kids playing homeless!"

The tour came complete with a celebrity sighting. Driving through Venice Beach there was a gray-haired man walking up the road. Just after we passed by, Justin screamed and turned around.

"Billy Madison! That guy was the old man in *Billy Madison*," he said. Then he stuck his head out the window and yelled, "Billy Madison!" Once back in the car, he googled the movie and showed us a picture of actor Larry Hankin.

"We have our first celebrity sighting!" Aaron declared.

As we neared the Playboy Mansion, I cautioned the guys not to expect further sightings. "It's right here," I told them as we approached a private drive protected by two female security guards, a gate and a 30-foot hedge. "Should I turn around and go by one more time?"

"No," Aaron responded. "The guard's looking at us funny. She'll think I'm a freak."

We found a French restaurant for our New Year's Eve dinner, then headed back to our motel room. As soon as the ball dropped in Times Square, I called to wish Tammy a Happy New Year and set an alarm for 5:00 a.m.

◆ ◆ ◆

The early morning traffic to Pasadena was lighter than expected and finding the route did not require Google Maps.

"Follow the blimp!" Aaron shouted.

Parking for the Rose Bowl is on a golf course located adjacent to the stadium. We followed directions and parked near a tree. I did notice the balloons, the closest bearing the numeral 2. We meandered across the golf course in the direction of the stadium and found the will call tent.

"How long until the tailgate?"

"About an hour."

"What do we do for an hour?"

Part of me wanted to stand and soak in the atmosphere, standing in the shadow of the Rose Bowl and the iconic sign I'd only seen on television. I sent a picture to Tammy and my mom.

"Just like on television," my mom replied. "Wearing green and drinking white wine," she added. Tammy, wearing green of course, sent a picture of Boogie and Dolly wearing Spartan shirts.

We bought a souvenir football and found a spot on the golf course to play catch while waiting for the alumni tailgate. I hadn't seen that many people decked out in green in a long, long time—33 years to be exact.

Justin was taken aback by the crowd's fanatical reaction to the video promo featuring voice-overs from the movie *300*.

"That really fires up the crowd," he said. "I'm worried they might charge the other school's tailgate."

"If someone gives the word, I'm in," I said.

The university president was less inspiring, politely rallying the alumni base with a subtle pitch for donations.

Eventually Sparty and the band arrived, entering the grounds with the traditional march as the alumni chanted "Go State!" Next the band transitioned into the greatest fight song.

"On the banks of the Red Cedar, there's a school that's known to all, its specialty is winning, and the Spartans play good ball," we all joined in. "Fight! Fight! Rah! Team, fight! Victory for MSU!"

Fireworks went off just as we finished.

"That's the signal to head for the stands," the emcee announced. "But before we go, let's sing the song we all know—the 'Michigan State Alma Mater!"

"Do you know the words?" I overheard someone say.

"Something about shadows," came the reply.

I certainly didn't know the lyrics, and it did not appear that the cheerleaders did either.

I'd taken Aaron to other storied venues, such as Solider Field in Chicago, but marching with Sparty Nation to enter the Rose Bowl for the 100th anniversary of the game hailed as "The Granddaddy of Them All" was a moment I'll never forget.

The structure didn't look like it had changed in its 100-year history. Unlike modern stadiums with lounges, concessions and televisions throughout the concourse, the Rose Bowl consisted of rows of concrete and a grass field. All of the concessions and restrooms were outside of the bowl itself.

Spectators enter the bowl through tunnels that are no wider than the foyer in my house. Moving 95,123 people through 28 tunnels is no easy task. After waiting for nearly three minutes, we were at the entrance when the usher raised the "tunnel full" sign.

Once inside, we began our ascent to row 69. When we reached row 60, I began to wonder how many rows remained. It turns out the Rose Bowl has 77 rows. The view was spectacular: the manicured field adorned with a rose at midfield, the iconic "Rose Bowl" logo atop the scoreboard at the north end and the mountain ranges rising in the background of the opposite stands.

We found ourselves among the Sparty Nation, aided by the fact Aaron had the decency to hawk the extra ticket to someone clad in green. Looking across the stadium, it appeared that almost two-thirds of the fans were wearing green.

The Stanford band performed first, running onto the field as if practicing a fire drill.

"Isn't that for bands that can't march straight?" I said. Both alumni of the venerable Pride of Capital High, they nodded in agreement. Watching them critique the band, I couldn't help but think to myself, "They could've been marching at the Rose Bowl."

Stanford's team name is the Cardinal and the band's mascot is a pine tree. When a costumed pine tree entered the field, the guys looked at me for an explanation. All I could do was shrug my shoulders.

We continued to scream "Go Green, Go White" and "Beat Stanford." Seeing the opposing mascot, a fellow rabid fan raised the stakes. "Cut down the tree!" he shouted. Someone added, "Burn the tree!"

Justin turned to me with a look of panic coming across his face. "Burn the tree? There's a human being inside that costume!"

The Spartan Marching Band marched on in S formation as we chanted "Go State!" Next the band broke into the MSU formation and played the fight song. The band veterans nodded with approval.

The coin toss was conducted by Vin Scully, a legendary broadcaster from Los Angeles. Aaron and Justin stared quizzically when I joined a handful of others from my generation to stand up as a sign of respect.

The Spartans won the toss and deferred until the second half.

"Good choice," Aaron said, explaining his reasoning to Justin.

Two plays into the game, Stanford completed a long pass to the MSU 30 and scored a few plays later.

Aaron was not impressed. "They need—" he began. "I know, I know," I interrupted. "If we don't start tackling, it's going to be a long day."

Things didn't look much better for the offense, which stalled around midfield. Stanford came right back at us (literally—our seats were near the end zone) but this time the defense rallied and held the Cardinal to a field goal.

The Spartans rarely make a win look easy, and the crowd knew the game would probably be decided late. No sooner had the teams switched goals at the start of the second quarter than the Spartans were right in front of us, knocking on the door. After a few tries, an MSU running back cut back the other direction and crossed the goal line.

"Touchdown MSU!" Justin yelled as he exchanged high fives with the two blondes sitting in front of him.

A few minutes later the Spartans had the Cardinal pinned down close to the goal line and we cheered at an apparent sack. The officials, however, ruled the runner down at the two-yard line. A couple of plays later the defense gave up another long pass and the Cardinal was on the move. The defense rallied and forced a punt, leading to the worst play of the day.

Connor Cook had been under pressure. Thus far he had managed to avoid any interceptions, but his pass hurled down the middle to no one in particular was easily picked off by a Stanford linebacker and returned for a touchdown.

"That may have cost us the game," I thought.

The offense regained its composure. Just before halftime Cook rolled to his right to avoid the pressure. This time he found his man—in the end zone.

Stanford 17, Michigan State 14 at the half.

The Spartans received the kickoff to open the second half and marched toward our end of the stadium. They settled for a field goal to tie the game at 17. The rest of the third quarter was a blur, with defense ruling on both sides. The Spartan punter shanked a couple of punts, giving Stanford better field position, but the defense continued to hold. Near the end of the quarter, the Cardinal quarterback launched another long pass, but this time a Michigan State defensive back reached in for the interception.

The quarter ended with the score tied at 17, but the Spartans were driving. A few plays later I jumped up. "He's in there!"

"Touchdown, MSU," Justin typed, updating his Facebook status.

My iPhone was well below 50% power, so I refrained from posting updates. Plus, I knew my mom and Tammy were watching the game. At some point Tammy asked my mom, "How did Ky become such a sports fan anyway? These tight games are tense!" She nonetheless stayed glued to the television and provided text updates to her step-father and a high school friend of mine.

Meanwhile at the Rose Bowl, Aaron asked, "Aren't we ahead?"

The digital scoreboard still showed Stanford 24, Michigan State 17. This used to happen all the time during Aaron's youth league basketball games, but I expected more from the Rose Bowl.

Aaron only knew we'd taken the lead because of the roar from the crowd. He had been out getting drinks when MSU had scored. Justin asked me where Aaron went. I said, "I don't know, but either way, text him and tell him to keep doing what he's doing." When I saw Aaron making his way back up, I stood up and waved my hands and yelled, "Go back!" Aaron, respecting my superstitions, smiled and started to turn back.

Thirteen minutes remained, too long to start counting our roses.

The sun had gone down and the cool night air was coming in, but I refrained from putting on my long-sleeved Spartan pullover. You don't change shirts when you're ahead. You don't even button up the one you're wearing.

With six minutes remaining, Stanford crossed midfield and was gaining ground. Once again, the defense held and the field goal unit came on the field. We were all on our feet as the ball was snapped. And we all gasped when the holder took the ball and ran to his right. We stood in stunned silence when the pass was completed for a first down at the five-yard line.

Then we noticed the flag on the field.

"Ineligible receiver downfield," the referee announced. Football fans know what this means, and the further announcement that the foul was on the offense was drowned out by our cheers.

Stanford kicked a field goal, making the score 24–20.

At the same time the official in the red jacket signaled that the media time out was over, I noticed an official coming over to the MSU coach.

"Please reset the game clock to 4:15," the head referee intoned.

"That's critical," I told Aaron. "That's 50 seconds we don't have to kill."

Following the kickoff, MSU made one first down before punting the ball back to Stanford with just under three minutes remaining.

With 1:50 left, the Spartans stopped Stanford a yard short on third down. With 1:50 showing on the clock, Stanford took a time out. Without question, they were going for it.

"This game's going to be 27–24 or 24–20," I thought, keeping this notion to myself.

As the players reentered the field, MSU called time out.

"They're trying to get our adrenaline up," a white-haired fan said.

"I don't think mine can go much higher," I said. Then I turned to the guys, both of whom are certified in CPR, and told them to be ready. Justin appeared to be contemplating whether his EMT certification was valid in California. Aaron continued to chant, "Go Green!"

The players took the field and we started screaming at the top of our lungs. From our vantage point we couldn't tell whether the runner was stopped short of the first down line, but we could see the Spartan defenders jumping up with fists pumping.

"We stopped them!" I screamed as high fives ensued.

Then the official announced that the "previous play is under further review." The 30-second review seemed to last forever, but upon hearing the words, "The call on the field stands," the Spartan Nation erupted.

With 1:45 left on the clock and Stanford out of time outs, the game was virtually over.

I wrapped my arm around Aaron and screamed. "We just won the Rose Bowl!"

The final three snaps seemed to take longer than a minute and 45 seconds, but finally players from the bench were running on to the field.

The Michigan State Spartans. Rose Bowl champions.

"This is the first time State has been to the Rose Bowl in 26 years," I told the guys. "We're staying for the trophy presentation."

Nearly two-thirds of the stadium stayed.

Leaving the stadium was an adventure, mostly because Aaron's phone was dead and mine was below 10%. I needed to save power to stay in touch with the guys in case we were separated finding our way to the car, so I resisted looking as the texts and messages flowed in.

We became separated as the throng of people emptied out of the tunnel, but Justin and I managed to rendezvous outside the stadium.

"We're parked in Area 2," Justin said.

"I know," I replied. "Any idea how to get there?"

"Across the golf course," he answered.

In the dark.

We eventually spotted one of the balloons, but then fog rolled in and covered the number. Finally we saw the balloon had a number 2.

"We were near a tree," I said. "Not that that means anything on a golf course."

Soon we found the car, with Aaron sitting comfortably in the front seat charging his phone and texting his girlfriend.

By that point my iPhone was down to 4% battery power, but I couldn't resist checking the multitude of texts and FaceBook messages.

"Mazel tov," said the Maestro.

"Congratulations!" my mom texted. "The white wine did it!"

"Way to go Spartans! The defense won it!"

"Congrats!"

"I know you're going nuts right now... Congrats Sparty!"

"What an awesome game! U have to be in heaven! Enjoy it!"

"Looks like your team won and I'm making an album." Yes, even Sierra had been following the game.

Justin took the wheel and I opened my iPad to respond to the messages. Realizing how many friends who were following the game, I posted a global thank you on Facebook: "Thanks for all the likes, comments, messages and texts. Watching my alma mater win the Rose Bowl was great, and it's an incredible feeling knowing how many people were watching the game and pulling for MSU on my behalf. Now if we can just find our way off this golf course..."

ON PAGE 75 OF THE ROLLING STONE

THE CALL CAME OUT of the blue on a Friday in July 2014 as Justin and I were getting off the interstate downtown.

"Hey Ky! How are you?" Sierra's cheerful greeting heightened my level of apprehension.

"Fine, and how about you?" I said, bracing myself.

"Great," she replied. "Can you find the current issue of *Rolling Stone*?"

My instructions to take a detour to the mall sparked Justin's curiosity.

"You've heard of the song, 'The Cover of the Rolling Stone'?" I asked Justin. "It's not the cover, but how about on the inside of the *Rolling Stone*?"

"What?" he shouted. "That's incredible!"

As soon as we reached the mall, we headed directly to the book store.

"There it is," Justin pointed to the music magazines. We each grabbed a copy. "It's probably in the Nashville article," I said. "Probably something about Todd Snider." Justin excitedly pointed out the picture on page 75.

There was my girl, wearing her cowboy boots and the leather hat, sitting casually with East Nashville's music elite.

◆ ◆ ◆

Several months earlier, Sierra's face came across the screen. I instinctively set aside a draft brief and tapped on my iPhone.

"Hey, what are you doing?"

"Just working. That's what I do on most Tuesday afternoons," I said with a hint of sarcasm. "How about you?"

"I can't talk long. I have to be in the studio in 40 minutes."

"You're really recording an album?"

"Yeah. I've already recorded like 18 songs and I'm doing more on my own."

"What are you doing with these recordings?"

"Todd's going to send them to bars to try and get me gigs," she said.

"Todd who?"

"Todd Snider! He listened to my music on Facebook and he says my voice needs to be heard." She explained that Todd performs at Mountain Stage and other venues. More importantly, he owns a recording label. "Not just a studio, a label" she stressed.

Sierra told the story about how she met Todd. "Mike Pushkin took me to Todd's show at the V Club and I started talking to his roadie," Sierra said. "He was sitting up by the speaker. Anyway, he invited me to come back to the green room—Todd only does shows where there's a green room—and I hung out with him. I guess he wants to talk about recording me."

"Is this for real?" I asked.

"I don't know," Sierra responded in an exasperated tone. "I hope so."

While I was in Pasadena for the Rose Bowl, the Maestro called to make sure I understood the magnitude of Sierra's opportunity.

"He's for real," Mike assured me. "I talked to him about Sierra when he was in town last month."

◆ ◆ ◆

Sierra returned from Nashville later in January. Her first order of business was to try on her various boots.

The antique shoes, circa 1940, looked as good as new. "I replaced all the buttons," the cobbler had told me when I picked them up. "My uncle left a bunch of antique buttons when he handed over the business. I doubt I'll have any other use for them so I went ahead and put them on." He had also refurbished the leather cowboy boots and replaced the soles.

"I really appreciate this," I said. "My daughter needs these for a photo shoot."

"Really?"

"Yeah, she's in Nashville. Recording an album."

"You know, when Taylor Swift is in town I work on her boots too," he added.

While Sierra changed boots, I listened to her recording on her iPad.

"I love the sound," she said. "I've never been recorded like that. The studio has like a hundred thousand dollars' worth of equipment."

Tammy asked about future plans.

"They still have to master the album," she said. "And I have to do that photo shoot."

"So what will you do with this album?"

"Todd's going to try and get me more gigs."

"By the way, you haven't signed anything have you?"

"No. But he says I will have to sign something eventually."

"Don't sign without asking me first," I instructed.

Sierra rolled her eyes.

"Eric's getting me a manager," she added. "And wranglers."

"Wranglers are a good thing," I said, looking at Tammy who nodded with approval, privately wishing them luck.

"Do you have any gigs coming up?" I asked.

"Yeah, I have one in Chattanooga." Sierra answered nonchalantly. "It's with Todd."

"When?"

"Not for a while," she replied, fixing her eyes on the iPad. "Like March 1st or something."

"Sierra," I intoned, "that's in two weeks."

Getting no response, I picked up my iPad and googled Todd Snider, located toddsnider.net and opened the "tour" tab. The entry was three lines down: "Sat Mar 1, Track 29, Chattanooga, TN, with Sierra Elizabeth Ferrell."

Track 29 is located on the "campus of the famous Chattanooga Choo Choo Hotel." Setting aside the irony of Sierra playing her first big show at a railroad siding, I booked a room and bought tickets for the show.

A couple of days later, I asked Sierra about her schedule. "I've got a gig at Black Sheep in Huntington this weekend," she told me. "And then I'm leaving for Chattanooga."

"That's over a week away," I said. "Why so early?"

"I'm planning to hop a train," she said nonchalantly. "I think it will be cool. I'll tell the crowd, 'I just arrived on the train.'"

"And how is the Gretsch making it to Chattanooga?"

"I don't know," she responded tentatively.

"You know," I said. "I was thinking of coming down to that show. I could bring it."

"That would be great! Just don't dress too fancy."

"Maybe you should take me shopping."

◆ ◆ ◆

Sierra's plans for a signature arrival at Track 29 proved to be tentative, and on the Tuesday before the show she announced that I was her ride.

"Justin gets off at 8:00 that morning, and we'll leave as soon as he gets off," I told her.

"OK," she responded. "Pick me and Wasabi up at Amy's."

As we loaded up, Justin asked. "Is there a food plan?"

"Yeah, I'm hungry too," Sierra added. I pulled up to the Tudor's drive-thru. The cashier smiled when she saw Wasabi.

"What a cute dog!"

"Thanks," I said.

"Where are you going?"

"Chattanooga."

"Are you staying a few days?"

"No, just overnight," I said. "She's got a gig tonight."

"What kind of music?"

"Acoustic Americana," I said authoritatively. "It's a mix of country and bluegrass. When she makes it big, you can say, 'I served her when she had her first gig.'"

"That's what I was thinking too," the cashier said with a smile.

◆ ◆ ◆

When we stopped for gas in Virginia, Sierra took Wasabi out in a field next to the gas station. Justin offered to drive and I climbed in the backseat.

"Where's Sierra?" I asked.

"She's out with Wasabi." We looked over and found Sierra yelling at Wasabi. "Get back in the car!"

"You may need to help her," I said.

Next thing I knew, Wasabi was running back and forth between Justin and Sierra, stopping inches short of their outstretched hands. Clearly she was the only one enjoying the game. I clambered out of the back seat, walked over to the edge of the lot and kneeled down.

"Wasabi," I said in a calm tone. "Come here, girl." She ran straight over and I grabbed the leash without hesitation.

"What are you, the dog whisperer?" Justin asked.

◆ ◆ ◆

Just under four hours later, the kids were asking for directions to the hotel.

"Todd's staying in the same hotel," Sierra said as she started doing her makeup. "Can you hand me my boots?"

The hotel was located on what appeared to have been a bustling main drag in its day. As we navigated to the main entrance that day, however, many of the storefronts were boarded up. The lobby was spacious, adorned in rich hardwood tones and green foliage. Our room was located in one of the units in the rear, closer to the performance hall. We drove past the train cars being used for a restaurant and hotel suites and parked outside the building. It appeared to be of 1970s vintage.

As we entered the elevator with Wasabi, Justin gave me an inquiring look. I just stared back, my way of saying, "I don't know if dogs are allowed and I'm afraid to ask." As the elevator doors opened on our floor, a man wearing a Chattanooga Choo Choo maintenance uniform was waiting to get on the elevator. "Hello there, pooch," he said with a smile.

Justin and I were famished and headed to the bar for a quick appetizer before the show. While we feasted on appetizers, Sierra and Wasabi walked with Todd and the roadies over to the green room to get ready for the show. "When people saw Wasabi they all yelled, 'That's the girl from the magazine article.' Apparently there was some article about me," Sierra told us later. In the article Todd recounted telling his wife that he was bringing home "this girl with an incredible voice—and her dog."

After finishing the appetizers, Justin and I walked along the old rail tracks to Track 29. I put the ticket stub back in my jacket pocket as we entered, a tradition I inherited from my dad. The ticket stub took its place alongside tickets to *The Lion King* (Aaron, 2002), *Phantom of the Opera* (Sierra, 2010), and *The Glass Menagerie* (Frieda, 2013).

Track 29 is billed on the website as a "world-class entertainment venue." In reality, it's a prefabricated steel building with a stage at one end, a bar at the other and 150 chairs sitting out on a concrete floor. Shortly before 8:00 p.m. the seats were full and the rest of the crowd stood back near the bar.

I sent Sierra a text wishing her good luck, adding "PS, this place looks for real!!!"

Shortly after eight o'clock Sierra walked on stage followed by a tall man who sat down at a steel pedal guitar. Sierra picked up her guitar.

"Hey, it's good to be here. Great weather we're having today," she began. "I wrote this song outside of Walla Walla. It's called, 'You Don't Have a Hold Over Me.'" The next song was also a product of her famed journey of whimsy and longing, this one from Portland. Before beginning the song she added, "My name's Sierra Ferrell, by the way. I'm from Charleston, West Virginia."

She played for just over 30 minutes with "Mr. Moon" providing the climax and a song by Paul, a friend who died a couple years earlier, as an encore. She left out that Paul died jumping off a train.

A few minutes later I saw Todd Snider for the first time, wearing a brightly-colored sweater and his signature fedora. The crowd came to its feet and stomped to the beat.

"I'll be playing two sets tonight," he said. "And I want to thank Sierra for opening up for me tonight. She'll be joining me for the second set."

Justin and I admired Todd's guitar skills and agreed that Sierra needed to work on her guitar playing.

Todd concluded the set with his version of meeting Sierra.

"I was at Mountain Stage in West Virginia and I saw these kids out by the rail tracks," he told the crowd. "And they all seemed to be listening to this one girl. So, I said I want to meet her. They told me, 'Oh, we know her, you don't want to let her in.'" Pausing for effect, he added, "Then I wanted to meet her even more."

During the set break Sierra came over. Her smile was as bright as the stage lights.

"You did great," I told her. "Did you enjoy it?"

"Are you kidding? It was awesome!" she replied. "I gotta go—I'm singing with Todd this set. And I'll see if I can get you backstage after the show."

I looked over at Justin. His jaw dropped about as fast as mine.

Sierra joined Todd for several songs, including a crowd-pleasing "This Land Is My Land." Later I asked Sierra if she knew the words. "Enough," she smiled.

◆ ◆ ◆

The next morning, Sierra and Wasabi came up to the room. "I bet you're hungry," I said to Wasabi. She answered by reaching for the food before I could set it down. When she finished, I offered to take her on a walk. Ironically, Wasabi trotted around the railroad tracks before I found the dog walk area. When she was sufficiently tired out, I came back to meet Justin and Sierra. She was on the phone with Todd's manager.

"They want me back in Nashville to do more recording," she told us.

Justin and Sierra volunteered to drive, so I climbed into the backseat with Wasabi, who rested her head on the guitar. Within six hours we were back in Charleston and Sierra was reporting to Amy's house. "The show was awesome!"

◆ ◆ ◆

"What time does Cabela's close?"

Looking around the dinner table, I winced at the looks on Tammy's and Justin's faces. We all knew what a trip Cabela's meant. When Sierra went downstairs to grab her bag, I whispered to Tammy, "I'm not thrilled with this any more than you are. But it's her money and I can't stop her from traveling."

"I know," Tammy sighed. "I was just hoping..."

"It's hard for me, too," I said. "I'm trying to balance enabling her and letting her make her own choices. And it's her money."

Shopping with Sierra at Cabela's is no different than shopping at Charlotte Russe or Cache. She randomly moves about the store in search of the right item at the best price. First we looked at cook stoves. I couldn't muster much interest in whether the Coleman or the MSR performed best under interstate bridges.

"Stop worrying, I'll be fine."

"Look," I responded, "I realize that you're 25 and it's your life."

"So just let me live it," Sierra cried, her eyes both pleading and defiant.

"That one looks good for camping," I offered. "But does it require a propane tank?"

"Oh my God, why does it have to be so complicated?" Sierra said in an exasperated tone. "Let's look for a backpack."

I thought back to our trip to Gander Mountain two years ago. "The last one was too big for me," Sierra said, as if to infer that I was responsible for choosing her first one. For the record, that one did make it back and forth to California. Twice. Setting aside my doubts about the traveling lifestyle, I relented and offered some fatherly advice. "This one seems to ride better, closer to the lower back."

"And it's got all kinds of pockets," Sierra added. "Those are cool."

Next we looked for a rain cover. "Do I need a large or an extra large?" Never having been a Boy Scout, I was of no assistance.

After walking through boats, guns and arrows, I happened upon the hunting dog department. Dog vests, dog beds, dog treats, but no saddlebags. We eventually found a sales clerk who responded, "That would be a good idea. I could use one for my dog."

Last, but by no means least, came the hat. Sierra tried on countless hats, looking into the mirror and adjusting her hair for each one.

"How about this one?" I handed a dark brown leather hat that closely resembled Indiana Jones' hat. Sierra switched back and forth between the leather hat and a canvass hat with the bent brim. On one rotation, I examined the leather hat and noticed metal pieces on each side. Sure enough, a metal tab on the brim clasped in, allowing the wearer to secure the brim for that Aussie outback look.

"Hey," Sierra shouted with excitement. "How did you do that?"

"Just trying to take care of my girl," I said with a smile.

◆ ◆ ◆

Sierra called for a ride two days later. Wasabi jumped to greet me when I came through the door, ignoring Sierra's shouts of "Down Wasabi, down!" After calming Wasabi I saw Sierra sitting on the futon by the new backpack, which was not bulging at the seams.

"Help me get my stuff," Sierra said. Though Sierra had only been at Amy's for a couple of months, it took us two trips to carry her belongings out, filling the rear of the Skunkmobile. Back home, I unloaded the car, setting boxes down wherever I could find space in Sierra's bedroom.

While I made one last trip from the car, Sierra came upstairs to search the fridge for leftovers. She sat down at the table to eat warmed-over pizza with ranch dressing and turned on my Macbook. She and Justin were still talking and surfing Facebook when I went to bed.

When I came home the next day Sierra said. "Hey, a friend of mine is in town. Can we go pick him up?"

That afternoon I met Tome, 27 years old and in his seventh year on the road. He wore jeans and a fashionable shirt. Judging by the odor, the shirt had not been laundered recently.

"I was in college in California and working as a graphic artist," he told me. "One day I was sitting in my apartment looking at a stack of credit card bills. I asked myself, 'Is this what it's about?'"

While I figured earning a degree in a field you enjoy and having a job sounded pretty good at that age, I kept silent and let Tome continue with his story.

"My dad's a lawyer. He's been with the California DMV for 10 years. He has a house payment and a car payment. So I asked my grandmother what to do. She told me to follow my heart and see the world.

"I've learned a lot," he continued. "I used to be trusting of everyone, but then a couple offered to record my music and they tried to take advantage of me. Now I've learned to see people's hearts."

To me this sounded like a euphemism for recognizing a soft touch when panhandling.

Later that evening Sierra came out of her room lugging her backpack. "Can you give us a ride downtown?" she asked.

I pulled out of the garage and waited for the kids. They came out to the car, but Wasabi ran back to the front door. (Tammy remains convinced that Wasabi preferred the comfort of the green room.)

"Wasabi!" I heard Sierra scream.

"Wasabi," I said softly. "Come here, girl." Wasabi came running down from the front door. I petted her playfully before grabbing the leash and "loading up," as the traveling kids say.

It took a couple of minutes to unload the two backpacks from the back seat of the Mini. I handed the guitar to Tome, who thanked me as he started to close the door. "Wait," Sierra yelled. She came back to give me a hug.

The following evening I received a text: "I'm leaving tomorrow to head to sc for 12. I'll be there before then but want head start there." At least she remembered the date of her show, opening at a weekend festival for Todd Snider.

Sierra and Tome hitched rides to Carrboro, North Carolina, a town that "knows how to party," according to Sierra's Facebook update. "The bars even let me in with my dog." After a few days of "making music," Sierra posted that they had caught a ride to South Carolina. Kitty, Sierra's traveling companion from her first season and the owner of Wasabi's parents, asked the obvious: "You back on the road? Did you bring Wasabi?" Following the festival, Sierra returned to the East Nashville recording studio, writing songs with Todd Snider and showing Todd around the internet with her iPad. Turns out she was taking the stage, too.

"Sierra Ferrell, a busker pal of Snider's, surprises everyone by singing a sad ballad about a boyfriend who died after jumping off a moving train," the *Rolling Stone* reported on page 75. A Nashville music writer summed up Sierra's performance: "She nailed it."

"YOU TWO MUST BE BROTHERS"

NEITHER AARON NOR JUSTIN were giving any ground as they debated the proper nails for repairing a deck. They stood toe to toe in the hardware aisle at Home Depot as each argued his case.

This lasted nearly 45 minutes. Two 20-year-olds arguing about nails. Finally, a clerk approached them. "Can I help you guys find anything?"

"Yes," Aaron said. "We're looking for stainless steel nails."

"Excuse me?" Justin interrupted. "We're looking for galvanized nails."

After watching the debate go on for a couple minutes longer, the clerk politely pointed to the stainless steel nails on one shelf and the galvanized nails on the shelf below. Seeing the debate growing more heated, the clerk smiled and said, "You two must be brothers."

"No, we just live together," Justin said.

"OK," the clerk said with a raised eyebrow before making a quick retreat.

"Great," Justin sighed. "He thinks we're gay."

"Chill out, man," Aaron replied. "Wait, what did you say?"

Since that incident they tried to be more careful, but they can't help themselves. One night eating out at Chili's they heard "Born to Run," the same song they'd blasted from the car stereo on the drive over.

"Hey, they're playing our song," Justin said.

"Don't say 'our song,'" Aaron pleaded.

More than living together, Aaron and Justin really are brothers.

◆ ◆ ◆

The guys first met in sixth grade band, and they forged a friendship as teammates on the middle school golf team.

"Wait, let us tell the story," Aaron always says.

"We're picking up golf balls after practice," Justin begins, "and I say to Aaron, 'Do you see that guy?'"

"I'm like, 'What guy?'" Aaron says.

"The guy over in the corner, the one wearing the purple suit," Justin continues.

"You said he looked like Barney," Aaron adds. (In hindsight, wearing my bright purple River City Runners warm-up suit to Elkview Middle School was not one of my better fashion decisions.)

"Yeah," Justin says as he breaks out laughing. "Ky was standing over by the far end of the bleachers."

"No he wasn't," Aaron interrupts. "He was over by the door near the hallway."

"He was at the far end of the bleachers."

"He was by the hallway."

"May I please finish the story?" Justin will inevitably ask. "I asked Aaron, 'Who is that guy?'"

"And I said, 'Uh, that's my dad.'"

"I was like, 'No, don't play with me.'"

"And I'm like, 'I'm serious. You're riding home with him.'"

Justin lived with his grandparents, who were not much older than Tammy and I. Justin had been playing golf for a couple of years, he played trumpet in the band, and he carried a briefcase in lieu of a backpack.

"I know, it's weird," Aaron laughed.

"Excuse me," Justin replied indignantly. "I prefer to be organized."

◆ ◆ ◆

Before long, Tammy and I were chauffeuring Justin and Aaron on a regular basis.

That summer Justin went with us to Parkersburg to watch Sierra in *Oklahoma!* My mom let him borrow one of my dad's ties. He seemed to enjoy the occasion to wear a tie as much as Sierra's performance. I think he slept with the tie on.

For the rest of the summer, Justin stayed over so often that he became a fixture. After school started in the fall, Sierra came out of her room and asked, "Where's Justin?"

"He's at his house. It's a school night." Tammy answered.

"Oh. I'm so used to him being around," Sierra said.

The following summer Justin joined the family vacation, a week-long stay at a cabin on the Greenbrier River. One night we took a bike ride on the trail. Halfway into the ride, Tammy half-jokingly warned the kids to be on the lookout for bears. Justin was not amused. At some point Justin mentioned that he needed to use the facilities, a polite euphemism they learned from me.

"OK," I said, pulling off to the side in a vacant stretch.

"Where do we go?" Justin asked.

"In the trees," I said. "Haven't you ever gone in the woods?"

"No!" And so, for the first time in his life, Justin "used the facilities" in the woods. He grimaced most of the way back, rushing to wash his hands as soon as we reached the cabin. The next day he and Tammy were back out on the trail and saw a black bear. He held his bladder until he got back to the cabin.

For the next two years, Tammy and I watched the band march in fall parades, play at football games and perform at school concerts. Often we'd pick up both guys from school. At their final spring concert, the band director individually recognized all the Elkview Middle graduates, telling a story about each one.

"Justin Hannigan!" he bellowed. "I refer to Justin as 'Valves' because he always played with his trumpet valves during class."

In our house, Justin's been "Valves" ever since.

The guys both enrolled in Capital High School and joined the band. In August we loaded Aaron's trombone, insulin supplies and a fan and took him to band camp. The camp was held at Glenville State College. The kids would be staying in dorm rooms with no air conditioning and shared facilities.

Justin had never resided in such spartan accommodations. He and Aaron were on the same floor, and I directed him to the bathroom. Looking around the bathroom, he shouted, "Oh my God. Community showers? Are you serious?"

I offered little sympathy. "Don't pick up the soap," I said.

"Don't worry," he said glaring back. "I won't."

We saw Justin at band performances and football games, but the guys started hanging around less during high school. Aaron changed schools after sophomore year, and the only time we saw the guys together was at the funeral for a family member of Justin's who died from complications of Type 1 diabetes.

"I wish we could get the guys together again," Tammy told Justin's mother. She replied, "I think he's afraid of getting too close to Aaron for fear he'll lose someone else to diabetes."

◆ ◆ ◆

Justin and Aaron reunited after high school. With Justin and Brooke dating again, the kids revived their *Three's Company* routine for the summer. Aaron invited both of them to our cabin one weekend, and two weeks later Justin and Brooke were dating. Being old enough to drive, they didn't ask us to join them on any double dates. That fall, Brooke went off to school at West Virginia University in Morgantown, about three hours away.

"I haven't heard from Brooke today," Justin often said at dinner.

"I'm sure she's busy," Tammy said in a reassuring tone.

One day I came home and bragged about my first FaceTime call. "Brooke called to check in," I said.

Justin dropped his iPhone and looked up with a stunned look on his face.

"She hasn't answered my texts all day."

"I think maybe she had to go to the library," I improvised.

Later that evening Tammy and I talked privately. "I've seen this movie before," I warned. "When I went to college, every guy that had a girl back home dropped her by the end of the first semester."

It was the same feeling I had when Aaron was learning to ride his bike, going down the hill and about to lose control. "I feel like Justin's on the bike and he's going downhill fast."

A few days later I was doing dishes when Justin cried out from the kitchen table. "She texted me," he cried. "She broke up by texting me!"

Keeping any clever remarks about Brooke's propensity to text to myself, I said, "I've got to take the dogs out." As I picked up my cell phone along with the dogs' leashes, Tammy nodded and sat down next to Justin. When you've been married 25 years, words are often unnecessary.

I held both dog leashes in my right hand and tapped on Brooke's contact information with my left thumb. She answered on the first ring.

"Hey there," I said. "I'm outside with the dogs and Justin is inside talking to Tammy and Aaron, so I've only got a minute."

"Did Justin tell…"

"Yes. Listen, I understand, you've got to focus on college," I continued. "I just wanted you to know we love you."

I hurried the dogs back in the house. After handing the dogs their biscuits, I acknowledged that breaking off relationships via text seemed a bit caustic. "But that's the way you kids seem to communicate," I added.

A few minutes later Justin had a confession. "I guess I did break up with my last girlfriend with a text."

◆ ◆ ◆

A few months earlier, Tammy and I had watched Brooke march at the Capital High School graduation. Justin was listed among the graduates, but we were told he went to the beach in lieu of the ceremony. Then we heard rumors that he still needed to finish additional classes through the online credit recovery program. Our efforts to talk about his future education plans failed. "I may take a year off" was his standard reply.

Aaron deftly brought the question to a head. While we were eating supper one evening, Aaron asked, "So Justin, is there anything you'd like to tell us about school?" Justin looked up with a stunned expression.

"I know it may be awkward for you," Aaron said. "So I thought you might want to get it off your chest." Once he overcame the shock, Justin explained that he needed to finish three courses through credit recovery, including math.

"Ky can help you with math," Tammy offered.

"When we're done eating, we'll log on and get started," I said without hesitation.

We worked on math almost every night for several weeks, taking a break at Christmas. The interruption turned out to be fatal—we missed the semester deadline. Justin promised to finish out the credit recovery when school started in September.

In August, I took Justin to find out what he needed to do to finish the credits. "They've changed the program," the counselor informed us. "It will take at least a semester for you to complete the credits. You may want to consider getting your GED."

I explained Justin's options in an e-mail, complete with a table outlining his options. "Don't jump to a decision," I advised. "Take time and consider the alternatives."

Two days later, Justin announced, "I'm going to drop out and get a GED." I directed Justin to the adult education center and explained the process. He qualified for the test after the first week of classes and he passed with flying colors.

Except for math.

❖ ❖ ❖

That spring Justin was living with his mother. His grandmother had moved out of state and he spent many evenings at our house. We could tell that he and his mother didn't always see eye-to-eye. In fact, he and Aaron often carried on conversations about who had the more irrational mother.

"I like your mom," Aaron often said. "She's not like Tammy."

"What are you saying?" came Justin's reply. "Tammy's a wonderful person. My mom is being so illogical."

One day Justin joined us for lunch. His phone chimed as soon as we found a table and his facial expression changed instantly. He narrowed his eyes and clenched his teeth as he tapped on the screen.

"Mother... I don't care... geez, why do you always have to complain... Fine... Look, I can't talk now. We're ready to order. Goodbye."

The waitress approached cautiously as Justin slammed his phone on the table. "All three of us will have the buffet," Tammy said politely.

"You know, Justin," I said, "at this rate you're going to ruin any hope of having a relationship with your mother."

Before Justin could say anything, I added, "You're always welcome to chill at our house. Hell, most of your clothes are already there. Feel free to bring over any other essentials."

Out of the corner of my eye, I saw Tammy nodding in agreement.

The next day the guys came in carrying an Xbox and a 40-inch flat screen TV.

I often came home to the sounds of Aaron and Justin yelling into their headsets from their respective bedrooms as they played Xbox online. "I'm coming your way, over by the tanker." "Get that guy!" "Oh man, where did he come from?"

"GTA?" I ask.

"Yes," Justin tells me. "We're running from the police." He interrupts to yell into his headset. "Aaron, I'm heading to the subway tunnel." Then he looks back at me and says, "In a Mini Cooper!"

"And you wonder why I won't let you drive my Mini?"

◆ ◆ ◆

The Xbox is the only similarity between their bedrooms. Aaron's room is typically littered with paper plates, empty soda bottles and dirty clothes. Justin vacuums once a week. Aaron's jeans and hoodies are in the laundry room, stuffed into whatever basket one of us placed them upon removal from the dryer. Justin's polo shirts hang in his closet.

"I can't believe you," Aaron shouts as they bring out hampers of dirty clothes from their respective rooms. "You always sort everything."

"I like to follow the care instructions," Justin retorts. "Is that OK?"

"You're such a freak!"

"Oh my God! Clothes last longer if you follow the care instructions."

"And you're so fussy about how many clothes you put in the washer," Aaron continues.

"If you put too much in..."

"Oh my God," Aaron interrupts. "I just stuff it full and run it."

"You're such an idiot," Justin scolds. "If you fill the washer too full, the water won't circulate enough to wash off the soap," adding, "you dumb #@%."

In Aaron's defense, he does like his American Eagle shirts to be ironed before he crumples up the sleeves. "Hey Justin," he'll say as Justin heads down to the laundry room, "iron my shirt while you're down there."

"Iron your own damn shirt!"

"Come on, help a guy out."

❖ ❖ ❖

"I need to go over to my grandfather's this afternoon," Justin announced one Saturday morning. "I have to take care of his dog while he's out of town."

"No problem," I said. "Thanks for letting me know."

That afternoon I returned from the store to find Justin sitting in the front yard with a dog. My first thought was, "That's not what I had in mind when I said, 'No problem.' When I greeted Bo, however, I said, "Have you taken him in to meet Dolly and Boogie?"

Bo, a mountain feist, was just over a year old and full of energy. When we brought him in the house, Dolly headed back to the bedroom while Boogie and Bo chased each other around. When they were out in the back yard, Boogie completed the orientation by tackling Bo to avoid any question as to the hierarchy within the pack.

Justin often left Bo in his crate when leaving for work. However, neither Tammy nor I could bear to leave him there. Most evenings were spent trying to make sure none of the dogs became overzealous about a toy.

Bo stayed until Justin accepted a full time position that entailed three 24-hour shifts per week. At that point, Justin's grandfather found another family member to take in the dog.

❖ ❖ ❖

When people ask, "Who's Justin?" I like to say "I'm not an ambulance chaser. I've got one of my guys on the ambulance."

"You really say that?" Justin asks incredulously.

Justin obtained his certification—EMT-B according to the shirts hanging in the laundry room—in 2013 and started with the county ambulance authority that summer. Ever since that day our text exchanges have been littered with EMS lingo like "roger," "negative," and "sitrep."

Often we're among the first to know that a bad batch of heroin has hit the streets of Charleston. "We ran our third overdose this week," Justin told us one night. It seems that the overdose calls come in batches. "It's because the heroin is either laced with something or it's stronger than usual," he explains. The staff at the office still looks at me askew when someone mentions reading about an overdose and I say, "I heard a bad batch hit town last week."

Justin and I both like a good debate, so the issue of whether EMTs should carry Narcan, a shot that counteracts opium overdoses, has been the subject of heated discussions. "These people are taking drugs, and they expect us to come and give them a shot to save themselves," Justin argues.

"It's an addiction, an illness," I counter.

"But we're paying for it!"

If the arguments become too heated, I bring up Sierra's ambulance bills from Utah for comic relief. "And who paid those, I wonder?"

"I can't believe you still get those," he says with a smile.

◆ ◆ ◆

Justin shares my intense interest in both politics and history. We're both JFK aficionados. I have a multitude of Kennedy biographies, along with pictures, posters and the original *Life* magazine cover following the assassination. Justin is interested in the biographies, but also wants a pair of sunglasses like what JFK wore at Martha's Vineyard.

One night I was soliciting Aaron and Justin to vote for my running partner in the Congressional race. Justin followed through by reading up on the contested races and candidates. He sent me a text the following day.

"I would like to meet Nick Casey." Later I replied by telling him to be at my office at 930 hours on Friday.

"Why?" he asked.

"You said you wanted to meet Nick Casey."

Justin came to the office in his Brooks Brothers jacket and creased Ralph Lauren slacks. At Nick's office I sat at the far end of the table and watched. Nick asked about the EMT business, listening carefully and then making a subtle pitch. That evening Justin asked me if it was legal for the candidate to find out who contributed. "Absolutely," I told him. "In fact, I was always taught to make sure the candidate knows you've contributed."

Two weeks later Justin joined me for Nick's birthday fundraiser. "How do I make out the check?" he asked. "Why don't you ask Nick," I suggested. "Ah, I see," he replied with a sly grin. "I'm catching on to your tricks."

Justin also accompanied me to a fundraiser for the Maestro, who was running for a seat in the state House of Delegates. "Why is it you go to these?" Justin asked.

"I view my role as showing that a man with streaks of gray hair who wears a suit and tie supports the cab driver/musician," I said.

Justin nodded his head and grinned.

◆ ◆ ◆

Being a good brother, Justin also used his EMT training to help tutor Aaron when he took the EMT class. That resulted in more comical arguments.

"What's BAC?" I asked one night at supper.

"Breathing, airway, circulation," Aaron answered. "It's the order you check a patient."

"That's not the way we do it in the field," Justin said.

"I'm sticking with what the book says," Aaron responded.

In addition to written work, the coursework included hands-on practice. One night I volunteered to serve as the dummy for Aaron's practical test. Under Justin's watchful eye, I lay down on the floor.

"OK," Justin announced. "You're responding to a call. An old man has just fallen on the floor."

Aaron took over in a measured tone. "White male, middle age, approximately mid-fifties," he said as he put on the blue latex gloves.

"Wait a minute," I shouted. "Who are you calling old?"

The training also included ride time with a crew. Aaron managed to sign up for some of his ride time with Justin. "I have sympathy for the patient," I said when I found out they'd be riding together. "Some guy with shortness of breath and you guys will be arguing about how to do your laundry."

They were scheduled to work the 8:00 p.m. to 8:00 a.m. shift one Friday. Shortly after seven o'clock—Justin would say 1900 hours—both guys were running back and forth between the family room and their bedrooms gathering their EMT gear. As Aaron opened the car door I heard Justin ask, "Did you remember your Xbox controller?"

Tammy and I met the guys for breakfast the next morning. When the kids were in school, we learned that the best time to get a full report is right after they get off the bus.

"We ran two calls," Justin said.

"Yeah, one of them was to the restaurant," Aaron interjected.

"Do you mind? I'm telling the story!"

They explained that the call came in as a cardiac arrest. Aaron was excited, Justin worried. "I grabbed everything on the truck," Aaron said. "When we came in, I froze," Justin said.

"We came running in and the person was conscious," Aaron lamented.

"What if she hadn't been? What would you have done?" I asked.

"I'd do compressions and Justin would bag her."

"So, you start that immediately..." I began.

"I'd first clear the airway," Aaron explains.

"What?" Justin shouts. "You'd clear the airway?"

"That's what the book says," Aaron retorts. "I know you don't go by the book."

❖ ❖ ❖

Aaron obtained the certification needed to be a transport driver and took a job with the ambulance service in Doddridge County. The guys' uniform shirts were distinguishable, but they both wore standard issue pants and belts. This posed a problem.

One morning Justin rushed out of his bedroom in a panic. "Have you seen my belt?"

"Look on the dog kennel," I said.

Justin breathed a sigh of relief. The respite turned out to be short-lived. "Oh my God! Aaron took my belt," he screamed, holding up the size 38 belt. Tammy and I broke out laughing as we imagined the scene in Doddridge County of Aaron picking up Justin's size 32 belt.

❖ ❖ ❖

While Tammy and I admire the work Justin performs, we also know his first loves are history and the law. "I respect the EMT profession," I often tell him. "But for years you've said you want to be a lawyer. And I know how much you like expensive wine and cheese."

"You guys don't know your limits," Aaron will tell us. "You're putting too much pressure on him."

"He needs to hear it," we respond.

"It would be easy to tell you what you want and be your friend, but that's not why I'm here. I'm going to keep telling you what I think you need to hear." At the same time, I recognize that Justin has turned 21 and he's free to chart his own course.

Sometimes our "encouragement" causes Justin to return to his mom's house or stay with a friend for extended periods. In that event, Tammy pastes Justin's picture on the milk carton and strategically places it in the refrigerator to ensure he'll see it when he returns.

◆ ◆ ◆

I've provided for both guys in my will. Aaron gets the golf clubs, Justin gets the library, and they can divide the ties—except for the JFK tie. All of my Kennedy paraphernalia goes to Justin.

I'm tempted to leave a hundred dollars in Kennedy half-dollars. Aaron will say that all the cash goes into the residuary to be divided among all the kids, and Justin will interrupt him.

"Excuse me? Those have John Kennedy's bust on them. Everything with JFK on it goes to me."

"Seriously dude?"

The fiduciary officer will probably smile and say, "You two must be brothers."

48 HOURS

7:45 P.M., MONDAY

"On the night before an exam, relax and go to a movie," was Professor McFarland's advice to first-year law students. So, on the night before a significant court hearing, I was searching for a movie on my iPad, eventually tapping on the BBC's *House of Cards.* Justin was midway through his 24-hour ambulance shift. Aaron was packed and ready to leave in the morning for work in Doddridge County. Tammy was sitting at the table filling out time sheets.

The tranquility lasted for almost 10 minutes.

"Get me a bottle of water and a trash can," Aaron said as he came out of his room. "My teeth are hurting, so I'm sure my blood sugar's high."

I handed him a bottle of water.

"I'd get him a trash can," Tammy advised.

"Do we have Gatorade?"

"We have Propel," I offered.

"We need Gatorade," Aaron added with a look of disbelief.

"Gatorade has carbs. He needs carbs for the insulin to work," Tammy said, adding, "I'll go to Olin's."

Aaron hacked for several minutes, eventually coughing up some fluid. "I hate the dry heaves more than puking," he said.

I offered a wet washcloth.

Tammy returned with Gatorade and asked Aaron if he'd checked his sugar.

Aaron's response was boilerplate: "I don't know where my kit is."

"Have you at least covered?" I asked.

"Yes," he insisted as he took out his pump and started punching buttons.

Two minutes later he stood up and screamed. "Oh my God! I just smelled the insulin." Pointing to the damp cushion, he added, "My site is leaking."

Tammy helped gather supplies for a new pump site.

"You should go to bed," Tammy told me. "You need a good night's sleep."

11:15 P.M.

My sleep was interrupted by the sounds of projectile vomiting.

Two minutes later Tammy announced, "We're going to the hospital. You might want to change out the trash bags."

"We should call the ambulance," Aaron insisted.

"I already checked with Justin," she said. "We're better off driving."

"Then help me stand up," Aaron said.

"I'm here," I said. "Just put your arm around me. I can't carry you."

He stood up and put his arm around my shoulder and pointed to the door. After a pit stop on the front porch, I walked Aaron to the car and went back inside.

I collected three trash bags of regurgitated Gatorade.

1:00 A.M., TUESDAY

My sleep was again interrupted, this time by Tammy's ring tone.

"You'd better call Aaron's work and let them know he won't be in," she said. I heard Aaron in the background, saying, "My phone's on my bed. The number is listed as 'Joyce, work.'"

I found the number and called.

"Doddridge County EMS. This is Joyce. How may I help you?"

"Hi, this is Ky Owen, Aaron's dad," I said, garnering the best lawyer voice I could at that time of night. "Aaron's in the ER and I don't think he'll be there for his 10 o'clock run."

"OK," she responded. "Thanks for calling."

6:00 A.M.

I woke up and rolled over and checked my iPhone. "Room 217," Tammy's e-mail read. "But we won't move until 7:00 because they're short-staffed." I turned to Facebook for details. Tammy had posted:

> *Have I mentioned lately how much I HATE dia-*
> *betes??!!??!! Ugh!!! Aaron had a bad pump site*
> *but didn't realize it. He has been north of 600...*
> *After lots of insulin and puking he is down to 578.*
> *Worried about a sudden drop since he threw up*
> *all the carbs... Very worried about DKA. They are*
> *admitting him.*

Seeing that Tammy was online, I assumed she was awake and able to take a call. She sounded exhausted.

"Is he awake?"

"Yeah, do you want to talk to him?" After a moment, I heard Tammy say, "Hey, Aaron, it's Ky."

"Hola, Senor," he said.

"Hey, how's it going?"

"I'm not throwing up anymore."

8:00 A.M.

I headed to the hospital before going to the office. Aaron and Tammy both looked wiped out. Tammy filled me in on the details. They had been moved from the ER less than a half hour earlier. Aaron's readings had dropped from the potentially lethal 600s to just under 300. Nausea remained an issue and the nurse had just started a different anti-nausea medicine.

"If you can stay five minutes," Tammy said, "I really need to go to the bathroom."

Tammy returned a few minutes later with her breakfast, a muffin from the hospital cafeteria. Aaron was sound asleep. Tammy handed me her time sheets and I headed over to the office.

"How's Aaron?" was the greeting of the day, followed by, "Don't you have that hearing today?"

I recalled my psychology professor at Michigan State telling us that running late for an exam is a good idea because "you'll be so stressed about being on time that you won't stress about the test." Maybe having my son in the hospital was a good way to get ready for my oral argument.

After staring at the briefs for half an hour, I decided that the hour I had available would be better spent with Aaron. I called Tammy and suggested that she come to the office. When we crossed paths between the buildings, she told me Justin had arrived, having canceled his golf trip.

"Your blood sugars are looking better," I heard the staff doctor telling Aaron as I entered the room.

"I'm Aaron's dad," I announced in my best lawyer voice. I'm sure finding that the patient had a lawyer father was not how the doctor wanted to start his day. He turned back to Aaron. "Dr. Sankari will be following up with you later this morning."

"Great," Aaron moaned. "She's not going to be happy with me."

"There's a reason for that," Justin said sternly.

Aaron rolled over and closed his eyes.

I left for Beckley.

2:15 P.M.

The hearing started 15 minutes late and the judge spent the first 10 minutes addressing other motions. Then I spent the next hour focused on arguing my motion, listening to opposing counsel's argument, and then in rebuttal. The judge eventually rendered a tentative ruling and the hearing concluded around 4:30 p.m. Thirty minutes later, I was on the turnpike entrance ramp, talking to Tammy through the bluetooth speaker in the Mini.

"He's doing better, but we'll be here another night," Tammy reported. "How did the hearing go?"

6:15 P.M.

By the time I returned to Charleston the office was closed, so I went directly to the hospital.

I walked in to see our family doctor talking with Aaron.

"I'm getting another lecture," Aaron told me.

"I'm not as strict as Dr. Sankari, though," Dr. McClung said with a grin.

"Ah, the good cop/bad cop routine," I said. "You must be the good cop."

"Oh, that's nothing compared to what I got from Amanda!" Aaron said about the lecture he got from his girlfriend.

We debated who would stay the night. "Ky should stay," Aaron said. "Tammy, you stayed last night." Tammy insisted that she would stay, though she did want to go home and change clothes first. She returned just before visiting hours ended at 8:00 p.m.

Justin and I went to dinner. Justin admitted that he was concerned, in part because his father died from diabetes complications.

"It just kind of freaks me out," he said.

1:20 A.M., WEDNESDAY

I woke up and saw a text from Tammy. "I am going to run home soon for pump supplies for Aaron—I didn't want to startle you and have you think I was breaking in. Aaron's site must not be working because he is high again." She must have realized that I hadn't seen her midnight e-mail asking me to bring pump supplies, not that it mattered—I'm never sure what supplies are needed. Tammy barged in five minutes later. "His site is bad," she said as she pillaged through a box. "He's back in the 400s."

Apparently the hospital didn't have any pump supplies in stock.

5:18 A. M.

My alarm went off right on schedule, and I got right out of bed and took the dogs out. Seeing no news on Facebook, I called Tammy from the car.

"I'm meeting Nick for our run," I said. "I'd come by first, but we're too close to the half-marathon to miss a day."

After the run I went home to shower and get ready for work. I checked my text messages on the way out the door. "If you haven't left home yet, bring a vial of insulin," the text read. Rather than asking if the hospital stocked insulin, I just took a vial from the butter drawer.

When I arrived at the hospital, Aaron sat up with the excitement of a kid at Christmas. He'd been without insulin for several hours, awaiting a delivery from the hospital pharmacy that had been reported to be "on the way" for some time. "You have my insulin? I've got to get that bike today or else I'll die!"

I noted Tammy's involuntary flinch at the mention of the motorcycle.

"He's doing better," I said to Tammy, "Why don't you go to the office and I'll stay this morning."

"Yeah," Aaron said. "Ky can stay. You've done enough."

"Let me know when they say anything about discharge and I'll come back," she replied.

"Ky can take me home."

After Tammy left I asked, "Is there anywhere to get coffee here?"

"You can't leave me."

"I need my coffee," I replied. "You'll survive."

Soon after I returned, a woman with a white lab coat entered the room, clipboard in hand. "I'm the nutritionist," she said. "I need to ask you some questions. Have you had any recent weight loss?"

"No," Aaron said, glancing over at me. I politely nodded, though my first thought was, "That's not what you told me when we were at American Eagle last week because you needed new jeans."

"Is the nausea better? Good. Then we can take off the GI restriction."

"So I can get chicken fingers," Aaron said. "That will be nice."

"And you're on the diabetic diet?"

Aaron picked up the "room service" menu without comment. "You order your food. It's like being in a hotel," he told me. "Just not as much fun."

"Yes, this is room 217. I want to order lunch," he said politely. "I'd like chicken strips and fries... They took off the GI restriction... Then what can I have?" He said thank you and handed me the phone.

"Apparently chicken strips are not allowed on the diabetic diet," Aaron moaned.

"Go buy me a Coke Zero," Aaron bargained. "Or else I'll tell Tammy you left me for coffee."

"Then I'd better not leave you again."

Before Aaron could lash out with a snarky comeback, I stood up to leave.

When I returned Aaron told me to get the nurse.

"It's time to check my sugar," he added.

"Why don't you press the call button?"

"Tammy just goes out and tells them."

"Use the call button on the remote," I told him.

◆ ◆ ◆

A nurse finally appeared and asked what we needed. "They were supposed to check my blood sugar at 9:30," Aaron said, glancing over at the clock on the wall. It read 9:45. Aaron's waiting, although not of his own volition, brought good things. By the time his nurse arrived a few minutes before 10, his blood sugar was nearly within normal limits.

"Hopefully you'll get to go home today," I said after the nurse left.

"I need to get that bike today."

"I know," I replied. "And we want to make sure you're healthy."

Justin stopped in a few minutes later. He joked that he had considered using his EMT badge to garner some scrubs and a face mask.

"I was going to wait until Aaron was almost asleep," Justin said "And then put my hand on his right leg and say, 'Are you ready for the amputation procedure, Mr. Owen?'"

"That's OK," Aaron said with a grin. "I shift with my left leg."

The nurse returned a few minutes after 10:00 and announced that the doctor was satisfied with the latest reading. "I'll begin working on the discharge papers," she said. "We should have you out of here after lunch."

Lunch on the diabetic menu consisted of a salad with no dressing, roasted chicken and mashed potatoes with stagnant gravy.

"I'm starved!" Aaron complained. "After we get home and I take a shower, we're going to Red Lobster."

"Why Red Lobster?" I asked.

"Crab legs are low-carb and filling. Plus it's near the motorcycle shop."

1:00 P.M.

The nurse arrived with discharge papers and a return to work slip. Discharge instructions were straightforward: "Manage your diabetes." Aaron signed all the papers and handed them to me. I left to get the car.

3:15 P.M.

Boogie and Roscoe, the lab mix we rescued from the shelter after Dolly died, jumped with excitement as Aaron came through the door, while Justin was more reserved.

"I'm glad you're alive."

"Me too," Aaron said.

They stood for a moment and then Aaron stepped forward. "Come on, give me a hug."

I interrupted the tender moment, asking, "Are we going to Red Lobster?"

Tammy and I met the guys at the restaurant. As we sat down, Aaron pulled out his kit and checked his sugar. "168, close to normal," he pronounced.

"Thanks for checking," we responded, avoiding the temptation to cheer a more reasonable reading.

After we finished eating, we drove to the motorcycle shop. Getting out of the car, Aaron padded the sides of his leather vest. "Did you get my kit at Red Lobster?"

"No," we responded in unison.

"Can you go pick it up?" Aaron asked. "I'm trying to avoid four-lane highways and intersections with four-way stops."

"Let's go to Red Lobster," I said to Justin.

6:00 P.M.

Ironically, my ringtone for Aaron's cell is an old motor-cycle horn.

"Hey," he said. "Can you come and get me?"

"Where are you?"

"At the dealership. This bike is bigger than I'm used to."

"I'm on my way."

Aaron was standing outside the dealership, holding his helmet and vest. The bike looked bigger sitting by itself. As Aaron got in the car he said, "The clutch is different than I expected... That bike has a lot of power."

7:45 P.M., MONDAY, JULY 30

We ate leftovers for supper. Aaron and Justin retired to their respective bedrooms, probably to race virtual Mini Coopers and Vegas 8-Balls on Xbox. Tammy and I finished doing the dishes, took the dogs out and enjoyed the respite before the next 48 hours.

NICE INK AND A BIKE NAMED ROXANE

THE SOUND OF AARON'S motorcycle boots pounding across the hardwood floor interrupted my concentration. When I looked up, I saw Aaron standing in the foyer looking for the car keys. He wore a red bandana wrapped around his head, a black leather vest and tattered jeans. The entirety of his full sleeve tattoo was in plain sight.

"Trying to make a good first impression on her parents, I see."

"Mind your own business," Aaron growled as he hooked the metal clasps on the vest.

"It's your choice," I said. "But since you're meeting her parents for the first time, I'd go with the jacket. Not all dads my age are as accepting of tattoos."

"Oh my God!" Aaron exclaimed.

"I'm just saying," I said as Aaron walked out the door shaking his head.

◆ ◆ ◆

Tammy and I were not fans of either motorcycle apparel or tattoos. As a matter of fact, we had forbidden Aaron from getting a tattoo, sternly exercising our parental rights in the hope that he'd change his mind by the time he turned 18.

Tattoos were just not for me, I guess, and I worried about Aaron making a youthful mistake that he'd be stuck with forever.

Tammy often mentioned that Type 1 diabetics are more at risk of complications from tattoos.

Talk of a motorcycle fell on deaf ears. Whenever Aaron mentioned wanting a motorcycle, I simply tuned him out. Tammy visibly cringed and told me, "The thought of him riding a motorcycle kills my soul."

Eventually, Aaron just stopped asking permission to get a tattoo, and he realized that until he had a job a motorcycle was out of the question.

◆ ◆ ◆

On the eve of turning 18, Aaron asked Tammy how to spell his grandmother's name, along with the dates of her birth and death.

"I'm getting that as part of my tattoo," he explained.

Tammy looked as though she was going to cry.

"I'm glad he wants to remember my mom," she lamented. "I just wish he'd find another way."

The next evening Aaron came home late with a bandage on his right shoulder. "Do you want to see my tattoo?" he asked. Tammy bid a goodnight and headed to the master bedroom, but I hesitated. I was as unhappy about the tattoo as Tammy, but at the same time I knew how much the tattoo meant to Aaron.

"Sure," I said. "Let me see it." It looked like any other modern tattoo as far as I could tell, but just the same I complimented the artwork.

"Be sure to keep the moisturizer on it," I said. Seeing the startled look on his face, I smiled and said, "The mayor's son got his first tattoo the summer he and Sierra dated."

Three years later, Aaron's tattoos had grown in size and scope. His forearms are emblazoned with "Primum familae," Latin for "Family First." His chest displays the names of his four siblings—Robert and Sierra on his birth mom's side and Haley and Jaxon on his birth dad's side. And his left arm is covered by a sleeve that's topped off by a Chinese Fu dog.

I've admittedly come to admire the Fu dog, maybe because he reminds me of Aaron's dog. Boogie won the adoption lottery because he looked like he had some pit bull in his lineage and Aaron wanted a big dog to match his hard guy image. But, in contrast to Aaron's tattoos and leather vest, Boogie wears colored polo shirts. Just like Justin.

Aaron's most recent tattoo is his own version of a diabetic alert symbol.

My mother, in keeping with her status as "the coolest grandmother," tells her college students with tattoos that her grandson has "nice ink."

One night I came home from work and found Aaron sitting at the table, his eyes narrowed as he drew on the sketch book. "It's a tattoo for a friend," he said. "I've ordered a tattoo gun online."

From the perspective of a liberal arts graduate, I admired the artwork. But from the perspective of a law school graduate, I worried about the liability aspect.

"Just don't give any tattoos in my house," I ordered.

"You should let me give you a tattoo," he replied, keeping his eyes focused on the drawing. "You said you like my Fu dog."

"I don't think so," I laughed. "Plus, if I ever got a tattoo it wouldn't be Fu dog, it would be grumpy Sparty."

"I can draw that," he volunteered. I politely demurred.

"Come on," he always says. "I can put it where no one sees it."

"Why would I want a Spartan tattoo if no one can see it?"

"Exactly!" he responds. "That's why you should let me put it on your shoulder."

◆ ◆ ◆

In addition to a tattoo, Aaron yearned for a motorcycle. "You don't understand," he once told me. "This has been my dream since sixth grade."

A few months before his 21st birthday, Aaron found a job that offered close to 40 hours a week and paid better than minimum wage. On payday he came up to my office and asked me to come downstairs to the bank to make sure he handled the deposit correctly. When we were done, Aaron came back up to the office and sat down in one of my client chairs.

"What's the payment on a motorcycle loan?" he asked.

"Well that depends," I said. "It depends on price, loan term and interest rate."

"The bike costs $6,000," he answered. "How long should I take to pay it?"

"Two years," I advised. "Three at the most."

"What's the interest rate?"

"Aaron," I said with a sigh. "I have no idea what kind of rates they're offering."

"Well, are you busy?"

Internally I debated the relative merits of ignoring the impending reality versus helping Aaron learn about how to manage a vehicle loan. "I need to send a couple of e-mails. Give me five minutes."

At the Victory dealership, Aaron showed me the used Vegas 8-Ball that he wanted to buy, and then we went to talk to the finance person. I asked about down payments and interest rates, repeating the answers to be sure Aaron was listening.

On the way home I set aside my concerns about motorcycles and used the mortgage app on my iPhone to calculate monthly payments. "Don't forget that you've got to pay for insurance on top of that," I said.

"Insurance shouldn't cost that much," he responded.

Having no idea about insurance costs, a few days later I called our agent to see what I could find out. "It depends on how many ccs the engine has," the agent told me. "I recommend he stay below 1,000 ccs to start." I thanked her for the advice and since I had no idea as to the specifications of a Vegas 8-Ball I asked a range of the cost based on ccs.

I called Aaron for more information.

"It's got 1,600 ccs," he told me.

"Do you think that's a good idea?"

"I'm not buying a minibike," he told me.

"Well, in that case, here's the insurance quote," I said, adding that the total monthly outlay exceeded his budget.

"First of all, I'm going to save money on gas because of the mileage," he persisted. "Plus, I've researched insurance costs. It shouldn't be that much."

"I don't know what research you've done," I argued. "But I've got the quote from an insurance agent."

"I'll take care of this," he said, plainly exasperated.

"Why don't you," I said. "I've got to get back to work."

Within the hour Aaron came to the office to tell me in person that he'd obtained insurance at half the rate I'd been quoted. I didn't believe it and I continued to press him for details.

"Let me see the dec sheet," I insisted.

"The what?"

"The sheet that has the terms, limits and whatnot," I said. "Just give me what you have."

Scanning the dec sheet I realized he was right. Apparently he really had researched motorcycle insurance.

"I told you so," he said when I handed back the paperwork.

A couple of weeks later Aaron attended the loan closing out-fitted in his motorcycle vest. His helmet and gloves remained in the backseat of the Mini, because the owner insisted on waiting until the check cleared. By that time Aaron was in the hospital with blood sugar readings in the 400s. He was released from the hospital on Wednesday afternoon, and shortly after five o'clock, Aaron strapped on his helmet and mounted the shiny black Vegas 8-Ball.

The mechanic stood nearby, looking on. He appeared to be in his early 60s, balding with skin worn from years of riding in the wind, old-school tattoos on both arms. "Don't do anything crazy," the mechanic advised. "That bikes got more power than you'll ever need."

Another customer, outfitted in a leather motorcycle vest emblazoned with the Victory logo, chimed in. "Take it slow," he said. "And watch for the deer. Look for the eyes."

Just in case I hadn't heard enough, the customer's wife added, "My brother rolled his over on its side once."

"What have you been riding?" Someone else asked.

"A dirt bike," Aaron responded.

An ominous silence followed.

"Be careful," I said before I got in Justin's car.

Justin looked at Aaron, waiting for him to leave. Aaron just stared back, obviously waiting for Justin to leave first. The two locked eyes like two gunslingers in one of the *Gunsmoke* episodes that always seemed to be playing when I used to drop Justin off at his grandparents' house in middle school. Aaron waved for Justin to leave first, to no avail. Finally I conceded and said, "Let's just go." Out of the corner of my eye I saw the owner standing in the doorway, his brow furrowed with concern.

"Aaron's nervous," Justin said. "And that makes me nervous."

"Same here," I sighed. I thought it best not to mention the dialogue among the graybeards and the owner.

Back at the house we reported to Tammy that Aaron was on the bike. "A lot of the old guys were giving him advice," I said with feigned comfort, offering no further details.

Within the hour Aaron called for a ride. All he said was, "That bike's got a lot of power."

The next day I dropped Aaron off at a shopping center parking lot a few miles from the dealership. The owner had offered to bring the bike up to the lot so Aaron could drive it in an open space before taking to the streets. A few hours later, Aaron strutted into my office carrying his helmet. A smile crossed his reddened face.

"That bike is awesome! I'm gonna name her Roxane."

◆ ◆ ◆

In the days that followed, Aaron spent his days off driving all over town, in traffic, two-lane roads and the interstate. That Sunday, he left early for Doddridge County so he could stop and show off his dream to his grandmother. Later in the week, he texted and compared notes on the forecast. He ended up staying an extra night at the EMS station waiting for the weather to clear.

The rain had passed by the following Sunday, so Aaron boldly headed out to go see Amanda. They'd been dating for several weeks despite Aaron's audacious first impression. I headed to the mall on an errand.

The text came while I was walking through the mall. "911 emergency call me." As I tapped on Aaron's contact information to place the call, I thought to myself, "He had better not be asking me to bring lunch."

"Hey," Aaron moaned.

"What's up?" I asked, still not sure if this was any semblance of a true 911 emergency.

"My bike slipped where there's a wet spot on the hill and went out from under me," he said. "Can you come and give me a ride?"

"I'm on my way," I said, picking up my pace. "Just tell me where you are."

Aaron told me enough that I realized he was still on Crestwood Road.

By the time I arrived, the neighbors had helped move the bike out of the road and provided Aaron with paper towels and a bottle of hydrogen peroxide. Aaron grimaced, but insisted he was okay despite the blood running down his arm and across the concrete.

"I'm just sore," he insisted. "But I lost a taillight and the tank is scratched."

"As long as you're not hurt, that's what counts."

"You might need to help me get this boot back on. I had to pull my foot out of it to get out from under the bike."

Once in the car, Aaron recounted the details—hitting the slick spot, feeling the back tire slide, knowing he was doing down. "I didn't think it had rained," he pleaded. "There was only one wet spot in the curve."

When we pulled into the driveway, Aaron admitted to shoulder pain. "It may be dislocated," he admitted.

"Do you want me to take you to the ER?" I asked.

"No, we'll wait until tomorrow."

Aaron gingerly got out of the car and headed upstairs, almost colliding with Justin on the stairway.

"I may need an EMT," I said.

"What is happening here?"

"Motorcycle accident," I said. "Aaron thinks he may have a dislocated shoulder."

"I'm more worried about the bike," Aaron said. "There's a scratch on the tank."

I'm sure Justin's heard this spiel at accident scenes before. He immediately took Aaron's pulse and carefully felt the shoulder.

"It's not dislocated," he concluded.

"Just help me get my shirt off," Aaron said. While Aaron showered, I scoured the house for hydrogen peroxide, Neosporin and bandages. We had just enough to wrap his arm. Fortunately, the wound was no longer bleeding profusely.

"Thanks for coming to get me," he said sincerely. "I really appreciate it. Just don't tell Tammy."

"Aaron," I said. "I can't not tell Tammy. Plus she's going to find out eventually."

"Amanda's going to be pissed. She told me not to ride today. I thought I was OK. I didn't know it rained."

Amanda arrived 10 minutes later, storming through the front door. As expected, she was not happy. "There's water in the driveway," she said. "That's all I'm going to say." She walked straight back to Aaron's bedroom, and I heard her ask in a much calmer voice, "How are you, baby?"

Later she came out to get another dose of Advil. "He sent me a message saying he couldn't come over today," she explained. "I thought, 'If this is another diabetic coma thing, he's in big trouble.'" Based on her tone, I surmised that Aaron was still in trouble.

I'd sent a preemptive message to Tammy to ensure she'd hear the news from me before seeing it on Facebook, trying hard to downplay the situation. Tammy was concerned, but she let Amanda take care of both first aid and lectures. Privately, she reiterated her displeasure at Aaron's dream of owning a motorcycle.

◆ ◆ ◆

The accident was a wakeup call for Aaron. Since that day, he has paid close attention to road conditions. And on the few times I've followed him when he's riding, I've noticed that he's more careful driving the bike than when he borrows my Mini Cooper. And, to be honest, on one occasion I was more concerned by the Monster energy drink—54 carbs in a 16-ounce can—riding in his cup holder. Diabetic or not, watching your kid cruise down the interstate is not for the faint of heart.

"If you want to come to the cabin for the weekend you can ride with me," I told Aaron.

"I'll just ride the bike," he said. "But I'll follow you down."

As we veered to the right in a curve at 63 miles per hour, I saw Aaron put his right foot out. It almost touched the pavement. My heart skipped a beat. Then he did it again, swinging the leg confidently out as he navigated the turn. This time I plainly saw the heel of the boot as it made contact with the asphalt. I pulled off at the next rest area and Aaron followed suit. "Are you putting your foot out for a reason or are you just trying to irritate me?" I asked.

He laughed and said, "No, that's how I check to see if the road is slick. Oil seeps up through the asphalt, you know. If my boot sticks, then I know the road is clear."

I liked it better when I thought he was just playing with me.

Getting back on the road, traffic picked up on the turnpike. I recalled my high school driver's ed teacher telling us that the West Virginia Turnpike had a reputation as the most dangerous highway in the world. And there I was, watching as Aaron weaved in and out of the traffic.

Coming out of a tollbooth, Aaron pulled out with an 18-wheeler in the next lane. Motorcycles look a lot smaller when merging onto the highway next to a tractor-trailer, even more so when it's your kid on the bike.

Finally I passed him and pulled ahead so I didn't have to watch.

At one point I fell behind a truck and couldn't pass immediately because a group of motorcycles was coming up in the left lane. Like seeing a freight train going by, I glanced over, wondering if my kid was traveling through.

Sure enough, the last rider was Aaron.

I caught a glimpse of his tattoo as he cruised on by with the rest of the cycles.

"WHO IS THAT GIRL AGAIN?"

"YOU DIDN'T BUTTER THE bread, did you?" Tammy asked as she was getting ready to put supper on the table.

"Yes, why?"

"Haley can't have butter. She's vegan."

Haley had become a vegan since her last stay with us. I knew something about the vegetarian diet, but had no clue as to the restrictions of a vegan diet. Unlike vegetarians, who only avoid meat, fish, and poultry, vegans avoid any food that has an animal source. That includes dairy products. Like butter.

◆ ◆ ◆

In the fall of 2014, Aaron and Justin were both working busy schedules and Sierra had remained in Nashville for several consecutive weeks. Sensing an empty nest on the horizon, Tammy and I focused on transactions and litigation respectively. In between conference calls, Tammy took a call from Aaron. Her text to me arrived while I was in the midst of defending a deposition.

"Haley wants to come back to our house for her senior year. She is so anxious she called Aaron. I'd like to put her in Sierra's room. Is that OK with you?"

This was the second tour for Haley. Two years earlier, she stayed with us while her mother was in the hospital.

"Who is that girl again?" Sierra's friend Monk had asked.

"It's a long story," I said, trying to think of the easiest way to describe the family tree. "Aaron and Sierra have the same mother. Aaron's biological father is Tammy's brother, who had Haley with a different woman. In other words, she's our niece and Aaron's other half-sister."

"OK," Monk said with a glazed look in his eyes.

◆ ◆ ◆

Justin and I were relentless in teasing Haley about her vegan diet, so much so that Tammy warned us to back off.

"It's how we show we care," I said.

In time, Haley learned that the best tact is a tart response. Like when I told her that Tammy was working late, so Justin and I were going out to eat. She slapped back with "I'm fine. I just ate. You guys have fun and go to a steak house or something lol."

Tammy devised a solution for pizza nights by convincing the neighborhood pizza guy to make a pizza with banana peppers, pineapple and no cheese. When I told Haley that Tammy had ordered vegan pizza, I added, "Don't worry, she also ordered a most definite non-vegan for me." Haley said thanks, adding, "That's good. I was worried about you for a second."

When it comes to Aaron's preference for steakhouses, the only solution we've devised is a good sense of humor. One night at LongHorn Steakhouse, Haley couldn't find anything on the menu other than salad.

"You've got to have more than a salad," the waiter said.

"I'm vegan," she replied.

The waiter, who appeared to be in his 40s, looked at me and said, "You brought a vegan to a steakhouse?"

"Yes, but I doubt she'll miss curfew again." The poor guy momentarily froze until Haley's laugh broke the silence.

◆ ◆ ◆

We moved Aaron's old dresser down to the green room, named for its Spartan green carpeting, that had last been occupied by Sierra. Although Haley stayed up until well after midnight, we always heard the garage door at 6:30 a.m. and never received any calls from the school attendance officer. She also managed to find vegan food options.

Haley spent a lot of time in her room, either on homework or Snapchat. She tried to explain Snapchat to me, going so far as sending a message from me to one of her friends. I still don't get it.

We often asked Haley to join in family activities. One Friday I invited her to join Aaron, Justin and me for a movie. She declined. "I checked out the rating on Rotten Tomatoes. It's not worth two hours of my time," she announced.

"Oh," Justin shouted with feigned indignation. "Spending two hours with us requires a higher rating?"

Haley just laughed, flashing a vibrant smile.

◆ ◆ ◆

Since her last visit, Haley had obtained her driver's license. Rather than face the logistics of transportation scheduling, we decided to let Haley use the Skunkmobile. She couldn't do more damage to it than Sierra had.

Haley typically communicated via text message. If her bedroom door was shut when I came home, I sent a text instead of knocking on the door. Likewise, requests for the car keys came via text. "Quick question: will the FJ still be okay for me to drive to church tomorrow with that light on?"

One snowy morning I was just about to head out for work when I heard Haley coming up the stairs. I walked out to say good morning. Haley was standing with her winter coat buttoned up.

"OK," she said with a sigh. "I wrecked the FJ."

"Are you okay?" I asked.

"Yes."

"Is the FJ drivable?"

"Yes," she said. "I drove it back up the hill."

"You're okay," I said calmly. She nodded.

"That's what counts."

"OK," she said with a sigh.

"By the way, how bad is the car damaged?"

Not surprisingly, Haley couldn't offer much of a description.

"Do you want a ride to school?" She accepted and managed a smile when we came across the circle of tire tracks at the bottom of the hill.

◆ ◆ ◆

Haley proved to be a good student who didn't need me to read any of the classic literature that I had skipped over during my high school days. I did, however, join my English teacher mother in quizzing her about *Hamlet* during Thanksgiving dinner.

I was of greater assistance when her civics class engaged in a mock trial competition. The case involved a woman who had killed her husband and raised a defense based on battered spouse syndrome. Haley was on the prosecution team. I offered tactical advice.

"We have to stay within the bounds of what's on the paper," Haley said in response to one of my ideas.

"OK, then ask the question another way. 'So you never saw the deceased hit the accused?'"

"The paper doesn't say she didn't see that," Haley argued.

"It doesn't say her friend ever saw the man hit her. That's within the paper," I argued in rebuttal.

"I don't know," Haley said. "I feel guilty prosecuting a battered wife."

"Allegedly battered wife!" I shouted. "Get on the right side!"

"I don't know how you do this," she said.

Despite my best efforts, the defense carried the day.

◆ ◆ ◆

Haley turned 18 in October. Within a few days of her birthday, Tammy brought her home with a voter's registration card.

"But I don't know who to vote for," Haley said at supper.

"Everyone who lives in this house is voting for Nick Casey," I deadpanned.

"That's right!" Justin said with a sly grin.

"Who's Nick Casey?"

"He's Ky's running partner," Tammy said, "but he also happens to be the best candidate."

To her credit, Haley read over Nick's campaign web page before deciding to cast her first vote for Nick.

Other times, Justin and I discussed current events and whatever issue was trending on Twitter. Sometimes these discussions morphed into heated debates. For the first few days, Haley ignored us while exchanging Snapchat posts. Later she started to listen without saying anything.

"Their discussions are really interesting," Haley told Tammy, "but I don't know what to say." Eventually, Haley gained her confidence and started asking questions and offering her own opinions.

"I think I've learned more history and social studies listening to you guys than I did in 12 years of school," she decided.

Just to be sure, when we went out to eat on December 7, Justin and I quizzed Haley. I mentioned, "This is a day that will live in infamy."

"Wait, I think I should know that," Haley said. "December 7, 1941. Pearl Harbor?"

"Oh yeah," Justin said indignantly.

She'll never forget that date again.

◆ ◆ ◆

Tammy took the lead in assisting Haley on the college front. She encouraged Haley to check into various schools and took several campus visits. Justin got in the act too, taking Haley on a trip to visit Shepherdstown. Tammy took Haley and a friend to Berea College in Kentucky for their campus visit and admissions interview. She also offered tactical advice on how to give an interview. "Don't hold back," she advised. "Tell the whole story. You guys are the kind of students they are looking for."

In early December, Tammy mentioned to the admissions counselor that if Haley was admitted in the first wave, she'd like to buy her a Berea t-shirt for Christmas. Tammy got the call a week before Christmas.

"We can't tell Haley," Tammy said. "But Berea is accepting her!"

◆ ◆ ◆

Haley began spending more time in the family room, coming up early for supper and staying longer. She seemed nonplussed by the NFL playoffs. While Justin and I raucously cheered replays of the winning score, Haley looked askance and said, "The game is over. Why do they keep showing that play?" She declined to watch the game, though she asked me to let her know who won.

"There's this guy," she said. "He's a fan and I'd like to be able to say something." At the end of the game, I texted her the winner and a one-line summary of the game.

For the Super Bowl, Haley was most interested in watching the national anthem. "Idina Menzel!" she shouted. She was shocked that Justin and I were both clueless about and utterly disinterested in Ms. Menzel. Midway through the first quarter, Haley headed downstairs. "Someone text me who wins so I'll know what everyone's talking about."

Haley learned not to panic when she heard me jump up and scream during Michigan State games. After the U of M game, I apologized if I had scared everyone.

"It's all right," Haley said. "I've gotten used to Ky yelling and screaming on Saturdays."

Privately she confessed to Tammy that "I never know if Ky's home on the weekends, unless there's a game on."

◆ ◆ ◆

Late in the spring Haley decided to look for a part-time job. "My friend told me that Charlotte Russe is hiring," she said at the dinner table one night.

"Feel free to use me as a reference," I said. "I was a reference for Sierra and she got a job there."

"I don't think I'd mention that," Tammy cautioned. "Sierra left without giving notice."

"I can still help," I said. "One of the questions is, 'If you were an animal, what would you be?'"

"Seriously?" Tammy and Haley said in unison.

"Yes," I insisted. "So, what animal would you be?"

"A peacock."

"Good answer."

At supper the next day Haley reported on the job interview. "I got the job," she said. "But they didn't ask me the animal question."

Haley was nervous on the first day of work, particularly running the register. "They'll teach you," I said reassuringly. "Plus, they'll probably just have you refolding clothes at first."

In fact, Haley turned out to be a stellar salesperson. One night she bragged that she had $5,000 in sales. "I was on my game," she boasted.

"Every girl who lives in the green room can sell Charlotte Russe," I bragged.

"Oh my God," she said. "Our manager is named Sierra. I told them I have a sister named Sierra—don't really know what else to call her. They said, 'Really? We used to have a Sierra that worked here!' I was like, 'I think I'll go back and check the dressing rooms.'"

◆ ◆ ◆

As the school year came to a close, only one hurdle remained: math. Haley left the house at 6:30 most mornings for math tutoring. On the Monday of finals week, the math teacher noticed that Haley was wearing a black dress. When asked why she wasn't wearing the latest spring colors from Charlotte Russe, Haley deadpanned, "I'm mourning the loss of my GPA."

By midweek I had stopped the jokes about converting the graduation announcements to "save the date" cards. Instead, I repeatedly assured Haley that she'd pass.

"You don't know how bad it is," she replied.

"If Aaron and Sierra can pass math, you can too," I insisted.

"Seriously, you don't know how bad it is," she repeated. But on Friday word came that Haley had passed math, though her math grade left her just shy of graduating with honors.

We watched with pride as Haley marched into the Civic Center as the band played "Pomp and Circumstance" and she crossed the stage to receive her diploma. Though it was tempting, I refrained from shouting, "Our graduation rate is up to .500!"

The next day Tammy left with Haley for the traditional post-graduation trip to New York City. In keeping with family tradition, they attended *Phantom of the Opera*. Aaron offered additional advice. "Go to Madame Tussauds and get a hot dog from a street vendor." Haley opted for the Metropolitan Museum of Art.

And she reminded Aaron, "I don't eat hot dogs."

TURNING 21

WHEN AARON WAS 15, I talked about taking him to Las Vegas for his 21st birthday. "We could go the day before your birthday," I had waxed romantically, "and at midnight we'd have a cocktail and hit the casino."

"Going to Vegas on my birthday won't work," Aaron told me six years later. "Justin's birthday is 12 days later. We'll have to wait until then."

"Are you seriously taking those guys to Las Vegas?" Tammy asked.

"I didn't realize that he'd remember," I said. "But he's counting on it. And we can't go without Justin."

◆ ◆ ◆

Aaron and Justin turned 21 within 12 days of each other. They both showed some modicum of responsibility on their respective birthdays. They had their DMV paperwork in order and were out of the house by 9:00 in the morning to renew their licenses.

"I decided not to get the federal ID," Justin told us. "I would have had to wait two weeks."

Aaron had restrained himself up to that point, simply making it a point to buy a beer every time we went out to dinner. "I don't need to see your card," one waitress said when Aaron reached for his newly minted license.

"Please, look at it," Amanda said. "He's so excited about it."

Justin's birthday fell on a Saturday, and Tammy and I were at the river for the weekend. Tammy was obviously nervous.

"Don't worry," I assured her. "Before I texted Justin a birthday greeting, I sent him Mike Pushkin's cell number." Mike often drives his cab on the night shift, and he's been kind enough to bring Sierra home on occasion.

"Sometimes I wonder about you," Tammy said, clearly not amused. "I seriously wonder about you."

"Tammy, they're 21."

No sooner had we turned out the lights than Aaron called.

"Hey, what's up?"

"Not much," I replied. "We just went to bed."

"Oh, sorry," he laughed. "Justin and I are at the Tavern waiting for the band to start."

"Make sure to introduce yourself to Washboard Dave," I said. "He's probably tending bar." The longtime bartender used to join the Sin on occasion, strumming spoons across an antique washboard.

We returned home the next day to find two tired young men. Aaron excitedly told us about the band at the Tavern, comparing it to the bands at the other bars on Capitol Street.

"We ran into Matt and we bar-crawled all the way up Capitol Street," Aaron boasted.

Tammy was not amused.

"Hey, do you remember Erin?" Aaron asked. "The girl from our basketball team?"

"Of course," I said, recalling a tomboyish third grader who wasn't shy about blocking out under the basket.

"I saw her last night," Aaron said. "She's a stripper."

Tammy's jaw dropped.

"Yeah, I paid $20 for a lap dance so I could have a conversation."

Justin remained unusually quiet.

"And how about you?" I asked Justin.

"I don't know..." he began.

"Dude," Aaron interjected. "You emptied your money clip!"

"You took a money clip to a strip club?" I asked, feigning indignation. "Didn't I teach you anything?"

◆ ◆ ◆

We had formally celebrated Aaron's birthday two weeks earlier. Tammy had flown in deep dish pizza from Gino's East in Chicago, served with an ice cream cake. The candles were a 2 and a 1, and after Aaron blew them out, I told him to save them for Justin's cake.

In contrast, we surprised Justin with an elegant dinner.

"Tell Justin we're going to dinner tomorrow night," I instructed Aaron. "We're going to the Chop House, so find your suit and be sure to tell Amanda so she knows to dress."

"Are we telling Justin where we're going?"

"It's up to you," I said.

"Let's surprise him," Aaron said. "But when I tell him we're wearing suits, he's going to be suspicious."

Justin was indeed suspicious, the anticipation growing as we pulled into the parking garage. He didn't allow himself to smile until we made the final turn off the escalator in the direction of the restaurant. Once inside, I noted Justin taking in all the details, looking over the mix of customers that ranged from well-dressed couples to a bombastic group of 40-year-olds in golf shirts.

The waitress arrived with menus and a wine list. "Would anyone like a cocktail?"

"This is a 21st birthday celebration," Tammy announced. "So I think the answer is yes."

For me, the wait was over. I enjoyed a Johnnie Walker Black Label on the rocks with my son. Legally. Justin chose an old fashioned. Tammy scoured the wine list and suggested a Cabernet.

"There's a wine called 'Justin,'" she said. Reading from the review, she added, "Beautifully balanced, with attractive aromas of black fruit and spice."

In the days that followed the celebrations, the guys eventually stopped ordering a beer with every meal. On occasion they left the house at 10 o'clock "to head downtown." On those nights Tammy tossed and turned until she heard the front door open. I took it in stride.

After all, they're 21.

And they've got Mike's number.

◆ ◆ ◆

July and August court dates delayed the Vegas trip until September. The day before our departure, I stopped in the bank to get cash for the guys' gambling allowances. At the bank I ran into Brooke.

We chatted about her newborn baby and married life. She mentioned that she might be changing nursing jobs, and I confirmed that she could continue using me as a reference.

I explained why I was stuffing cash into two envelopes. Her reaction mirrored Tammy's.

"Are you serious?" she asked, her eyes widening as she spoke. "You're taking Aaron and Justin to Las Vegas?"

"Of course, they just turned 21," I said with false bravado.

"Good luck," she said, shaking her head as she gave me a hug.

◆ ◆ ◆

When we checked in at the airport, Aaron declined to check his garment bag. "I can't afford the chance of it getting lost," he said.

"Good point," I replied. "That bag has the insulin."

"No, it's got our suits."

Shortly after we boarded the first flight, I heard Aaron ask Justin "if the stewardess would be serving drinks."

"She's a flight attendant," Justin exclaimed. "What is this? 1958?"

Both guys purchased a beer from the flight attendant. When they saw me look back, they smiled and said, "Come on, we're going to Vegas!"

The flight to Charlotte took approximately the same amount of time as the trip from the runway to the terminal. "Can I go to the restroom?" Justin asked.

"Not until we reach the terminal," I told him. "Seriously, it's a federal law."

"I don't think I can make it that long!" he said. "I'll never order a beer on a plane again."

We stopped in a couple of clothing stores in the terminal, but the guys refrained from making any purchases, instead saving their money for the blackjack tables. Shortly after four o'clock we boarded the flight to Las Vegas. Three hours and two cocktails later, Aaron spotted Vegas out the window. Justin leaned over Aaron to look out the window and mentioned his first flight into Las Vegas, although "we didn't leave the airport."

I tenuously kidded Aaron about his first flight into Vegas. He took my jibe in good humor. "Funny," he said. In response to Justin's inquisitive look, he explained that the first time he flew into Vegas was with an escort taking him to Turn-About Ranch.

When we got off the plane, I half expected that the guys might start playing the airport slot machines. Instead we made our way to the baggage claim and eventually our bags came through.

We reached our hotel at around 8:00 p.m. local time, which meant 11:00 p.m. body time. I quickly changed clothes, expecting the guys would be anxious to get going. Instead they needed some prompting.

"Look," I said, "My body says it's 11 o'clock, too, but we're in Las Vegas. Get changed!"

Ten minutes later we were boarding the southbound monorail. Next stop, the MGM Grand. We found a casual bar and grill for supper—just burgers and beers—and then cruised the Strip. It didn't take long for the guys to realize that Vegas doesn't prohibit open containers. After a block and a half we stopped for refreshments. We strolled on the Strip until we reached the Bellagio, which the guys know from the movie *Ocean's 11*.

"The article I read says to find a $5 table," I advised. "That way your money lasts longer."

Aaron settled on a $15 table. Justin stayed back with me to watch the scene unfold. Aaron looked the part, confidently pulling up a chair and grabbing an ashtray for his cigar. Within a few minutes he was reaching for his money clip.

While Aaron took part in live action, Justin started feeding dollar bills into the video blackjack machine. I tried to be a good sport, losing $5 to the machine in less than five minutes.

After an hour or so, Aaron got up and came over.

"How'd you do?" I asked.

"I lost $75," he said. "That's harder than it looks."

"That's why I'm sticking to the machines," Justin said. "I made $5."

I offered some fatherly advice. "Why don't we call it a night?"

◆ ◆ ◆

On Saturday night we went to a see Louis Anderson, a comedian who bridged the generation gap, then to dinner at the Eiffel Tower, an elegant restaurant atop the Paris Las Vegas Hotel and Casino.

The waiter offered the standard inquiry. "Would you like something to drink other than water?"

"Definitely," I answered. "They're celebrating their 21st birthdays."

I ordered a gin martini, straight up.

"I'll have the same," Aaron said. Justin ordered some concoction from the menu of specialty cocktails.

"What's 'straight up'?" Aaron asked.

I explained the difference between "straight up" and "on the rocks."

When the drinks arrived I offered a toast to turning 21. Aaron winced when he sipped the martini and made a face reminiscent of the first time he ate asparagus.

"Give it a chance," I said, adding, "Just wait until you taste the olives."

"Oh my God!" he exclaimed a few minutes later. "The olives are incredible! Why doesn't Tammy buy these?"

"It's the vermouth," I explained.

The waiter came back to notify us that the chef needed time to prepare the soufflé in case we wanted that for dessert.

"It's up to you guys," I said. "Assuming Aaron brought insulin." Justin chose the soufflé while Aaron decided to wait for "something chocolate."

Aaron turned his attention to the wine list, asking what everyone was ordering for dinner. Red meat was the clear consensus.

"Then I think we should get a red wine," he said. "What's our price range?"

"I'd prefer to stay under three figures," I said.

A couple of minutes later Aaron handed over the wine list. "Here, see what you think."

I immediately grasped his problem, raising my threshold to the $200 range.

The sommelier came over to see if we needed assistance. I politely asked for her thoughts on two Bordeaux varieties.

"May I make a suggestion in that area?"

"That would be fine," I said, relieved that the guys thought I had some semblance of my parents' wine expertise. The wine was a hearty Bordeaux, a fine complement to the various filet dishes.

After the soufflé and a chocolate concoction, the head waiter strolled over with fanfare and laid out two plates with chocolate mousse with "Happy Birthday" written in chocolate.

"This is not real," Justin said to Aaron as they stared at the plates.

"What's the plan for the evening?" Justin asked.

"First I need to pay the bill," I said, reaching for my wallet.

"How much was it?" they asked.

"Under a thousand." Both guys' eyes got wide as they interpreted my enigmatic response.

"Start saving now and next year we'll get the $500 bottle of wine."

"Are we going out?" Justin asked. "I'm exhausted."

"Me too," Aaron said. "But I still want to go back to the tables to say I sat at the blackjack table with my dad."

I took the opportunity to practice my poker face and without a hint of emotion simply said, "Shall we try our luck at the Bellagio?"

Aaron and I found two open chairs at a $25 table. I had decided on a $200 budget but decided to start with $150. After a couple of early wins my luck turned and I put down another $50 bill. Aaron seemed to fare better, aided by hitting blackjack three times. After about 20 minutes, Aaron asked how long we were going to stay.

"I'm down to two chips," I said. "So next hand I lose I'm done."

"OK," he said.

At that point my luck changed course once again, and I won five straight hands. I lost on the sixth.

"That's it for me," I said.

"Me too, I guess," Aaron said, throwing a $5 chip to the dealer like a regular.

We met Justin on the way to the cashier.

"So, how'd it go?" he asked.

"I broke even," I said. "Can't beat that."

"And I made up for what I lost last night," Aaron bragged. Then he turned to me to say, "Thanks for stopping when you did. You probably saved me!"

We finished off the night by riding the Ferris wheel that overlooks the Strip, marveling at the number of hotel rooms and casinos.

❖ ❖ ❖

On Sunday morning we checked our bags at the hotel and headed to the Strip for lunch. I was nervous about leaving my computer, so I lugged my carryon to the monorail and through the casino.

Lunch took longer than expected and we were rushing to catch the monorail. We were passing by the Bally's sports book area where bettors watched a dozen NFL games when Aaron stopped. "My site fell out," he reported.

"Will you make it to the hotel?"

"Not unless you want me running high." As luck would have it, I had packed his insulin and supplies with my computer. I watched the bettors while Aaron changed his site and Justin bought souvenirs. We made it back to the hotel just before noon and caught a cab.

We all felt exhausted, but looked forward to another visit.

❖ ❖ ❖

About the only way to get to Charleston is through the E Concourse at Charlotte Douglas Airport. "There's only one flight to Charleston," I warned, "so we need to head straight to the gate." The flight left right at 10:05 p.m.

Shortly before midnight the plane reached Charleston.

"This is your captain speaking," said the voice over the intercom. "We've been circling over Charleston hoping the fog would lift, but it's still too dense and our fuel is limited. We'll be returning to Charlotte."

Hearing the news, I looked back and saw Justin sitting upright with a look of panic on his face. "Justin has to be at work in 20 minutes," Aaron said. "He needs to call the station."

"He'll have to wait," I said. "Federal law."

Once on the ground Justin frantically called in, and I found the first flight back to West Virginia.

One of our neighbors who drives for a limo service met us at the airport.

"How was the birthday trip?" he asked.

The guys grinned sheepishly and said, in unison, "What happens in Vegas stays in Vegas."

Scott looked back at me inquisitively.

"Like I tell Tammy, they're 21."

SIERRA: A TALE OF TWO CITIES

NASHVILLE

"Looking for Sierra? You'd better look out West."

I glanced at my phone to check the address. The thought that maybe she'd changed plans and hopped a train within the past 10 minutes crossed my mind.

"You might try one of the other houses," the man standing in the door suggested.

As I turned to leave, he stopped me. "Hey, wait a minute." Looking back through the house he shouted, "J.R., is that girl's name Sierra?"

"Sure is," a voice replied in a pronounced Southern drawl. "Hey, Sierra, your godfather's here."

A few minutes later Sierra came strutting through the kitchen carrying a pair of antique boots. I had not seen her since she left five months earlier to hitchhike to South Carolina to play a festival.

"I bet you thought I'd left traveling again," she said, laughing as she laced up the boots. "This is J.R. We've been busking together. We made $115 last night. Each."

"Yeah, it was a good night," J.R. said.

"Are you hungry?" Sierra asked. "There's a place downtown that I've seen that looks like the kind of place you'd like. Plus I saw Jack White in there once."

"Sounds good to me," I said, trying to recall whether Jack White is a recording artist or an actor.

The restaurant was located in an old building in the heart of the downtown district. The wait for a table was 30 minutes, so we walked across the street to shop for a belated birthday present. Sierra found a coat she liked, but hadn't made up her mind when I received a text saying our table was ready.

Sierra was right about Merchants. The building once housed a hardware store, a drug store and Nashville's premier hotel rooms. I liked the style as well as the food. We sat near the grand black and white bar, and since I was in Tennessee, I decided to have a bourbon. The bar carries Smooth Ambler bourbon, distilled in Greenbrier County by one of my clients.

Between the appetizer—an iceberg wedge that Sierra thought I might like, thinking it was a potato—and bacon cheeseburgers, Sierra made up her mind on the coat.

"I'm afraid that other woman who tried it on will take it," she said, looking wistfully out the window.

"Go across and ask if they'll hold it for you," I said. "Tell them Richard Gere will be over to pay for it. Hopefully they've seen *Pretty Woman.*"

The staff was happy to hold the coat for Sierra.

"You're not performing today," the sales clerk said.

"Too rainy. I like this corner though. I like singing to the mannequins."

"We enjoy it too," the clerk said.

◆ ◆ ◆

Busking in Nashville is serious business. J.R. carries business cards. Performers run the gamut from a homeless-looking vagabond using a tub as a drum, to guitar players promoting their CDs, to the man with silver body paint portraying a Confederate statue. Performers are governed by the Nashville city code, which prohibits sitting and amplifiers, and their own performers' code, as J.R. explained. "My rule is to stay far enough away that I can't hear the other musicians. It works well for those of us playing guitar or banjo, but it's hard to stay far enough away from that trumpet."

The job pays well during the season, lasting from spring through October, plus the holiday season. "I try to make enough so I can save something to get through the winter," J.R. told me.

Sierra says the money is better in Nashville, but Asheville has better musicians. Plus, the people are "way more cool."

"There are a lot of tool boxes here," she said.

"What's a tool box?" I asked.

"Guys in polo shirts." Seeing me look down at my shirt, Sierra added, "but you're not a tool box. You're cool."

After shopping, we went to check on Wasabi, who was staying at a recording studio in East Nashville. The area has recently become the "place to be" for Nashville yuppies, which is apparent by the mix of old houses in varying states of disrepair and newly remodeled houses. Eric's falls into the former category. Inside lay a menagerie of recording equipment, instruments and computers.

Eric has been in the music business for about 20 years, both as a performer and a producer. Years ago he had played the bar scene. Now he spends most of his time producing records. He's done a lot of work with Todd Snider, which is how he hooked up with Sierra. Talking about his studio, he casually mentions artists like Loretta Lynn.

"You worked with Loretta Lynn?" I asked.

"Yeah," he said nonchalantly.

As we talked, Sierra played music on her iPad and Eric thumbed his steel guitar. Sierra mentioned that Eric had played the show at Track 29.

"That was you?" I said. "You looked taller on stage."

Sierra and Eric talked about details regarding the album. "You need a name for your publishing company," Eric reminded her.

Eric explained that Sierra needs to register her songs with one of the publishing companies, either BMI or ASCAP. Those companies collect royalties in the event music is used in movies, television shows, commercials, et cetera. Producers pay thousands of dollars just to use a snippet of a song. Eric mentioned that he had shared some of Sierra's music with a friend who works as a "music supervisor." He said the guy took a 20-second piece from "Little Bird" and looped it for his elderly father who listens to it constantly.

I learned that the name of the publishing company isn't important, except that it should be something out of the ordinary.

"I guess 'Sierra Ferrell Music Company' won't do," I said. Both Eric and Sierra rolled their eyes.

Eric mentioned that some famous recording artist chose the name for his company by opening the dictionary three times.

"Got a dictionary?" Sierra asked.

I asked more questions about publishing and royalties. "I guess you've got all the players in Nashville—producers, agents, managers, lawyers?"

"Actually," Eric said, "the best entertainment lawyers are in New York, but I use a guy in Atlanta. The only problem is lawyers can't write a contract in less than 20 pages."

"I've heard that before," I replied.

◆ ◆ ◆

The next morning the weather looked gloomy, with predictions of scattered showers. I walked around the District and found that a couple of guitar players were out busking along with the general. Sierra called around noon to tell me she and J.R. were playing down on Broadway.

I had circled the District several times when I came upon a van that looked to be J.R.'s. Out of the corner of my eye, I saw a girl carrying a guitar case across the street.

"Hey," she said.

"What are you up to?" I asked.

"Out looking for you," Sierra said. "We're playing down the street."

"I walked that way," I told her, "but I didn't see any buskers."

"We're playing inside," she said. "It's his gig and I'm singing too."

I could hear the banjo outside as we came upon the Nashville National Underground, which is on street level despite its name. J.R. was playing the banjo alongside a fiddle player.

"We'd like to thank Mr. Ky for joining us," J.R. said between songs. "Sierra, why don't you come back up and sing a song?" Sierra took a seat on stage and grabbed her guitar.

The gig was billed as the "Brewgrass Brunch" from 10:00 a.m. until 2:00 p.m. Shortly before two o'clock J.R. announced, "There's time for one more song." They finished the song, packed up their instruments, and divided bills in three stacks.

"We made $140," Sierra said. "This is way better than playing outside."

As I got ready to pay my tab, I noticed the bar owner talking to J.R.

"I guess the other band didn't show," Sierra explained before returning to the stage.

"We'll be playing for the next three hours," J.R. told the crowd. They played a mixture of crowd favorites, led by reprises of "Rocky Top," "Dueling Banjos" and The Beverly Hillbillies theme. They also played some of Sierra's original compositions.

By the end of the set, Sierra lay back on the stage and fell asleep. I sat with J.R. and listened to his story. He told me how he gave up his truck driving job—"I had a good bread route"—to move to Nashville with his ex-wife.

"I stayed and started playing on the streets, trying to get recognized," he told me. "That's how I got this gig. The guy found me on the street."

"He's the real thing," the bartender interrupted. "A real Mississippi porch banjo player."

Then he asked, "Can you play another set?"

"Might as well," J.R. replied. "Gotta make it while you can."

"I understand," I said. "My business is the same."

◆ ◆ ◆

Busking and playing the bars have trade-offs. "Out on the street I can take a break. If I see people coming, I start playing," J.R. explained. "Plus, I don't have to play a whole set list."

"I guess you can just play one or two songs all day."

"Last Christmas I just played 'Jingle Bells' all day."

The season runs through late November and there's not much busking in the winter. "I try to make money in the summer and save enough to get through the winter," he said. "I was doing pretty good last year, but then I bought a motorcycle." He added, "I convinced myself it was a good deal because I'd get better mileage."

"I've heard that somewhere else," I said.

◆ ◆ ◆

A few minutes later they started their third set. Before long they were playing "Rocky Top" for the fourth time. "That's the Tennessee anthem," J.R. said with a laugh.

"I'm not from Tennessee," Sierra told the crowd. "I'm from West Virginia.

"So are we!" shouted a woman sitting with a group of people at the front table. "Charleston. How about you?"

"I'm from Charleston," Sierra said. "He's from Charleston too," she added, pointing to me. "But he's originally from Michigan. He goes crazy when Michigan State is playing."

"Go Green!" came a voice from the bar. "We're from Michigan State."

"Go White!" I yelled.

"OK, I guess we'll get that 'go green/go white' thing going," Sierra said.

"Maybe it's a good time to pass the offering plate," J.R. said. Sierra smiled and walked through the tables with the tip jar.

When Sierra got back on stage, the woman from Charleston asked, "Do you know 'Country Roads'? That's our anthem."

"I should know it," Sierra said. "People ask me to sing it all the time."

A quick Google search on the iPad came to the rescue. Sierra held up the iPad and belted out the lyrics while J.R. strummed the chords. The front table sang along raucously and then dropped some bills in the tip jar before leaving.

◆ ◆ ◆

On Monday I picked up Sierra from J.R.'s place and headed to Eric's house. Eric inquired as to Sierra's plans

"I'm going back to get my ID and then I'll hitchhike back," she told him.

The route to Charleston took us past Elizabethtown, Wasabi's birthplace. Proving my theory that dogs are smarter than we think, Wasabi sat up in the back seat and sniffed the air anxiously as we passed the exit for Kitty's house.

Once back in Charleston, Wasabi ran up to the front door to find Boogie. They immediately began chasing each other around, picking up where they left off in April. Roscoe entered the fray with excitement.

Sierra logged on to Facebook to make plans for the evening. She had already posted her impending arrival and a friend mentioned that there was an open mic at the Glass. After dinner James Brown came over to pick up Sierra and Wasabi to head to the Glass.

The following afternoon I gathered my file of "Sierra - Important Papers" and took Sierra to DMV to get a new driver's license. She was thrilled with the new picture.

"I have a gig on Saturday night at Black Sheep," she announced. "It's $100 plus a $20 bar allowance. I'm going to see if Mark Bates will share the gig."

"Isn't his dad the cardiologist?" I asked.

"I don't know," she said. "I guess."

"Small world," I remarked. "His dad treated my dad years ago."

"Anyway," Sierra continued, "since I'm not drinking I can split the gig with him and still make $70. So it's only costing me $30 and I don't have to play it on my own."

"Good point," I replied. "You could probably make it back for the brunch show with J.R. and make another $140."

"Hey, can you take me back?"

"Sure," I volunteered.

"We should just leave after Black Sheep," Sierra suggested. "Like the time we went to New York."

Shortly after 10:00 p.m. Saturday, I pulled up outside of Black Sheep. The place looked like a reunion. James came by as he left, then Amy came out with a group of friends, and finally Mike stopped by to talk. Eventually Sierra came out. Fortunately, before we left she looked around and asked me to call her cell phone. She went back to retrieve it, avoiding another text saying, "This is Sierra's phone. It's at Black Sheep in Huntington."

With virtually no traffic and a change in time zones, we reached the outskirts of Nashville by 3:30 a.m. When the Nashville skyline came into view, Sierra sat up, smiled and looked back at Wasabi.

"The lights of Nashville. We're almost home, girl."

NEW ORLEANS

The French Quarter was in full swing the weekend before Christmas, filled with tourists, football fans, locals, panhandlers and buskers. I turned the corner and headed south on Frenchmen Street, where I heard a familiar voice among the menagerie of sound.

"What's that smelling like fish, maw maw? Tell it to me, honey."

In the doorway of the Café Rose Nicaud stood Sierra, pulling on the string of a washtub bass and harmonizing with two other young ladies strumming on a banjo and a guitar. I joined the crowd in a round of applause and smiled when a woman placed a $20 bill in the banjo case.

◆ ◆ ◆

When I called Sierra on Thanksgiving, I assumed I'd be visiting Nashville for Christmas.

"Hey, Happy Thanksgiving to you," Sierra said. "I'm in New Orleans."

"For how long, may I ask?"

"For a minute," she answered. "They say it's really hot here in the summer, so I'll probably go back to Nashville."

She called back on the following Monday. "Hey, me and my friends are getting a house. It's a six-month lease. I listed you as a reference."

Where is the house?"

"Music Street."

I checked my work schedule and decided on a weekend in New Orleans. I sent Sierra a Facebook message letting her know my plans.

"Bring black fringe boots," she replied.

◆ ◆ ◆

When I arrived on Friday afternoon, I texted Sierra a picture of her boots. "Your boots are in the French Quarter. Are you?"

"I'm not far. Want to pick me up and go to Ladyland?" A Google search revealed that "Electric Ladyland" is the most famous tattoo parlor in the French Quarter.

With trepidation I replied, "Give me an address." Sierra gave me an address a couple of miles away. The area was a rundown mix of old houses and vacant lots. She came out carrying a guitar.

"Where to?" I asked.

"My place," she said. "It's on Music Street. I don't know how to get there from here. Sorry, I never drive." I breathed a sigh of relief as I realized that "Ladyland" is a house on Music Street occupied by the members of a lady jug band, known as "Ladies on the Rag."

We found our way to the house, a yellow structure on the corner across the street from a vacant lot. All but one of the windows had decorative wrought iron bars. The door led directly to the living room, which was furnished by a couch, coffee table, two chairs, seven guitar cases and a French horn case. The couch and chairs were occupied by a group of traveling kids. The dreadlocks, odor and guitars left no doubt. Wasabi and three other dogs pranced around on the hardwood floor.

"Hey," Sierra said. "This is my godfather." A couple of the guys nodded and one girl reached out to shake hands.

Then Wasabi recognized me. She whined in a high soprano pitch and rushed over, pushing the other dogs out of the way to reach me.

"I've never heard her whine like that," one of the kids said.

"I'm telling you," Sierra said. "She really likes him."

Sierra showed me her room in the corner of the first floor. The room was adorned with a washtub, two milk crates and a wrought iron gate on which several belts and scarves were carefully hung. A couple of coats and skirts hung in the closet. Hiking boots sat on the closet floor and antique white shoes and Sierra's antique boots were stored on the shelf. Sierra pointed out a cream-colored lace dress. "I'm going to wear that once I get a corset."

"How much is a corset?"

"Like $200."

"Frieda wants to get you a Christmas gift," I said. "I'm sure she'd love to get you a corset."

After hanging out for a few minutes, Sierra grabbed a skirt, the white shoes and a petite hat. One of Sierra's housemates overheard us discussing going to lunch and suggested Café Rose Nicaud. As we left, Sierra said, "Will someone be a princess and take care of my dog?"

On the drive over Sierra explained that the girls busk on the Café Rose Nicaud steps after closing. "My friend says they have great crocodile. Or alligator, I don't know," she said.

When we walked in Sierra asked, "Do you guys have crocodile?"

"We have alligator sausage. It comes with the southern break-fast and the eggs Benedict." Sierra chose the eggs Benedict and I ordered the southern breakfast, complete with grits. While we ate Sierra talked about New Orleans, repeatedly saying, "I love it here."

"How does it compare to Nashville?"

"There are way more good musicians down here."

Next we went shopping for the corset. Sierra looked around the antique clothing store with wide eyes and said, "I'm so materialistic sometimes."

The wall was lined from top to bottom with corsets ranging from brown leather to black velvet with gold embroidery. "I'm trying to decide between those two," Sierra said, pointing to one in brown leather and another with stitching.

"Oh my God, look at that one," Sierra said, pointing to the corset with gold embroidery.

Sierra first tried on the stitched model. It looked good, but I suggested that she try the embroidered one too. Seeing her in the mirror I concluded, "Don't even bother trying on the brown one."

"This would look great with that blouse," Sierra said, pointing to the wall. Seeing that the corset was coming in under budget, I asked the clerk if she had the blouse in a size small.

Checking out, Sierra asked, "How much was all that?"

"It doesn't matter," I said. "It's a Christmas present."

◆ ◆ ◆

Sierra mentioned that she'd met a guitar player. "Don't worry," she said. "I'm not ready for a relationship. I just like playing music with him."

"What's his name?"

"Shine," she said. "His parents were hippies."

We made plans to go to Café Sbisa, the bar where Shine played on Friday nights. The cafe, I learned, is one of the most historic restaurants in the French Quarter. Sitting at the bar, I studied the painting above the bar. Not surprisingly, the artist was known for his provocative nudes, typically male. We listened to the jazz trio: Shine on the guitar, Diablo on the stand-up bass, and Genevieve on the trumpet and vocals. She had a deep, raspy voice that matched the jazz sound. She seemed a little old for green hair.

Sierra joined the band for one song. By the time she reached the chorus, her voice had taken over, leaving the guitar and bass as a backdrop. Her tone was a mix of the raspy jazz sound and her natural soprano voice

Following the last set, we walked briskly through the Quarter. Sierra planned to perform at a house party later that evening. I decided that a house party might be too big a slice of New Orleans for me, so I dropped her off and stopped off in a bar on Bourbon Street.

◆ ◆ ◆

"I'm awake!" Sierra texted the next morning. "Do you want to come over? We have to go pick up this stove. And get some supplies. Mop wash rags pots pans."

When I arrived at the house, Wasabi ran to the door to greet me wearing the saddlebags I'd given her.

"She loves it," Sierra said. "Now she can carry her own food."

A few minutes later Sierra, Ali and I headed out with Wasabi in tow. Getting into the car we saw a couple of the traveling kids with their backpacks and guitar cases.

"I thought you were leaving?" Ali said.

"We are now. We decided to go to Mississippi."

Ali drove a white Honda minivan. I provided directions via the GPS on my iPhone. After a couple of missed turns, we arrived at a house located on a suburban cul-de-sac and the stove was loaded in.

"We should look for the pots and pans," Ali said.

We had seen a Walmart, but given the kids' animosity to corporate America, they preferred to look for a thrift store. I used my YP Mobile app to find a nearby thrift store, but when we reached the location we discovered that it had gone out of business. We ended up stopping at Walmart. Sierra picked out a mop, along with a rug, air mattress, pillow, sheets, blanket and jug of Mr. Clean.

◆ ◆ ◆

Sierra's Christmas present, in addition to the corset and blouse from Frieda and an Empty Glass hoodie and glowlight necklace from Tammy, was an iPad to replace her first generation model. I located an Apple store and we joined the throng of holiday shoppers. While we were completing the set up, Sierra's phone chimed with an incoming text.

"I need to get going," she told me. "I need to relieve Pigeon. She's holding our spot."

Sierra told the clerk that she needed to go to work.

"Where do you work?"

"I'm a busker."

We drove by the house to pick up Sierra's washtub bass and I dropped her off on Frenchmen Street. Later that evening, I walked over to Frenchmen to hear Ladies on the Rag. A crowd of about ten people was standing along the curb, some tapping their feet to the beat.

"You should do a Christmas song," a woman shouted from the curb.

"If we knew one," Ali laughed.

"Fall on your knees," Sierra began, perfecting each note like she was in the choir loft at First Presby. "Oh night divine, oh night when Christ was born. Oh night divine, oh night, oh night divine."

◆ ◆ ◆

Ladies on the Rag started when Sierra was hanging out at a friend's house. "I heard this awesome guitar player though the wall, and I said, 'I have to play music with her.'" Ali, the guitar player, is originally from Florida and most recently from Portland. She looks to be in her 20s, and except for the tattoo on her shoulder, she dresses more conservatively than Sierra. The banjo player, Pigeon (not her given name—that's Zera), is from Portland. "I don't do fancy," she says when the conversation turns to clothes.

In Nashville most of the buskers played solo or in duets. New Orleans is filled with larger groups ranging from trios to five- and six-piece jazz bands. The other difference is that New Orleans authorities do nothing to discourage buskers. Permits are required in a few areas, such as an open market. "We should get a permit, just in case we want to play the market," Sierra told the group. "You can get one for free any Wednesday."

◆ ◆ ◆

When I arrived on Music Street on Sunday, there were still three people hanging around, playing music and sketching. When Sierra mentioned that we were going to eat lunch, Ali and Pigeon decided to join us. Ali suggested Café Rose Nicaud. I thought it wise to continue patronizing the restaurant where Sierra borrows the steps every night. Wasabi and Pigeon's dog came along and we sat outside at the sidewalk tables.

"You guys played here last night," a man said. "You sounded great."

We also saw a fair number of traveling kids on the streets. Sierra spoke to one guy with a dog and told me, "That dog's going to have puppies with Wasabi's brother, Omelet."

Speaking of traveling kids, Pigeon said, "Those guys stayed for two weeks and didn't do anything."

"We bring home a mop and they all leave," Sierra added. "I wish these people who aren't paying rent would leave."

The ladies discussed plans for the day. Pigeon wanted to rehearse. "You need to know when to come in on the bass," she told Sierra.

"I should spend the day with my godfather while he's in town," Sierra said.

"It's okay with me if you need to rehearse," I said. "Maybe I'll stay and listen."

Throughout the weekend the ladies discussed new songs to learn and used iPad apps that showed chord progressions for jazz standards and harmonies. Sierra suggested they could do a song playing on the radio, and Ali suggested that they try it in a different key. They threw out chords and octaves like lawyers citing Latin legal phrases. "It's A, B minor, then C, but we should do it in a different key." Other times they broke into song. Once, while walking on the sidewalk after lunch, Sierra and Pigeon started singing. Sierra thought she was too low and they repeated the verse twice more until they found the right octave.

Musicians in New Orleans take their music seriously. And they make decent money. Shine told me one can make $3,000 during a weekend festival that follows Mardi Gras.

"It sounds like you make some real money," I said.

"My dad once sat down and figured out what I made, and it was like $60,000 a year," Shine said. "But that doesn't include expenses."

❖ ❖ ❖

On Sunday night I took Sierra and Shine to dinner at Port of Call, "the best burger place in New Orleans" according to Shine. We had an hour to wait for a table. Rather than standing in the cramped doorway, we walked down the block to have a beer at Bubba's, a neighborhood joint with eight barstools and a half dozen tables. The bartender offered a plate of cheese fries that another customer had sent back as our appetizer. "This kind of random thing only happens in New Orleans," they told me. Later we enjoyed fantastic burgers at the Port of Call, served with baked potatoes instead of fries. Leaving the tavern, I braced myself to drop Sierra off and say goodbye. But the kids had other plans.

"Want to come with us to a burlesque show?" Sierra asked.

"It's a slice of New Orleans," Shine said.

"And it's your last night in town," Sierra added.

"Give me directions," I acquiesced.

Shine guided me on a rather circuitous route that ended up on a dead end street. All I could see was a bus parked on the street illuminated by a flood light. We met a man in front of the bus who collected the cover charge.

I realized immediately why the show was billed as "Backyard Boylesque." The stage was set up in the backyard of a house, with the kitchen serving as the dressing room. The bar was built out of two-by-fours and choices were limited to beer, spiked eggnog and hot toddies. Seating ranged from an old couch to lawn chairs. The crowd numbered close to 20, a mix of Caucasian 20-year-olds and middle-aged African Americans. A three-piece jazz band sat perched on the second floor overhang.

The emcee announced the next act, titled "How Bobby rehearses in the shower." From behind the curtain came a young man clad in a bath towel. Bobby's dance moves were precise and practiced, all in touch with the beat and choreographed so that the towel moved to cover his genitals at the precise moment the audience expected the dancer to bare all. Other sequences included a disco duet, dancing with roller skates and a creative play on "I Just Want to Be King" from The Lion King. The dance moves were clearly choreographed and rehearsed.

I learned that the three dancers work a combination of day jobs and night gigs. I wondered privately what these guys' fathers thought of their sons' putting on a "backyard boylesque." Maybe they wanted their sons to dance on Broadway or become accountants, but clearly the guys were enjoying the show. Just as Sierra enjoys pulling on the string of a washtub bass and harmonizing with Ladies on the Rag on the steps of Café Rose Nicaud.

"What'd you think?" Sierra asked when we left.

"Clearly a slice of New Orleans."

I drove back to Ladyland. I gave Wasabi a pat and Sierra a long hug before heading back to pack for my flight the next morning.

As I got in the car, I could hear a banjo strumming and Sierra singing. I listened momentarily, and then pulled out into the late-night traffic, accepting that my girl is doing her own thing.

On Music Street.

EPILOGUE

WHERE ARE THE KIDS now?

Good question.

As I write this, Aaron and Sierra are charting their own paths: Aaron studying to work on motorcycles, probably doing tattoos on the side; Sierra traveling and busking as she pursues her music career on her terms.

Brooke is balancing a nursing career with being a wife and mother, texting on occasion—but much less than 5,000 per month.

Cody is a father to two kids of his own and one that's not his. He's starting to learn to bite his tongue, resulting in a promotion from driver to supervisor.

According to her Facebook page, Haley is "studying, not dying" at Berea College. She still frequents Taco Bell for special order vegan burritos.

Justin? He's still driving an ambulance. Probably looking in the rearview mirror to see if I'm chasing it.

While their courses are not what I envisioned, I'm proud of all of them.

And every time "unidentified caller" flashes across my iPhone, I answer. They're my kids and I'll always be here for them.

Even though none call me dad.

Acknowledgements

WRITING MY FIRST BOOK has been quite an undertaking, and I appreciate all of the support and encouragement that I've received. In particular, I'd like to acknowledge Frieda Owen, my editor, confidant and mother; Lorna Nakell and Poppy Milliken of Interrobang Collective, my publishing consultants and designers; Tara Lehmann of Endpaper Publishing, Cheryl Frey, and Ali McCart of Indigo Editing, my editors; Jens Kiel of Made In Germany, publicist; Michael Pushkin, Sierra Ferrell, Troy Schrek of Alfred Music, and Hal Leonard Corporation for lyrics permissions.

I'd also like to acknowledge Suzanne Jett Trowbridge and Shana Brown, beta readers; Carrie Goodwin Fenwick, proof-reader; Secretary Kay Goodwin, reviewer; and Jennie Baird, Janice Brand, Nancy Carlson, Holly Chen, Carol Dowd-Forte, Courtney Knowlton, Jane Kyte, Chris Rubin and Colleen Kinder, my Yale Writers' Conference workshop classmates and leader.

Thanks to Aaron, Sierra, Justin, Brooke, Cody and Haley.

And, most of all, to Tammy, my wife of 27 years and counting, who joined me for the roller coaster ride and allowed me to tell our story.

Richard D. "Ky" Owen is a lawyer with Goodwin & Goodwin, LLP, in Charleston, West Virginia. He earned a B.A. in journalism from Michigan State University in 1981 and a J.D. from Hamline University in 1984. Coming from a family of writers, he considers himself a "writer by birth." *None Call Me Dad* is his first book.